D0844929

Industrializing Antebellum America

Industrializing Antebellum America

The Rise of Manufacturing Entrepreneurs in the Early Republic

Barbara M. Tucker

Kenneth H. Tucker, Jr.

INDUSTRIALIZING ANTEBELLUM AMERICA

First published in 2008 by PALGRAVE MACMILLAN® in the US—a division of St. Martin's Press LLC, 175 Fifth Avenue, New York, NY 10010.

Where this book is distributed in the UK, Europe and the rest of the world, this is by Palgrave Macmillan, a division of Macmillan Publishers Limited, registered in England, company number 785998, of Houndmills, Basingstoke, Hampshire RG21 6XS.

Palgrave Macmillan is the global academic imprint of the above companies and has companies and representatives throughout the world.

Palgrave® and Macmillan® are registered trademarks in the United States, the United Kingdom, Europe and other countries.

ISBN-13: 978-1-4039-8480-7
ISBN-10: 1-4039-8480-8

Library of Congress Cataloging-in-Publication Data

Tucker, Barbara M.
Industrialization antebellum america : the rise of manufacturing entrepreneurs in the early republic / Barbara M. Tucker and Kenneth H. Tucker, Jr.
p. cm.
Includes bibliographical references and index.
ISBN 1-4039-8480-8
1. Businesspeople—United States—Biography. 2. Industrialists—United States—Biography. 3. Entrepreneurship—United States—History—19th century. I. Tucker, Kenneth H. II. Title.

HC102.5.A2T834 2008
338.092'273—dc22 2008004030

A catalogue record of the book is available from the British Library.

Design by Scribe Inc.

First edition: September 2008

10 9 8 7 6 5 4 3 2 1

Printed in the United States of America.

To the memory of our parents

Contents

Acknowledgments

The origins of this project are many. Though in different disciplines we share an interest in nineteenth-century history and its implications for today. We are happy that we were able to translate our interests into this book. But this study has a more specific genesis. Barbara Tucker's postdoctoral fellowship at the University of Pennsylvania many years ago acquainted her with the Roswell Colt papers housed at the Historical Society of Pennsylvania. Findings were presented to the Center for Early American Studies, but nothing further was done with the project at that time. A second input came from Professor David Brody, Emeritus Professor of History, University of California, Davis, who suggested that a work on Horatio Slater might be in order. That, too, was put on the shelf. Then came a query from Professor James Huston, Oklahoma State University, to write an article on the current state of entrepreneurial history during the Early Republic. Thus the project was set into motion, and it provided an opportunity for collaboration.

There are several people who deserve special mention for their assistance on the project. Christopher Clark read several chapters of the manuscript and made astute and valuable comments. He was able to grasp the internal arguments of the chapters, an impressive achievement for a reader. Both James Huston and John Larsen provided insight and encouragement for this study. Sherry Tucker read the entire book and shared her comments with us.

Barbara Tucker wishes to thank Eastern Connecticut State University for its continued support. Anka Stanley-Gorling, the interlibrary loan office at J. Eugene Smith library, was able to secure the most obscure materials, and her steadfastness is appreciated. For Kenneth Tucker, a grant from Mount Holyoke College provided some funds for research. He thanks members of the Mount Holyoke College Department of Sociology and Anthropology who heard a presentation on the material and made helpful comments. He is particularly grateful to Sherry, as always, for her graciousness, support, and intelligence. Finally, we wish to thank our sister, Carole Apra, who reminds us of the importance of family, which is such a central feature of this book.

Unlike some collaborations that can be a nightmare, working together was a pleasure. Research, discussions, writing, and deadlines all are made easier when working with someone who shares the same goals, discipline, and values. Our parents had much to do with this bond, and to them this book is dedicated.

Introduction

The rise of manufacturing entrepreneurship in the United States from the late eighteenth century to the aftermath of the Civil War can be explained in large part by focusing on Samuel Colt, Horatio Nelson Slater and John Fox Slater, Amos Adams Lawrence, and their families. These men epitomized the different visions of capitalism and manufacturing that arose at this time. Colt dominated the firearms industry, and he embodied the freewheeling, patriotic yet internationalist entreprenurial spirit of "casino capitalism" combined with elements of "crony capitalism" as he and his family cultivated and sometimes bribed government officials for contracts and favors.[1] Horatio Nelson Slater and John Fox Slater, leaders in the textile industry, fused philanthropy and paternalism, imagining a manufacturing capitalism based on small-town American values. Amos Adams Lawrence, the textile magnate, developed a view of a national American culture defined by a commitment to capitalism and Protestantism. Fearful of immigrants, he proclaimed the virtues of a nativist, Anglo-Saxon America yet was also a major opponent of the extension of slavery into the West. Though these men were enormously successful and influential businessmen, they were also cultural innovators intimately involved in the political disputes of their day.

Given their centrality to the economic and cultural history of the United States, it is surprising that these men and their families have not received more attention from historians. There have been few good histories of these families or examinations of the transmission of management attitudes, business practices, and cultural beliefs from generation to generation. More broadly, few historians have investigated the cultural, social, and economic differences among manufacturers in this era, and fewer still have analyzed the cultural dimensions of entrepreneurial activity and how manufacturers were influenced by and helped influence the distinctive emerging culture of antebellum America. Moreover, the importance of the firearms and textile industries that shaped early manufacturing in the United States has not been sufficiently addressed. As the renowned economic historian Alfred Chandler states, until the 1840s "the factory . . . appeared in substantial numbers only in the textile industry. The one other type of manufacturing enterprise to have similar characteristics was that producing firearms for the American army."[2]

Colt was the leader of a firearms industry that pioneered the technology of standardized parts and mass production. He engaged in international sales, established overseas offices, and perfected lifestyle advertising that made the romance of the gun integral to American life. The Slaters and Lawrences led a textile industry that forged the mass production of inexpensive, standardized woolen and cotton products, laying the groundwork for the rise of readymade clothing. This industry transformed the American household and freed women and girls from the time-consuming tasks of spinning and weaving sheeting and shirting.

Samuel Colt, Amos Adams Lawrence, and Horatio Nelson Slater and John Fox Slater, born within one year of one another, shaped their generation's manufacturing ethos. They represented a second generation of entrepreneurs. Samuel Colt's father, Christopher Colt, worked at a textile mill in Ware, Massachusetts, and his great uncle Peter Colt served as a superintendent for the Society for the Establishment of Useful Manufactures in Paterson, New Jersey. Amos A. Lawrence was the son of Amos Lawrence and the nephew of Abbott Lawrence, two of the wealthiest textile manufacturers in New England. Horatio Nelson Slater was the son of Samuel Slater, the "father of American manufactures," and John Fox Slater was the son of Samuel Slater's brother John Slater, also a successful mill owner. Family connections were essential to the operation of their businesses; they trusted one another, sought advice and economic support from relatives, and used the political contacts of relatives to further their business enterprises. The Slaters, Lawrences, and Colts used their positions, knowledge, and contacts to create or supplement their fortunes. In intensely competitive industries, they succeeded through creativity and innovation.

They were among the first manufacturers to employ immigrant labor, to adopt cost accounting, and to pioneer the use of brand names to sell their products. Their outlook extended beyond the region in which they operated and encompassed a national and even an international worldview.

Yet the different values of these men demonstrate that any common vision of the economic, political, and cultural future of America, fragile at best in the post-Revolutionary era, began to fragment by the first third of the nineteenth century. These manufacturers represented divergent views of the American project. Their differences show that shared beliefs about the nature of capitalism or the social responsibilities of entrepreneurs did not automatically arise from the emerging manufacturing economy. Indeed, capitalism itself is an amorphous concept. Many economic historians of the Early Republic see the rise of entrepreneurial activity as a rational response to market opportunities, as *homo economicus* enters the American economic stage. Like many contemporary economists who view globalization and its associated Wal-Marts and McDonalds as the only possible expressions of capitalism, economic historians of this era often narrow the possible trajectories of capitalism and the different ways that a capitalist economy might be structured; they focus almost exclusively on the influence of market conditions on economic activity. But Samuel Colt, Amos Adams Lawrence, and the Slaters were not simple rational economic actors, puppets of a market economy. They had to constantly experiment with new approaches to economic pursuits in the unstable boom-and-bust market conditions of the Early Republic. More important, their social and economic practices and beliefs were influenced by the culture in which they lived and the values that they adopted.

Samuel Colt, for example, embraced the risk of the market, endorsing an individualistic and expansionist vision of capitalism. He was a typical example of the striver after fortune, endemic to the American character as described by Tocqueville in *Democracy in America*.[3] He was an exemplar of the liberal individualism that Louis Hartz and several generations of historians view as central to American history. But Colt, taking a cue from his cousin Roswell Colt, represented a distinctive version of this individualism. He was a new kind of American manufacturing entrepreneur, much like today's "rock star" CEOs, such as Virgin Airlines owner Richard Branson—flamboyant, self-promotional, and intensely patriotic, while internationalist in his approach to marketing. Though asserting the benefits of laissez-faire, Colt was also a precursor of "crony capitalism," where government and business were intertwined with one another. He actively pursued government contracts and saw no moral problem in bribing government officials. Colt became an American icon because of his understanding of the new, emerging popular culture in the United States. Unlike other manufacturers, Colt honed his entrepreneurial skills in this popular culture of illusion of the 1830s, epitomized by P. T. Barnum and the rise of the penny press promoting sensational stories of crime and corruption. Seeking publicity wherever he could find it while creating a cult of celebrity about his own life, he made his six-shooter an integral part of the emerging mythology of the American West while contributing to shaping that very mythology. Colt placed popular symbols and promotional techniques at the center of the manufacturing economy. His advertising was based on the emotional appeal of his revolver; he described his pistol as a man's "one true friend, with six hearts in his body."[4] He tied the lifestyle of the freewheeling Westerner to ownership of his gun some seventy years before lifestyle advertising became an everyday part of American culture in the 1920s. Colt believed that technological advances such as his six-shooter ensured that the United States would take its rightful place as a world power, which reinforced his vision of America as a new empire.

John Fox Slater and Horatio Nelson Slater advocated an early version of moral capitalism with elements of social responsibility that built on the paternalistic beliefs of their respective fathers. If Colt symbolized the fusion of individualism and empire, John Fox Slater in particular represented "Christian republicanism," in the historian Mark Noll's terms.[5] The Slaters' economic innovations were substantial, from the introduction of cost accounting to the centralized control of many geographically dispersed mills throughout New England. Yet their economic activity was shaped by their moral values. While the Slaters invested in many ventures outside of textiles and supported Western expansion, they sought to fuse the small-town values of America with industrial change. For example, John Fox Slater tried to keep his native-born workers on his payroll even in difficult economic times. Influenced by the paternalistic values of his father as well as by the rise of a post-Puritan Protestantism that emphasized the gospel of social duty, his prudent vision of capitalism took local values seriously. He believed that manufacturers should be committed to promoting the welfare of their communities in addition to making money. Yet the Slaters attempted to mold their workforce in the shape of their own values, eventually jettisoning any pretense of care for their workers as immigrant labor replaced the native born. The Slaters not only distrusted the Catholicism of many of the immigrant workers but also the emerging popular culture of Colt and Barnum. They believed that these twin evils could undermine the virtuous character of Americans.

Their approach to these issues was complex. John Fox Slater recognized that the welfare of the dispossessed, the African Americans and Native Americans, could not be separated from the concerns of the majority of white men. His post–Civil War creation of the million-dollar John F. Slater Fund for the education of African Americans demonstrated his commitment to these causes. Like most people, many scholars believe that widespread philanthropic endeavors by businessmen began in the late nineteenth century with figures such as the Rockefellers and Carnegies. They often ignore the culture of philanthropy that arose in the Early Republic, one of whose most important representatives was John Fox Slater.

At first glance, Amos Adams Lawrence seems to share the Slaters' vision of an emerging industrial America, and there are important similarities between them. A second-generation textile manufacturer and philanthropist like John Fox Slater, Lawrence consolidated the business innovations of his family, invested widely and wisely, and turned his attention to politics and culture. Like John Fox Slater, he feared the spread of slavery; his strong sentiments derived in large part from the values of his father, Amos Lawrence, and his Protestant background, which emphasized the centrality of moral character in governing individual conduct. Yet if the good society for Slater could be found in a shared moral community, Lawrence took this idea one gigantic step further. He wished to dictate the moral and religious terms of this shared community to all Americans and develop a manufacturing society where talent could be recognized and rewarded through higher education. Lawrence rejected all populist sensibilities. For example, his philanthropy differed from Slater's, for he aimed at furthering an elite based on the possession of educational credentials, as his many donations to Harvard College and his contributions to the founding of Lawrence University in Wisconsin and the University of Kansas demonstrate. Lawrence's rabid anti-Catholic nativism and opposition to the education of women separated him from John Fox Slater's more communal orientation. The Slater vision was of a manufacturing economy based on small-town values; Lawrence believed that conservative, urban elites, such as those of the Bostonian upper class of which he was a part, could better guide the people than provincial, small-town Americans.

In many ways, Lawrence's character was the mirror image of Samuel Colt's. Like Colt, Lawrence advocated violence in the service of his cause, as he supported the murderous actions of John Brown in Kansas and may have provided financial assistance for the Harpers Ferry raid. Lawrence was a public figure, a visible presence on the national scene. Absolutely convinced of the rightness of his values, his temperament was much more like the publicity-seeking Colt than the behind-the-scenes style of the reticent Slaters. If Colt was the face of an emerging casino/crony capitalism, and Slater the ambassadors of a paternalistic manufacturing society, Lawrence was the public countenance of a moral, elitist, and nativist understanding of America. These different views of America and capitalism represented an incipient "culture war" in the nineteenth century. Religious self-righteousness, urban elitism, and individualistic capitalism continue to inform our seemingly incessant culture wars, even if today these values do not coalesce into the political and cultural positions of the antebellum period.

Indeed, as the second generation of powerful families, Colt, Lawrence, and the Slaters could not achieve their fortunes without confronting a number of social and cultural issues. They had to develop an understanding of their roles as manufacturers in a United States that was still largely agrarian. In doing so, they did not just draw on market principles of efficiency and productivity but wrestled with widespread American values of individualism, religion, nationalism, and democracy. The meaning of these values was in flux in the Early Republic, their definitions far from settled. For example, there was little consensus among Americans about the social responsibilities of individual entrepreneurs to their communities and whether the nation should be guided by commercial principles based on the expansion of trade and the encouragement of industry or remain an agriculturally based republic of small farmers. Western expansion posed problems, for it not only exacerbated tensions between the North and the South but also centralized power in the federal government, which diminished the roles of states and individuals in controlling their communities. Finally, in the eyes of many, the existence of slavery and the forced removal of Native Americans made democracy a sham while mocking the Christian beliefs so important to many Americans. Colt, Lawrence, and the Slaters held different views of these issues for the most part. These entrepreneurs, through their economic activity, contacts with government, and cultural influence, tried to create a social context where their vision of America could come to pass.

Certainly this story is not a simple dichotomy of virtue (the Slaters and perhaps the Lawrences) and vice (the Colts). For example, the second generation Slater clan and Amos Adams Lawrence attempted to "Americanize" their immigrant workforce through religious and other moral instruction, sentiments at odds with our contemporary multicultural sensibility. Samuel Colt, on the other hand, celebrated the ethnic distinctiveness of his (white male) immigrant laborers, going so far as to construct replicas of Prussian villages complete with beer halls for his German immigrant workers. Balzac's famous dictum that "behind every great fortune there is a crime" is also appropriate here. Samuel Colt built his empire as a gunmaker, a merchant of death; the fortunes of the Slaters and the Lawrences were due in large part to slave labor, which supplied the cotton for their textile mills. Marxist historians also remind us that capitalists did not embrace values that would harm their economic interests, and this is certainly the case for Colt, Lawrence, and John Fox Slater. These entrepreneurs shared many economic convictions, from the defense of private property to a belief in the natural harmony of all classes. But these economic interests could be expressed in manifold ways and were to a great degree shaped by distinctive cultural beliefs.

Historians of antebellum manufacturing have not pursued these insights. In a recent article, James Huston writes that "commentary on entrepreneurs is limited to theoretical standards-*homo economicus*" that ignore the "cultural norms" informing "the pursuit of self interest." It is this gap in entrepreneurial history that this study hopes to fill.[6]

Much of this book is based on primary sources. Company records for the three families were examined in detail. The Slater and Lawrence company and personal records can be found at the Harvard Business School, Massachusetts Historical Society, Rhode Island Historical Society, Slater Mill (Pawtucket, Rhode Island), and the Dodd Center, University of Connecticut. The later depository contains many of the papers for the S. & J. Slater Companies in Connecticut. For the Colts, the material can be found at the Historical Society of Pennsylvania, the New Jersey State Library, the Connecticut Historical Society, the Connecticut State Library, and the University of Rhode Island Special Collections. In particular, the Pennsylvania and Rhode Island collections have not been well utilized by historians.

The scholarly work available on these men and their families is meager, simplistic, antiquarian, or nonexistent. Nothing of significance has been written on Peter Colt, Christopher Colt, or Roswell Colt. Horatio Nelson Slater, son of Samuel Slater; John Slater; and John

Fox Slater also suffer from a lack of scholarly attention. When historians discuss John Fox Slater, they limit their examination to his benevolent activities.

While Samuel Colt has been the subject of a few biographies, they are primarily in-house, uncritical versions of his life. Ellsworth Grant and Jack Rohan, among others, tend to merely summarize or embellish the work of nineteenth-century author James D. McCabe in his book *Great Fortunes, and How They Were Made; or the Struggles and Triumphs of our Self-Made Men.*[7] More recently, in an attempt to promote their Colt gun collection, the Wadsworth Atheneum Museum of Art in Hartford has been behind the publication of several books including William Hosley's *Colt: The Making of An American Legend* (1996).[8] The latter provides a good narrative of Colt's life, but the author does not explore in depth the connections between Samuel Colt and his family, especially Roswell Colt. He also neglects Colt's immersion in popular culture and does not link him to a wider culture of individualism that was developing in the United States. Finally, his biography of Colt does not explore him in a comparative context with other entrepreneurs.

Most importantly, these works do not adequately examine Colt's enormous cultural influence. This lack of attention to cultural context and cultural influence extends to scholarly interpretations of the Lawrences. Robert F. Dalzell Jr. discusses this family in his work *Enterprising Elite* (1987), as does Thomas O'Connor in *The Lords of the Loom: The Cotton Whigs and the Coming of the Civil War* (1968) and Richard Abbott in *Cotton and Capital* (1991). But these authors fail to place the Lawrences' lives into the context of larger and diverse trends within capitalism. While there is a biography of Nathan Appleton by Frances Gregory, there are few good sources on Amos Adams Lawrence or on other important figures associated with him, such as Francis Cabot Lowell, Amos Lawrence, or Abbott Lawrence. Materials relating to the latter tend to be privately printed pamphlets such as Bradford P. Raymond, *Discourse in Memory of Hon. Amos A. Lawrence* (1886); Hamilton Hill, *Memoir of Abbott Lawrence* (1883); or William Lawrence, *Extracts From the Diary and Correspondence of the Late Amos Lawrence with a Brief Account of Some Incidents in His Life* (1855) and *Life of Amos A. Lawrence with Extracts from His Diary and Correspondence* (1888).[9]

More broadly, Charles Sellers in *The Market Revolution* (1991) has attempted to replace Arthur Schlesinger's *The Age of Jackson* (1945) as the major interpretation of the era. But like Schlesinger, Sellers concentrates on political history and neglects the role of manufacturing entrepreneurs during this period. He tends to see early capitalists as stooges of the market economy. He also constructs a simple dichotomy of Jacksonian Democrats versus the money interests of a market society, which neglects the diversity of capitalist approaches to the market and society that is at the heart of this study. The only works to fully explore some of these issues focus largely on rural capitalism and include Christopher Clark, *Roots of Rural Capitalism* (1990), and Winifred Rothenberg, *From Market-Places to a Market Economy* (1992). While impressive, they do not analyze manufacturing entrepreneurs in any depth.[10]

To date, the field of entrepreneurial history has been dominated by Alfred Chandler and his emphasis on organizational-centered, large-scale enterprises and what he termed managerial capitalism. In 1977 he published his seminal work, *The Visible Hand*, and it had a significant impact on business and entrepreneurial history. Until the late 1970s, Robert Cuff argued, organizational-centered activity, not individual-centered activity, dominated the field. But now a shift has occurred, and "entrepreneurship as individual behavior" once again commands scholarly attention. More recent arguments have been advanced by Naomi R. Lamoreaux in "Rethinking the Transition of Capitalism in the Early American Northeast" (2003).[11] This represents a new beginning, for she notes the cultural influences on emerging American capitalism. This book takes this cultural approach a giant step further, examining in detail the social and cultural influences on Colt, Slater, and Lawrence and their contributions to shaping the ethos of the Early Republic.

Part I investigates Samuel Colt's vision of casino/crony capitalism, beginning with the Colt family, in particular his father, Christopher Colt, and his great uncle Peter Colt, who provided economic and political support for his ventures into the firearms industry. But Samuel Colt was most influenced by his wealthy cousin Roswell Colt, who introduced him to many political contacts and financed his early gun factories. This section examines Colt's innovative manufacturing, industrial, and managerial techniques; his forays into popular culture; the development of his distinctive approach to advertising; and his influence on the emerging understanding of the West.

Part II explores the distinctive vision of capitalism and culture developed by the Slaters. The Slaters inherited not only textile mills and managerial practices from their respective fathers John Slater and Samuel Slater but also an entire paternalistic worldview about the relationship of owners and workers. They helped initiate cost accounting and centralized control of diverse mills into American manufacturing and fashioned this paternalistic approach into an industrial version of small-town America. Animated by post-Puritan religious beliefs of social service and duty, they treated their native workers fairly on the whole but their Catholic immigrant workers deplorably. As paternalism faded, they became agents of the rise of a disciplinary society, instituting contracts, rules, and regulations in their factories and company towns, which became the new ingredients of social control in an industrial society. Yet these were complex men, and in particular John Fox Slater gave generously to his community and other philanthropic causes. This section also examines John Fox Slater's strong antislavery views and activities and how they contributed to his vision of a manufacturing society based on small-town values.

Part III explores the contributions of the Lawrences to American manufacturing and culture. Amos Lawrence and his brother Abbott became important economic, political, and philanthropic figures in the antebellum era. The son of Amos Lawrence, Amos Adams Lawrence, inherited his father's business and his philanthropic attitudes. Influenced, like John Fox Slater, by a post-Puritan religious worldview, he became a fervent Christian determined to prevent slavery from expanding into the West. The intersection of his religious persuasion, economic interests, and political activities are explored as well as how his religious fervor contributed to a range of activities and beliefs from his anti-slavery views that culminated in his support of John Brown to his virulent anti-Catholicism. We also discuss his attachment to the Brahmin elite of Boston, which contributed to his elitist vision of moral capitalism. In our conclusion, we compare and contrast the respective visions of America developed by Colt, the Slaters, and Lawrence and suggest that more attention to cultural issues can benefit the study of business history.

Part I

The Colts

Casino and Crony Capitalism

CHAPTER 1

COLT FAMILY VALUES

Samuel Colt may be the best-known member of the Colt clan, but his family represented a panorama of the economic and social prospects and problems of the Early Republic that reached far beyond entrepreneurship. While Samuel followed a manufacturing path like his father Christopher, Sam's brothers John, Christopher Jr., and James found it difficult to find their calling. The eldest brother, John Caldwell, first became a clerk and then a writer of accounting manuals before becoming infamous as a vicious ax murderer. A second brother, Christopher Jr., married into a family involved in the slave trade and led a wanderlust, dissolute life. The youngest boy, James, was involved on and off in politics, serving as an attorney, a judge in Missouri, and an official in Samuel's enterprises. Both James and Christopher Jr., as well as the ax murderer John, had bouts of depression and were sometimes estranged from their extended families. Throughout their lives, the specter of their sister Sarah, who committed suicide at the age of twenty-one, haunted them.

This represented just one line of the Colt family tree. The Peter Colt side of the family also exhibited a degree of eccentricity. Samuel's great uncle Peter Colt engaged in a variety of occupations, working closely with post–Revolutionary War state and federal agencies; there he developed warm relations with influential politicians and businessmen, an early version of the "crony capitalism" that influenced his son Roswell Colt and later Samuel Colt. Peter left another legacy for later generations. He was an early proponent of tying his business ventures to American patriotism. His motto "Buy American" would be taken by Samuel Colt to new heights of publicity, as Samuel linked his guns to Manifest Destiny while contributing to the origins of brand-name advertising.[1]

Peter also set another example for later Colts: to ensure a wealthy existence, marry well. While the early nineteenth century saw the rise of the "cult of domesticity" in the United States and England, the Colts turned the stereotype of the woman searching for a wealthy and caring husband, embodied so skillfully in Jane Austen's novels, on its head. While a middle- or upper-class woman's vocation was home and hearth, her identity was essentially dependent on the man she married. The Colts appeared to be a team of Lotharios who secured their social position by marrying into prominent families. Thus, the Colt heritage is bound up with the fortunes of such well-known families as the Caldwells and Lymans of Connecticut; the DeWolfs of Bristol, Rhode Island; and the Olivers of Baltimore, Maryland. The Colts and many of their inlaws were ambitious risk takers who looked upon the landscape of the early Republic and saw endless bountiful possibilities. Although Peter and Samuel Colt sometimes failed, they used failure as an incentive to redouble their efforts to be successful. But the others allowed their misfortune to overwhelm them: John Colt committed murder, while Christopher Colt Jr. and James Colt reacted to their distress through possible suicide, depression, and even madness.

The Colt family confronted an emerging American capitalism that was replacing nonmarket, traditional values with the centrality of wealth as a measure of social position. As Tocqueville observed, "Distinction based on wealth is increased by the disappearance or diminution of all other distinctions."[2] Status and reputation became increasingly tied to success in the market; the second and third generations of Colts evidenced no embarrassment in their ambitious pursuit of wealth, indeed reveling in the hunt. Yet two important factors tempered this relentless quest for riches. First, the boom-and-bust cycles of early capitalism meant that not only the pursuit but also the maintenance of wealth was precarious at best, as Colt family members, like other Americans, made and lost a great deal of money in antebellum America. Economic risk was prevalent in all areas of life, as small entrepreneurs often experienced failure. Businessmen dealt with this new risky market economy by cultivating personal networks, sharing risks, and developing new types of bookkeeping.[3] The Colt family and their relatives would be innovative in all these areas.

Second, given that there was no aristocracy to ensure the transmission of wealth, family and personal contacts became increasingly important. Sociologists from Emile Durkheim to Francis Fukuyama remind us that market activity, no matter how widespread, is dependent on nonmarket values such as trust to ensure its efficient functioning, and early American capitalism was no exception.[4] Trust was grounded in the noneconomic relationships of family life, which remained central in a burgeoning capitalism. Family firms dominated a patriarchal era where trust of anyone outside of the kin circle was limited. In New England, the family was the foundation for the community, the church, the state, and the economy. The significance of the family carried over into the Revolutionary era and the rise of the Early Republic. Family networks, family business, and family firms directed economic life. The Browns of Providence, the DeWolfs of Bristol, and the Deanes of Wethersfield were among the most celebrated entrepreneurs in the latter part of the eighteenth century. In the epoch before widespread affluence or any kind of welfare state, only the family could take care of its members. Moreover, family and friendship networks and connections often resulted in economic and political opportunities for relatives. Family dynamics and values helped influence and in turn were shaped by an emerging capitalism. Yet this was a combustible mix, as the complex psychodynamics of family relations became bound up with the competitive pursuit of wealth. This unstable fusion of capital and family was played out in the relationships among Samuel Colt, his brothers, and his parents, and they could be seen in earlier generations as well.

The family, while a central component of business activity, was undergoing enormous cultural and social changes in antebellum America. Not only were spheres of men's and women's worlds becoming more distinct, but the agriculturally based, relatively fixed familial roles for parents and children were undergoing change. Affections began to narrow to the nuclear family as family celebrations centered on Christmas, birthdays, and anniversaries, supplanting civic celebrations as major yearly events.[5] Rather than adopting adult roles at a young age through farming and other chores, after 1800 "youth" became a more volatile category of the life cycle. Teenage boys began moving out of their houses in greater numbers to find their fortune Although young people were still expected to defer to their elders, there was much confusion about age-appropriate behavior. Schools mixed different age groups together; young men in particular began to have more choices about their occupation, residence, friends, and even spouses.[6]

The Colt family mirrored these changes. The unsettled beliefs and circumstances of the nineteenth century could be seen in the peripatetic activity of Samuel Colt and his brothers. The first generation represented by Peter Colt still lived in a world where not only the family but also noneconomic values, from patriotism to a reputation for moral probity, strongly circumscribed purely market values and activities and somewhat moderated entrepreneurial ambition. But the experiences of these men convinced them that the traditional world was fading, and a more dynamic and competitive world was taking its place. In the unsettled circumstances of post-Revolutionary America, Peter Colt in particular overcame economic failure and learned lessons from his hardships. Though relying on family contacts for economic and political opportunities, he began to adopt the ethos of the new capitalism. Whether cultivating government contracts, looking to the West as a source of wealth, or marrying well, Peter Colt discovered how to be flexible and to maneuver in a complex, emerging economic system. The second generation of Colts, including Peter's son Roswell and his nephew Christopher Colt, were transitional figures to the enthusiastic embrace of capitalist values represented by Samuel and his brothers. Roswell became wealthy through shady government connections, while Christopher was a manufacturer who both made and lost money and whose nomadic life in search of business opportunities would be followed by the restless activity of his sons.

Samuel and his brothers faced a more competitive capitalism than their elders, which only exacerbated rivalries between them. They confronted a world of mobility, choice, and opportunity, as well as the changing landscape of familial roles. The brothers Colt were neglected as youngsters, having lost their birth mother at a young age, and were sent away from their family to pursue a trade as Christopher Sr. remarried and moved from place to place in his quest for business success. Though Samuel retained a relatively cordial relationship with his parents, the ambivalent and often hostile family ties of the Colt brothers increased their insecurity, and they sought status and approval through the acquisition of riches. All were ambitious, desiring wealth in any way that they could achieve it, from bribing politicians to marrying wealthy women, and they traveled the country in pursuit of economic success and status. Their volatile temperaments guaranteed that they were competing constantly with one another. As Samuel became rich, his brothers were increasingly dependent on him, asking and occasionally demanding money from him, while simultaneously seething with sibling jealousy. For example, James Colt, like Golem in *Lord of the Rings*, careened between sycophantic praises of his brother when requesting loans to threats of litigation when they were not forthcoming. Christopher Jr. slandered his brothers while sinking into depression and alcoholism. Their disturbed mental state seemed to complement their activities in the seamy underside of economics and politics in antebellum America, including the global sale of guns, the slave trade, and political intrigue and bribery. Through all these travails, despite the amoral pursuit of wealth that defined their actions, they rather hilariously protested their good character and disdain of mere money-grubbing—family values indeed.

PETER COLT

The Colts were among the original settlers who migrated to Windsor, Connecticut in the 1630s. These fiercely independent early proprietors wanted to create their own church, worship their own way, and secure an economic future for themselves and their children. Windsor residents saw their community as a potential commercial port town, a center for trade whose foodstuffs could be shipped to the West Indies. But instead, the town proved to be a jumping-off point and not a permanent settlement for many early settlers. Benjamin Colt, for example, moved further east to Lyme, Connecticut; married, and had ten children. Two of his sons, Peter and Benjamin, became the patriarchs of families that played a pivotal role in both the American and Industrial Revolutions. Through the years, these brothers and their families formed a tight network that supported one another politically, economically, and socially. Benjamin was the father of Christopher Colt and grandfather of Samuel Colt. He fought in the Revolutionary War and was a successful landowner. But it was the activities of Peter Colt, who prefigured and influenced the later Colt clan, that gained early success.[7]

Peter Colt's rise to prominence in the new American Republic was tied to the fortunes of the new government, his family networks, and the influential people he met and cultivated. Born in 1744, Peter Colt was the tenth and youngest child of Benjamin Colt. After his parents died and left him as an orphan, he was handed from one relative to another and from one schoolmaster to another. Within a two-year period, he studied with at least five different men: Mr. Smith, Mr. Phelps, Mr. Parsons, Mr. Griswold, and finally Rev. Simon Ely, who taught him Latin and prepared him for entry into Yale. A precocious, intelligent youngster, by his sixteenth birthday he was independent and a college student in an era when few boys passed beyond a basic education. At Yale, he walked into a different world where money and status played a significant role.[8] At the time, Yale offered a classical curriculum that fit its graduates to take their places in the forefront of society, politics, and business. In the tradition of classical European *Bildung*, Yale graduates were expected to embody the virtues of a gentleman: integrity, honesty, responsibility, and piety. It appeared that Peter Colt learned those lessons well. A test of his integrity occurred immediately upon graduation with a Masters of Art degree in 1767. During his years at college, he had incurred considerable debt to pay for his education. It took him four years to pay off his creditors, and although, as he noted, I could "have avoided payment of by pleading that I was a minor at time of contracting them, but as I considered this plea utterly unworthy of an honest man not having been seduced into these expenses by my honest creditors I chose to endure any privation rather than defraud them of their just dues."[9] After Yale, he tried teaching, traveled throughout the north, and returned to New Haven to pursue a business career.[10]

New Haven offered many opportunities for the young Yale graduate. A small group of alumni dominated the economy, and Peter took advantage of these connections. Like Colt, many of them initially had come to town to attend college; some of them enjoyed the community and the opportunities it offered and decided to remain in town. Colt's future father-in-law, Daniel Lyman, Yale class of 1745, was a prominent member of this circle. Born in Northampton, Massachusetts, Lyman attended Yale, graduated, and married the daughter of the town's leading public figure Joseph Whiting. Although initially labeled an interloper by local residents, through hard work and Whiting's connections, he became one of the town's most celebrated residents, serving as county surveyor, justice of the peace, school trustee, and church deacon. He was elected deputy to the General Assembly eleven times and town moderator four times.[11] By the Revolution, he was counted among New Haven's leading businessmen. When Connecticut decided to support the patriot cause, men like Lyman were tapped to assist the new army.[12] Peter Colt would benefit from these political, commercial, and collegial connections, and he too would play a prominent role in the Revolution and its aftermath.

During this war, the Continental Congress looked to local merchants, especially commission agents with their established networks of suppliers, their local knowledge of resources, and their personal relationships with residents and government officials, to procure supplies and provisions for the new government and its army. The merchants recruited, however, were not expected to abandon their personal businesses but to merely take on another, albeit a significant, new client.

They mingled personal and government affairs. The businessmen continued to operate in traditional ways: they vetted suppliers who were often personal friends, family members, or their own partners; loaned money to prospective contractors; purchased, stored, and transported goods either using their own or government warehouses, wagons, or ships; and arranged payment sometimes using their personal funds and credit lines to pay for the materials and foodstuffs and then trying to recoup their expenses from the new government. There was little accountability or oversight.[13]

Peter Colt was drawn into this system and began his career in this intersection of business and politics while gaining influential contacts. With the outbreak of the Revolutionary War, in large part because of his father-in-law Lyman's contacts, Peter was appointed to the Committee of Inspection in New Haven and became involved in local and state affairs. His life became intertwined with that of Jeremiah Wadsworth, a Hartford merchant whose responsibilities included provisioning the Continental Army. By 1778 Colt had been recognized by Wadsworth as a promising and creative merchant, and he was recruited as his subordinate to provision American soldiers. The Connecticut General Assembly had ordered that the daily rations accorded troops include the following: pork, beef, beans, butter, milk, molasses, onions and vegetables, coffee, chocolate, sugar, and spirits. Providing these rations was no simple task. Each town had a quota to meet, and its contributions were coordinated and supplemented by the State Commissary General Joseph Trumbull, son of the Connecticut governor, and his staff. For their work, these men received a 1.5 percent commission on all supplies purchased for the state's militia. At the urging of George Washington, Congress appointed Trumbull commissary general for the Continental Army. Trumbull then tapped Wadsworth for the position of Connecticut commissary of supplies with the mandate to provide for the state's troops and militia and to confiscate whatever cereal crops he needed.[14] One of his lieutenants was Peter Colt. As Wadsworth's fortunes changed, so did those of Peter Colt.

In his governmental post, Joseph Trumbull centralized his department, hired men known for their business acumen, and selected former associates such as Wadsworth to assist him. Trumbull served until August 1777 and was first succeeded by William Buchanan and then by Wadsworth. When Wadsworth assumed the post, the department was in disarray, supplies were scarce, and funds were insufficient to provision the army. Wadsworth reorganized the districts and appointed Peter Colt to a region that encompassed the area east of the

Hudson River including part of New York, as well as Massachusetts, Rhode Island, and Connecticut.[15]

For Wadsworth and his associates such as Colt, service in the new government initially proved to be a nightmare. Food was in short supply, provisions had been stored in out-of-the-way or inconvenient locations, transport was difficult, and independent contractors often outbid army agents. Peter Colt pleaded with Governor Trumbull for help in securing food for the Continental forces. Trumbull ordered Colt to "take and seize any quantity or parcel which may be wanted for the use of the army."[16] Although he resorted to confiscation of supplies, the department was constantly short of wheat, cattle, and pork. Men deserted in ever increasing numbers, and Washington feared the demise of his army. Despite disbursements that totaled seventy-nine thousand dollars, Colt constantly complained of insufficient funding. Wadsworth, Colt and others in the department often used their own funds to purchase supplies. They fell into debt and received little relief from the Continental Congress. On the contrary, Congress demanded an accounting of dispersed funds and a list of all those who had cheated or committed other crimes against the department. Disgusted with the lack of funds and the increasing scrutiny, Wadsworth, Colt, and others resigned, and the procurement of foodstuffs reverted back to the states.[17]

But Wadsworth just exchanged one procurement post for another. He found more lucrative business elsewhere. Wadsworth together with his partner John M. Carter made a fortune provisioning the French forces stationed in Rhode Island. Wadsworth knew the area, had important contacts with local businessmen, and set up an efficient organization. His defection to the French was followed by others including Colt. Wadsworth, Carter, and Colt worked well together and continued their relationship into the postwar period. Colt served as an "attorney" for Wadsworth as well as for the firm of Wadsworth and Carter, a business that he also managed. [18]

Despite their success supplying the French, economic prospects in the immediate postwar period appeared grave. Britain dumped goods on the American market, and Colt lamented that the "the whole world [is] mad to ship English goods to America." [19] Colt faced this situation when he opened his own store in Hartford, Peter Colt & Co., where he sold all types of goods from linens and ribbons to tea, chocolate, coffee, and even steel.[20] Fellow merchant, privateer, and commissary agent during the war years Barnabas Deane was his partner. Colt was saved from economic hardship in large part because of his contacts. In 1789 he was appointed treasurer of the state of

Connecticut. For this position he received an annual compensation of only two hundred pounds sterling, less than half of his salary under Wadsworth. At the time he became state treasurer, he liquidated his share of the mercantile business, placing it in the hands of his nephew Elisha Colt. Immediately the business took on an American image. With Peter's support, Elisha Colt advertised that his goods were of "American manufacture."[21]

The risky and ever-changing economic and political conditions of the Early Republic demanded an experimental approach to business and government affairs. Colt reveled in this challenge and built upon the burgeoning sense of American patriotism that informed his approach to selling cloth products. He carried this patriotic sentiment into yet another field, manufacturing. With Wadsworth, Colt and others organized the Hartford Woolen Manufactory Company in 1788. This firm predated the celebrated cotton textile mill established by Almy, Brown, and Slater in Pawtucket, Rhode Island the next decade. Colt and Wadsworth were the largest subscribers to the firm, but businessmen such as George Phillips and Jesse Root and politicians like Lieutenant Governor Oliver Wolcott Sr. and Mayor Thomas Seymour wanted to participate. They proposed to manufacture woolen cloth equal to any available from Britain. These men set up their business in downtown Hartford, but the proprietors lacked the mechanical and managerial knowledge to make this factory profitable. Wadsworth and his team relied on English army deserters or former prisoners of war who had previously worked in the British woolen industry for information on how to construct and operate a woolen mill. Needless to say, this proved inadequate, and they continued their search for mechanical and managerial expertise. They were unable to find a man like Samuel Slater, the eventual "father of American manufactures," who had worked in and had extensive knowledge of the British factory system, its machines, labor force requirements, motive power, and product quality.[22]

Still, they persevered. Colt served as treasurer of the firm, and Captain Daniel Hinsdale, a local merchant, was left to manage it. When they began production, they had to find a market for what was considered an inferior product. Colt recognized that the people were prepared to "buy" American. As the nation-state consolidated its power and a burgeoning textile industry did likewise, they reinforced one another. By the 1830s, Tocqueville would recognize the enormous patriotic pride of the Americans, informed by a distinctive egalitarianism of conditions and attitudes (at least among white men). In an era where such patriotism was beginning to take hold, Colt and other manufacturers persuaded American politicians to wear American-made cloth. This ode to patriotism succeeded. Both Washington and Adams wore suits to their inauguration made of Hartford cloth. Colt convinced the secretary of war, Henry Knox, to purchase cloth for military troops. Even Martha Washington was induced to buy cloth for a riding habit. But this publicity could not cover up certain obvious defects and deficiencies in the American-made cloth: dye was not colorfast, and the Hartford cloth stained whatever it touched; the cloth was coarse; the prices were high, and fine grades of wool could not be easily obtained. The company struggled until 1795 when the stockholders held their final meeting. By then Peter Colt had severed his ties with the concern and had left for yet another position, this time in Paterson, New Jersey, to take charge of a manufacturing scheme devised and encouraged in part by Alexander Hamilton.[23]

Secretary of the Treasury Hamilton had taken notice of Colt and the Hartford Woolen Manufactory In his *Report on Manufactures*, he wrote, "A promising essay, towards the fabrication of clothes, cassimers, and other woollen goods, is likewise going on at Hartford, in Connecticut. Specimens of the different kinds which are made, in the possession of the Secretary, evince that these fabrics have attained a very considerable degree of perfection."[24] Although the positive assessment of this particular project was premature, Hamilton believed that the future of America relied on industry and not agriculture. He had been impressed with the enthusiasm and expertise exhibited by Colt as Connecticut state treasurer and as part-time company treasurer of the Hartford Woolen Manufactory. In his bid to support American manufacturing, Hamilton aided the struggling Society for the Establishment of Useful Manufactures in New Jersey. At the urging of Hamilton, Colt was persuaded to leave Connecticut and become superintendent of this new enterprise.

Taking up his office in Paterson in February 1793, Colt walked into a quagmire. The company had received a state charter to use the water from the Passaic River to power a textile factory. A new town, Paterson, was to be laid out and serve as a model of American ingenuity and progress. But when he arrived, there was no factory, no manufacturing center, no machines, disgruntled mechanics, and the few operatives they had worked in "wretched sheds." William Pearce, who had been employed to construct textile machines, was so disenchanted with the venture that he asked to be discharged. Colt pleaded to Hamilton that Pearce and a fellow mechanic Thomas Marshall were "perfectly masters of their Business; & very valuable Men to the Society, & that they cannot be discharged without the Society Sustaining great loss."[25] Given these circumstances, Colt requested Hamilton's assistance. "Knowing how much you have the success of this institution at heart has induced me to make you this communication," wrote Colt. Colt wanted financial guarantees from Hamilton as well as assistance and advice in governing the establishment. This included handling the temperamental Pierre Charles L'Enfant, the architect associated with the design of Federal Hall in New York City and the Federal District on the banks of the Potomac. L'Enfant was employed to plan the new industrial city and to develop the water privileges, but he viewed his assignment more broadly to include constructing the mill, a job that had been delegated to Colt. Colt appealed to Hamilton to intercede on his behalf. These differences and confusing lines of authority led L'Enfant to quit in June and leave for Philadelphia. Construction of the canal now fell to Colt.[26] The business continued its downward slide, and by June 1796 the scheme was discontinued, and the buildings and water privileges were leased. Peter Colt was now unemployed, but that situation did not last long.

The following year he was in New York working for the Western Inland Lock Navigation Company, but he also failed in this venture. Colt decided to change direction and become a farmer. Near Rome, New York, he purchased just over one thousand acres of land and moved most of his family to the farm. By this time, the Colts had six surviving children, two sons and four daughters. The eldest son, Roswell Colt, was left to finish his education in Hartford. For Peter Colt, education and appearances were important. He made sure that his children attended school, and he also counseled his wife to see that the children were "neat and smart in their dress—& a little finery is not amiss."[27] Colt's persistence paid off as investment opportunities opened up for him. He speculated in western and Oneida Indian land and held twenty-five thousand acres in Genesee, New York.[28] Although he had intended to remain in New York for the rest of his life, financial and industrial prospects reappeared in New Jersey. In 1810 he saw a magnificent opportunity to acquire the former land, buildings, and original charter of the once moribund Society for the Establishment of Useful Manufactures in New Jersey. Two of his sons, Roswell and John, joined him, and they entered an exceedingly successful business. Peter Colt regained the prosperity that he had lost, living well until his death in 1824.

Peter Colt's life experiences demonstrated the opportunities open to a hardworking, eager young man. The American Revolution made this orphan, Yale graduate, and New Haven businessman one of the leading commercial figures in Connecticut and among the most important entrepreneurs in New Jersey. A friend of Jeremiah Wadsworth, Jonathan Trumbull, Alexander Hamilton, and other important men, he used his abilities and contacts to advance the economic position of his family. Colt's patriotism and pride in American manufacturing presaged Henry Clay's famous enunciation of a distinctive American System of industry by some twenty years.

Peter Colt was part of a generation that valued education, had a steadfast set of values, and yet saw and seized the opportunities offered by the American Revolution. A small-town merchant in the prewar years, he was concerned with maintaining his reputation for honesty, integrity, and honor, all required in dealing with face-to-face creditors and debtors where one's personal reputation dictated acceptance and status. Yet these traditional values were under siege in the crazed world of war where privateering, greed, and duplicity brought status and wealth. While Peter Colt might not have been entirely comfortable in this context, as he left commerce for agriculture, he was able to maneuver and take advantage of changing economic circumstances. His sons, however, felt no conflict among different value systems and embraced the new order. Their world was the capitalist urban environment where economic success was the measure of a person, and almost any means could be employed to attain riches. Peter Colt's son Roswell fit that description. Speculator, sycophant, and swindler were the labels that best described Roswell Colt.

A few details about Peter Colt's sons are relevant here. Roswell had been born in Weathersfield, Connecticut while Peter Colt was engaged in the commissary service. Later Roswell entered the New York firm of Jacob Le Roy & Sons where he remained until his marriage to Margaret Oliver, daughter of the wealthy Baltimore merchant Robert Oliver. Peter Colt's second surviving son, John, also initially pursued a mercantile career working with the New York firm of G. & T. Meyer. Opportunities opened for him to serve as supercargo on a vessel that sailed to Europe and the East Indies. When his father and brother began to invest in New Jersey manufacturing, he joined them, becoming a leading factory owner and operator in Paterson. The Paterson business, however, belonged to Roswell Colt. With his father's urging, he purchased sufficient stock to control the Society for the Establishment of Useful Manufactures and subsequently became governor of the society. He envisioned himself not as a manufacturer but a businessman and speculator who owned and improved the waterpower sites on the Passaic River and rented or leased them to others. This model was later to be adopted by such textile manufacturers as Francis Cabot Lowell and Abbott Lawrence.[29] While engaged in his

Paterson works, he developed business values and connections that were to have an enormous impact on Samuel Colt. Samuel was also influenced by his father Christopher and his troubled relationships with his brothers. Their problems and troubles provide a perspective into the varieties of entrepreneurial life, its possibilities and setbacks, and its intersection with the family in antebellum America.

CHRISTOPHER COLT

Samuel Colt's father, Christopher Colt, represented a transitional figure in the Colt family with feet in both the world of agricultural society, based on personal relationships and shared ideas of duty, and the entrepreneurial world of a rising industrial capitalism. Christopher, the nephew of Peter Colt, moved from place to place and occupation to occupation in his search for economic stability, never quite attaining it. Like Peter Colt, his first marriage brought him some measure of wealth, status, and connections. His second marriage, however, represented a watershed in the Colt family, as Colt's second wife, Olive, convinced him to send his boys away to school and to work, which created conflict. While Olive represents a rather stereotypical evil stepmother for several of the boys, Colt's sons also had clearly ambivalent relations with their father and with one another.

Christopher Colt was born in Hartford on August 30, 1780, to Benjamin Colt, the brother of Peter Colt. The vicissitudes of Christopher Colt's life could not have been predicted from his early years. He was one of eight children; his male siblings included Benjamin Colt, a Vermont farmer, Elisha Colt, a Massachusetts farmer, and his unfortunate older brother Daniel. The latter traveled south to New Orleans where he opened a store that proved unsuccessful; rather than try again, he succumbed to gambling and alcoholism, a choice that would later be repeated by some of his relatives.[30]

Christopher followed Daniel into business, but he remained in Connecticut, purchased a store in Hartford, and by 1802 he was selling glassware, dishes, and looking glasses to both the wholesale and retail trade. His fortunes multiplied when he married Sarah Caldwell, daughter of the town's leading merchant, in April 1805.[31] Her father, Major John Caldwell, was involved in a variety of enterprises from shopkeeper, import merchant, manufacturer, to banker. In the 1780s, Caldwell managed a store where he sold European goods, rock salt, produce, and spirits including Madeira, brandy, and rum. He also served as a commission agent, purchasing, storing, packaging, and shipping local goods and produce.[32] His involvement in foreign and domestic trade was buttressed by other ventures including industry, shipbuilding, and marine insurance. Caldwell became a partner and executive in a distillery, B. Deane and Company, and in the Hartford Woolen Manufactory. He engaged in the lucrative West Indies trade as well as occasionally venturing into the European market. Because foreign trade was so precarious with captains confronting storms at sea, pirates, disease, and mutiny and because cargos could be delayed, spoiled, or looted, merchants sought financial protection for their ships and cargoes. Wealthy men including Caldwell were among the first to pool their resources and to insure or underwrite ships and cargos engaged in overseas trade. With friends Barnabas Deane and Caleb Bull, among other leading businessmen in town, Caldwell founded the Hartford bank. The bank was capitalized at one hundred thousand dollars, and 250 shares costing four hundred dollars each were issued. John Caldwell was elected president, a position he held until 1819.[33]

Throughout this period he interacted with the leading mercantile and political leaders of the community including Dean, Bull, and Oliver Wolcott, among others, to increase the prestige and importance of Hartford. Because its citizens played an important role in the war, influence passed from merchants and commercial men in New Haven and Norwich to those in Hartford. These Hartford men were going to exploit that advantage. In 1785 Caldwell was appointed to the Hartford Committee of Accounts and Directors of the City Funds to receive and settle all financial transactions conducted by the town. Later he was elected an alderman and was involved with commissions to construct the State House, to build a bridge across the Connecticut River, and to establish a school for the deaf; Caldwell and his friends also served on a board to establish a chamber of commerce modeled after one organized earlier in New York City, and when launched, he was elected its first president. Not limited to local politics, he was elected to the state legislature twenty times and was a major in the Governor's Horse Guard. Like many of his fellow merchants, Caldwell was a loyal Federalist. The local newspaper described him as "better known and more highly respected than any merchant in the State. He was nature's nobleman. . . ."[34]

Christopher Colt's father-in-law opened doors for him, initiated political contacts for him, and loaned him money to both finance personal ventures and to pay off his debts. In 1806 Christopher had a shop that handled fine and fancy items such as sherry and port wine, East India sugar, chocolate, coffee, and spices, and later included tobacco, nails, cloth, and various seeds.[35] By 1814 Christopher Colt and his family lived on Lord's Hill, a small, expensive district comprised of about one hundred people, among them his father-in-law John Caldwell.[36] With a growing family that now included three boys and two girls, Christopher Colt became interested in local affairs, especially education. In 1814 he joined the school committee and persuaded residents to construct a one-room schoolhouse to be funded through local taxes and tuition fees. His position in the community was enhanced when he became a trustee for the Society for Savings. This institution was the first of its kind in Connecticut and among the earliest savings banks in the country. Members of the governing board represented the apex of Hartford society: Daniel Wadsworth, Charles Sigourney, and the Hosmer, Goodwin, and Bull families.[37]

But the market at this time knew no favorites, and Christopher suffered economic hardship along with his father-in-law. Loans and gifts together with declining mercantile activities brought about by the Embargo of 1807 affected Caldwell's solvency and position in the community. Once the most respected man in Hartford, when he died in 1838, little was left of his fortune. The family home was about all that he managed to salvage. The fate of his son-in-law mirrored his own. Following Caldwell's lead, Christopher speculated in land, finance, and manufacturing, and by 1820 Christopher Colt was bankrupt. Income from a trust fund established by John Caldwell for his grandchildren kept the family afloat. Christopher's anguish intensified when his wife Sarah died in 1821. They were married in 1805, and she was just twenty-nine when she died. Trustees took over the fund and administered it supplying funds only to the children.[38] Sarah left Christopher Colt with a large family; in addition to daughters Margaret Collier Colt and Sarah Ann Colt, four sons survived her death: Christopher Colt Jr., Samuel Colt, James B. Colt, and John Caldwell Colt. Few could have anticipated the futures of these four men: an unsuccessful silk manufacturer who died estranged from his paternal family, an arms producer, a judge and potential political candidate for senator, and an ax murderer.

Several years after his wife died, Christopher married Olive Sargeant, daughter of a local jeweler, and began a second family. The family's financial circumstances were precarious, a situation that continued for decades. First the Colt family moved to Ware, Massachusetts in 1830. Christopher Colt assumed a position as an agent in a textile factory, a job he held only for a short time. Business failures followed. By 1834 he was again back in Hartford, this time planning to open a silk mill. Ever optimistic, he noted that although his last business had failed, "the wheel of fortune seems once more to be rolling in my favour. I am now engaged in organizing a new company, say the Connecticut Silk Mg. Co. to be located at the Stone building in Front St. formerly the Brewery & do expect to have the management of the concern with a salary that will afford a support." Still, funds were short. The Colts' home on Prospect Street was open to boarders, and Mrs. Colt took in four or five lodgers at a time to supplement the family income.[39] Christopher's pursuit of silk manufacturing did not work out, however. By 1841 he was selling his real estate as well as some equipment, including calendars, winding machines, and presses, to be used for calendering and packing goods.[40]

Christopher Colt's itinerant search for employment opportunities coincided with a change in the Colt family dynamics. His second wife Olive was practical, parsimonious, and a disciplinarian. One contemporary noted of her, "A step-mother's vocation, where there are any offspring nearly grown, is by no means enviable, even if her tastes and aims are in entire accordance with those to which the children she must adopt have been accustomed; but where the difference is radical, discomfort can scarcely be avoided, no matter how adroit the management."[41] At the time of this marriage, her stepsons included John, thirteen; Christopher, eleven; Samuel, nine; and James, seven. Although the boys from the first marriage all attended school, the new Mrs. Colt preferred to see them quickly settled into practical occupations rather than extending their education. For many of the sons, she became the epitome of the stepmother interloper who manipulated their father for her own ends. Whether or not that was true, all the sons except Samuel experienced difficulty with Olive and Christopher Sr., and the family began to break apart. It was during these years that Christopher and Olive Colt agonized over the future of the boys.

In 1834 their sons Christopher Jr. and James Colt could be found in Savannah, Georgia, one employed as a clerk in a grocery business and the other as a bookkeeper. After visiting Christopher Jr. and James, their father wrote, "They board together & both in one room, this makes it pleasant for them. If they plan I think they will do well for themselves but if they make a misstep it will be all up with them, but I hope for the best & trust there is yet in store some good fortune for my sons."[42] For James, relocation caused some despair. After leaving for Savannah, he stated, "I wish I could spend my existence beneath my father's roof-comforting him in his old age & shedding a tear over the graves of those dear friends (mother and sisters and brother) who have gone before me, but no it is impossible wishes, hopes can do nothing."[43] While the eighteen-year-old James was homesick, his older brothers appeared more estranged from the family. When in Hartford, Christopher Jr., for example, had stayed at a local hotel rather than with his parents. His family only heard rumors of his movements about town.[44]

John continued to be alienated from his parents after he left home. The only news of John arrived through his brothers, and that information was sketchy. When the boys were in Savannah and Samuel was about to travel south, it was rumored that John had left the area and was either in Montreal or perhaps looking for a position on the Mississippi or Ohio Rivers. While Olive offered little sympathy or concern for John, his father wanted all of his sons, including John, "well located & doing a business that afford fair prospects for a respectable living." He desired the same prospects for himself.[45] Christopher Colt was to live for another fifteen years. During that period, his financial situation remained strained as he tried to support his young second family and simultaneously assist his grown sons.

The boys reacted to their father's misfortunes in different ways. While Samuel was able to overcome the unsettled circumstances of his upbringing and create a fortune, his brothers were not so lucky. They seemed to suffer from Christopher Sr.'s peripatetic quests for a home and a successful business. Like Christopher Sr., they never achieved the recognition, success, or security that they were pursuing. These circumstances established the basis for sibling conflict and enmity.

JOHN C. COLT

After his mother died, John had a troubled relationship with his parents. He wished to attend West Point but instead found work as a clerk and later a bookkeeper in a nearby town. But he defied his parents, deserted his employer, and ran away to New York where he became involved with gamblers and criminals. Although he returned home, the situation was not harmonious, and he left again, vowing not to return. His travels took him to Baltimore, Wilmington, Massachusetts, and New York, where he found jobs ranging from business manager to clerking for a lawyer. He spent a short time at the University of Vermont where he established a reputation as a first-class debater. Like his younger brother Samuel he took trips around the country from Ohio to New Orleans, lecturing on chemistry and other scientific subjects. John was far from a failure. In 1835 he wrote a book on bookkeeping that became a major text going through eight editions. He also lectured and taught bookkeeping in Ohio and Kentucky from 1835 through 1837.[46]

But John ran into some difficult economic times, and by 1841 he was living in New York and working as a clerk. It was there that he became notorious for the ax murder of Samuel Adams. After an argument with Adams over his debts, Colt killed him, chopped up his body, and attempted to send it to New Orleans in a crate. The ship was delayed, and when the stench from the crate became unbearable, suspicious sailors opened it up and found the body parts. The New York papers created a sensation out of this murder, painting Colt as a scoundrel who deserved to be hanged. Reporters were fascinated with Colt's personality and depicted the story of his life as a prelude to this horrible crime. Digging into his past, they portrayed him as a professional riverboat gambler who had committed perjury to both enter and leave the marines and a criminal who had been arrested for burglarizing his employer's crockery shop. He was considered a sexual deviant who had a public affair with the wife of a rich planter and was currently living with a woman, Caroline Henshaw, who was not his wife. Samuel Colt, by that time somewhat famous, came to John's defense and hired a team of lawyers including Dudley Selden, a Colt cousin, former congressman John Morrill, who had defended an abortionist, and the Irish attorney Robert Emmett. They contrived various defenses for Colt, from self-defense to insanity (John's younger brother James claimed in a newspaper that insanity ran in the Colt family). The trial was spectacular and lurid. The prosecution argued that Colt had shot Adams in an act of premeditated murder. The defense disputed this claim, and Adams's severed head was exhumed and brought to court. Though the defense succeeded in showing that an ax rather than bullets had killed Adams, the very act of showing the jury the gruesome head probably sealed Colt's fate. On November 18, 1842, Colt was sentenced to hang. But before the execution could be carried out, Colt was found dead in his cell, ostensibly having committed suicide. A fire broke out at the hour when Colt was to be hung, and although never proven, rumors abounded that Samuel Colt had absconded with his brother, paid off jailers and the coroner, and even substituted a dead body in the morgue in place of John.[47]

Christopher, Jr., and James B. Colt

While John's fate was perhaps the most dramatic of the Colt band, his other brothers, especially Christopher Jr., also experienced hardship. Christopher Colt Jr. was born in 1812 as the second son of Christopher and Sarah Caldwell Colt. He entered the silk manufacturing business with his father, and following in the family tradition of advantageous matrimony, in November 1837 he married Theodora DeWolf of Bristol, Rhode Island, daughter of a leading merchant. His business career was a disappointing one, and much like his father, he moved from one town to another trying to find a permanent settlement: beginning in Savannah, moving to Connecticut during the 1830s, then to New York, Dedham, Massachusetts, Paterson, New Jersey, and finally back to Connecticut. Throughout his short life (for he died in 1855 at the age of forty-three), he could not establish a permanent home anywhere. During his stay in Savannah, the family was hopeful but cautious that Christopher and his brother James would succeed. Samuel Colt noted that "they are now in a good part of the country to make their fortunes," but he cautioned "they will require much self command to stear clear from all the dissipations of that country—gambling, and wine drinking are the two worst and as all the Colt young men not expected have a fashion for the former."[48] This venture did not work out, and by 1836 Christopher was again in New England, this time looking for opportunities in Norwich, Worcester, and Boston. His family knew not to question him about his prospects as he "[was] very sensitive & extreme caution must be used" when discussing his future.[49] Marriage did not seem to anchor him, though it gave him access to business contacts that promised both riches and infamy.

As in his father's first marriage, young Christopher's fortunes in life were tied closely to his inlaws. His wife's father was George DeWolf. The DeWolf family of Bristol, Rhode Island made their fortune from the slave trade, unlawful privateering, and rum dealings. They "had the largest interest in the African slave trade of any American family before or after the Revolution; theirs was one of the few fortunes that truly rested on rum and slaves." Even after Rhode Island prohibited its citizens from participating in the slave trade in 1787, and the Federal government banned the importation of slaves in the first decade of the nineteenth century, the DeWolfs continued in this business. They merely moved some of their operations from Bristol to Havanna Cuba. There James DeWolf owned a large plantation worked by over one-hundred slaves. George DeWolf entered this family business and the money he made secured him a prominent place in Rhode Island society.[50]

By 1803 George DeWolf owned one brig and soon thereafter acquired a share in another. During the initial years of his career, he operated his business with impunity, for penalties were few and those that existed were rarely enforced. In 1818 the situation changed when the U.S. Navy was authorized to track down slave ships and reward those who provided information on "blackbirding." Two years later, slavers were considered criminals and subject to capital punishment.[51] But this did not hamper George DeWolf. Even after the slave trade was outlawed, he went underground, continued his business, shifted his attention to Cuba, engaged in privateering, and led the life of a wealthy, respected Bristol businessman. Local politicians either ignored the law or accepted bribes to look the other way; town residents tolerated the business because much of their economy depended on it and other ventures conducted by the slave traders. Even when the federal government created a customs district in Bristol to control the slave traffic, the DeWolfs were able to install their own candidate as customs agent, a former captain of one of their slave ships, and thus they continued to circumvent the law.[52]

Yet George's fortunes declined, and in 1825 he was unable to deliver a cargo of sugar to its destination; his Cuban sugar crop had failed, and panic ensued. Banks called in their notes; creditors demanded payment; and local residents who had invested heavily in his schemes insisted on an explanation. Bristol residents rioted, looted his home, and demanded recompense. Rhode Island banks refused to accept notes drawn on Bristol banks, and the local economy collapsed. The situation became so dire that George DeWolf absconded to his father's Cuban plantation taking his wife and children with him. Other relatives had to leave town as well. One relative noted "the disastrous failure of a cousin, George De Wolf, by which the whole town of Bristol was wrecked and the whole family connection impoverished. . . . all the uncles and cousins suffered more or less."[53]

Christopher Colt had married seventeen-year-old Theodora with high hopes of economic fortune, but like so many of the Colt marriages, a seemingly fortuitous financial situation deteriorated as the DeWolf family lost its wealth. Christopher spent time in Cuba dabbling in the slave trade, but as the trade became illegal, the DeWolf family's problems intersected with his own. Christopher and Theodora were forced to move from town to town, living in Connecticut, New York, Massachusetts, and New Jersey, where Christopher tried to make a living as a bookkeeper, silk manufacturer, or pitchman.

By the 1840s Christopher could be found living in the small town of Dedham, Massachusetts. Their household consisted of several young children and Theodora's father. Never able to recoup his fortune or reputation, George DeWolf visited his daughter in 1844 and died inconspicuously in that rural, hard scrabble town.[54] He had not been able to return to Bristol, and for the next twenty years, his children remained exiles from that town. From Dedham, Christopher's family moved to Paterson and then back to Hartford in the early 1850s. By then Christopher was ill, and as one associate noted, he "has been sick of late. His liver is affected probably by the manner of his life heretofore."[55] He was broke and living with his wife and five children in a local Hartford hotel. His father, Christopher Colt, had died in 1850; his stepmother who had inherited a considerable amount of money avoided him; and he was estranged from his other siblings.[56]

Sick, indigent, and resentful, Christopher disparaged his brothers. Jealous of Samuel's success, he pressed his claim that he had made improvements to Colt's pistols and was not compensated for them. According to his brother James, Christopher "talks to much for his own or any body else's good, and with every body. . . . It is certainly rich to hear the town talk and speculations of the hour. They may get me ruffled in my temper—a very bad thing—in which event I shall be very apt to hit 'anything that is loose.'"[57] In May, Christopher Colt Jr. died homeless, alienated from his brothers, and impoverished. This estrangement continued even after death, for Christopher stipulated that he did not want to be buried near any of his relatives. Destitute, his wife and children were evicted from the hotel, and they "obtained cheap board in some family."[58]

Neither the DeWolf nor the Colt families wanted to take responsibility for Christopher Colt's widow and children. A protracted discussion began between James and Samuel Colt over the welfare of their nieces and nephews. Theodora announced that she wanted to remain in Hartford, but James told her "that she must look to her own family and friends for advice."[59] He described her as "very inefficient so far as taking care of a family and the most dependent woman I ever knew. I think she is a very pure minded woman but wants some one to direct and advise for she seems utterly incapable of going ahead Yankee girl fashion." James's interviews with her were "very unpleasant," but productive. It was decided that the family should be split up: two of the youngest boys were sent to New Hartford to attend school; the daughter Isabella was sent to live with Samuel Colt and his family; and the eldest boy resided with a Colt family friend Harry Brach. In an almost unbelievable turn of events akin to a fairy tale, Theodora's fortunes changed dramatically. Upon the death of her brother-in-law Samuel Colt, she challenged his will, won a large settlement for her family, and later returned to Bristol where as Madam Colt she dominated Bristol society. The family regained what they had lost including their magnificent mansion, Linden Place. One of her sons, LeBaron Colt, graduated from Yale, studied law, and later represented Rhode

Island in the U.S. Senate. Another son, Samuel P. Colt, became a successful businessman; and her daughter Isabella married well.[60]

But that was in the future. Christopher Colt Jr.'s death exposed many of the tensions within the Colt family, especially the sibling rivalries among the brothers. This was also true of James B. Colt, the youngest of Sarah Caldwell Colt's sons. Despite success as a judge and erstwhile politician, he depended on his brother Samuel for advice and support. He was unable to commit to any career, and his family chided him for idleness and implored him "to do something for his own support" rather than depend on the gifts of others. Throughout his life, however, he seemed unable to break away from Samuel, and his interests circled around the edges of his brother's life. Like Samuel, he sought to go to sea. In 1834 he went to Washington, DC hoping to secure a midshipman's appointment. His father despaired and believed that although "I hope he may . . . it is very doubtful if not entirely hopeless."[61] After that attempt failed, in 1836 James went off on a jaunt to Texas, returned, and decided that he wanted to be a lawyer or a politician and expected Samuel to support him emotionally and financially in that decision. His father cautioned Samuel against giving him money: "He has so long been idle or reading books that has given him a desire to be a politician or a lawyer or something that is to make a great man of himself that I fear it will soon be too late for him to make himself useful in any way."[62] His concern was prophetic. Christopher Colt Sr. tried to interest him in the silk business but to no avail and eventually relented and suggested that Sam might have to help him. James was placed with an attorney to study law, and in 1849 he was appointed to the bench in St. Louis, Missouri.[63]

Missouri was an exciting place to be in the 1850s, and it was a center for much of the national debate on slavery. Thomas Hart Benton, one of the state's senators, had earlier engaged in a contentious fight with John Calhoun over slavery and disunion. A slaveholder himself, Benton adopted the position that one could simultaneously support slavery and be a Free-Soiler.[64] The two men struggled over issues including abolition, recognition of Texas, the question of Oregon, military appropriations, protection of slavery, and national union. James Colt observed this debate, Benton's struggle for reelection in 1850, the ethnic riots of 1854, and the tumultuous demonstrations that occurred thereafter. James was attracted to this rough-and-tumble politics that rewarded quick thinking and eloquence, qualities that he believed he possessed in abundance. He put out feelers to his brothers suggesting that he might like to enter the U.S. Senate, and in that capacity he could be of considerable use to the family. He assured Samuel that he was "a sober, steady, industrious citizen" who eschewed high living and treasured family life. In fact, he went further and chided his brother's carousing and womanizing: "High living and excitement is not what it is cracked up to be. God knows how you have stood it so long. Sensible Sam don't get savage when I tell you that I don't have a wife in every port." What he wanted was "love and long life and as much money as you can reasonably spend."[65] Samuel was not forthcoming, however, which only increased his rage.

Though desiring a political life, James was involved in his brother's armaments business both in the United States and in England, which only increased the tensions between them. The British enterprise caused the first noteworthy rift in their relationship. For a time James had managed Samuel's English armory, and he believed that he and Samuel Colt had an arrangement whereby James was entitled to one half of the profits from the enterprise. James claimed that his brother had broken his word and failed to give him the promised money. Again and again James criticized his brother; for two years he tried to get Samuel to settle the claim: "And so ends my lost hope so ends two years of labor. It is true I thought you meant something when you talked a hundred times of your having done nothing for your own family yet. . . . God forgive you for the past."[66] Harry Brach, a friend of the Colt family, became so concerned about the simmering rift between James and Samuel that he cautioned the latter about the strange behavior of the former. When James was in Hartford for the funeral of Christopher Colt Jr., Brach observed the following behavior:

> During the time he was here and particularly at the time he left his mind was in a very excited state and in the opinion of his friends damned near deranged—his whole conversation and acts were more like a crazy man than James Colt natural. . . . He feels that you have not done right by him in not coming to a settlement or making some permanent arrangement in writing that he may know with certainty what he has to rely upon having lost the high position he had attained. . . . He will not be persuaded that he is wrong in his impressions and so broods over his imagination and has worked his brain to a fever heat making the wildest and insane speeches possible about past matters in your own family."[67]

As with Christopher, Samuel's success seemed to drive James to near insanity. A resentful James criticized Samuel's arrogance, warning his brother that "you don't seem to act towards me as you did before you had accumulated a large estate."[68] Furthermore, "you state that it is your wish to have me have an interest in the new organization—that you think I should have got sufficient insight into your business when engaged in it to enable me to do what would be required of me but there would be no use in my beginning again unless I intended to make it my business for life and settle permanently in Hartford."[69] If he was to work for Samuel again, he set certain conditions: first, he wanted the deed to the Wethersfield Road house and the adjoining lot; second, he wanted a salary of at least four thousand dollars annually. Samuel initially resisted these conditions, and for years the brothers fought bitterly. Eventually Samuel relented, and by 1860 James Colt was living on the Samuel Colt homestead. After Samuel's death in 1862, James successfully contested his brother's will, eventually settling with the executors for one hundred thousand dollars, and he received close to the remaining amount in dividends until his death in 1878.[70]

Samuel Colt

Samuel Colt faced the brunt of his brother's criticisms because he was the success in the family. Bright, charming, industrious, and rambunctious, he became a favorite of his parents. He even had a good relationship with his stepmother Olive. She and Christopher Sr. made special provisions for Samuel. For example, they thought that he would benefit from an education. In 1830 Samuel Colt was a student at Amherst Academy, a classical institution designed to prepare young men for college. His stepmother Olive was under the impression that he was there to acquire a knowledge of navigation, and she encouraged him to pursue his studies with "energy and vigour." She wrote, "You see then Samuel, that self-application is necessary to the gratification of your inclination in your favorite pursuit and a thorough knowledge of navigation will be a great advantage to you in a voyage upon the seas." She cautioned him,

> Now when making a choice of your occupation it is time to pause and reflect, you stand as it were upon an eminence, a given point of time, for you to take your stand. Look around on the one side you see the abode of wisdom and virtue enter in through her gates. On the other, that of vice and folly. Her habitation leads to misery and wretchedness pass not by her gates turn away, stop by on the other side. Give up the low frivolous pursuits of a boy and determine at once you will pursue the steps of manhood.

At the same time she let him know that he could set sail aboard a New London ship, which would be a more practical use of his time than attending Amherst Academy.[71] His stay at Amherst was short. He was suspended for pranks and other disruptive behaviors, allegedly setting off an explosion in the school.

Olive and Christopher Colt were undeterred, however, and made Samuel's career a priority. Using Olive's family connections, they learned that several ships were being outfitted for voyages, some to the Pacific and others to the South Atlantic. Samuel's father requested help from a New London relative acquainted with maritime activities. He wanted to know if Samuel could become an officer, and if so, how he would go about accomplishing this feat. Further inquiries were made into any vessels due to depart from New London and whether or not they had a full compliment of sailors. Christopher Colt was told, "Your son could get a whaling voyage all most any time in a months notice and some times immediately, but he would have to go before the mast one voyage before he could be an officer as it is required that the officers should have some experience in the business."[72]

For those engaged in seafaring, whaling was probably the least favored type of voyage. Sailors whose fortunes hit bottom, who could not find another type of ship, or who were escaping the law or other personal problems were those most likely to board a whaling vessel. Most of these voyages were long, and the one offered to Samuel Colt was to sail from New London on a three-year venture to the Pacific Ocean in search of sperm oil.[73] Samuel turned a potentially useless experience into a central component of the Colt myth, as Samuel's alleged time at sea plays a prominent part in Colt lore. While on a voyage to Calcutta, Sam ostensibly became almost dumbfounded by the churning of the paddle on the ship. In a moment of almost divine revelation, this motion gave him the idea of the possibility of a repeating pistol that could be fired continuously. The veracity of this story has been questioned by historians. Not only was the idea of a repeating weapon in the armaments air, so to speak, but it is unclear if Sam even went on this voyage. The conclusion to be drawn from this episode is that Sam recognized the value of a good story, and his ostensible sea adventures began the mythological construction of his inspirational genius that was to play a prominent role in the advertising and sales of his weapons. But what is clear from Samuel's childhood are the supportive efforts of his parents, which continued into his adulthood.

Back on land, Samuel Colt established his first major business venture in Paterson, New Jersey, the hometown of his cousin Roswell. In the 1830s, he constantly called on his father for financial support and advice. Christopher Colt supplied both. His son was always without funds. At one time he asked his stepmother Olive to make some shirts for him so that he could sell them. "I have not got a whole shirt to my back but the three sent to me from Connecticut or a dollar in my pocket to pay for the making of those now with you," wrote Samuel Colt to his father. "I wish therefore for charity's sake that mother would forward my shirts to me & I will be able to sell enough of them to pay the remainder of the bill for there making. Can you get any money from the Hartford banks?"[74] Although engaged in his own silk manufacturing business, Christopher Colt was able to provide some cash. In 1836 Samuel asked for eight hundred dollars and was told it was forthcoming. But his father also suggested that he turn to investors for funds, including his relatives Roswell Colt, Dudley Selden, and family friend H. L. Ellsworth, all of whom would play central roles in Samuel Colt's life: "To enable you to make the most out of the Fire Arms my opinion is that an act of Incorporation must be had & that some of the first men in this Country must be interested in the concern not forgeting our friends Mrss. Selden, H. L. Ellsworth, Roswell Colt & such public men as may hereafter be desired appro[priate]."[75] Roswell Colt proved to be a good friend to Samuel, and so would Ellsworth who was especially important as director of the federal patent office.

Samuel Colt received several patents for his armament inventions, which set him on the path to success. After Christopher Sr. died, Samuel would become the de facto substitute father of the Colt clan. But he had to contend with his dysfunctional family, including his jealous brothers, conniving inlaws, and various cousins and uncles who would become prominent actors in his life. This is not to say that Samuel was the benevolent patriarch of the family. He too was plagued by psychic demons, as he stepped on, ignored, or took advantage of relatives in his single-minded pursuit of success. The relations between Colt and his family represented a veritable witch's cauldron of psychic conflict, exacerbated by a new capitalism that was replacing all relations, even familial ones, with "callous cash payment," in Karl Marx and Friedrich Engels's terms.[76] This incredibly ambitious family demonstrated the perils and promise of an emerging industrial capitalism and its problematic relationship to the idea of a stable family. Samuel's success was the mirror opposite of his brothers' and father's failures, as the new freedoms of antebellum America destroyed as many people as it enabled. Such conditions forced many in the Colt family to take risks and embrace a dynamic, changing capitalist system that left little room for the traditional values represented by families such as the Slaters. Perhaps Samuel maintained his confidence in this turbulent time because of his father's and stepmother's clear favoritism toward him. In any case, like his father Christopher Colt and great uncle Peter Colt, he never gave up in his pursuit of riches and status. More substantively, he learned from his family that political and social contacts were an essential component of economic success and that personal charm could open doors. Like his great uncle Peter Colt, he developed a strong sense of patriotism that would inform his massive advertising campaigns for his guns. Yet Samuel's path to wealth and power was not easy or assured. He, too, would dramatically fail before achieving great success.

Chapter 2

The Education of Samuel Colt

Samuel Colt certainly knew how to throw a party. Shortly before his marriage to Elizabeth Hart Jarvis on June 5, 1856, Colt invited friends as well as his laborers to attend a gala reception at his new Hartford office building, known as Charter Oak Hall. Although ostensibly a party for his workers, it was in reality a testament to the ego of Samuel Colt. Upon entering the hall, visitors saw a staircase decorated with sixty muskets that Colt had refashioned as rifles. As the guests walked further into the space, they were met by a large portrait of Samuel Colt flanked on one side by an American flag and on the other by the state of Connecticut's coat of arms. Beneath the portrait, more rifles encircled a bronzed stallion fiercely raised on its hind legs, the symbol of Colt's manufacturing enterprise. Colt revolvers crafted in the shape of stars were centered between the windows, all of which were filled with rifles and pistols. Finally, when guests looked up to the ceiling, a cluster of revolvers attached to the gas chandeliers pointed straight down at them. As the *Hartford Courant* reported, "The general effect may be better imagined than described."[1] Colt's penchant for guns, ostentatious wealth, self-promotion, and spectacle was extreme even by present-day standards.

The guns and symbolism of Charter Oak Hall represented the fruits of Colt's burgeoning gun empire. A rugged, bearded six footer, Colt lived as a larger-than-life figure. He had come a long way from the boy who had gone to sea in search of adventure. However, a recurring theme from Colt's youth informed his personal approach to the arms industry. Colt, always confident even as a young man, realized that only those with ambition and abundant egos could make it in the ultracompetitive weapons trade. "You had better blow out your brains at once and manure an honest man's ground" than compromise your ambition, he had written to his half brother William.[2] His road to success had been a difficult one, and he surely believed that he deserved to trumpet his riches and fame. Yet Colt's path to success had not been easy: he had embarked on a youthful and ultimately unsuccessful venture as a fictional "Dr. Coult, lately of Calcutta, London, and New York," traveling throughout the nation from 1832 through 1835, demonstrating the astonishing effects of the new drug nitrous oxide (laughing gas) to mesmerized crowds, relentlessly pursuing profit and fame, and enduring many failures. Indeed, he would only enjoy his achievements for a scant six more years, for he died in 1862. But Samuel Colt was not a man to question his motives or rethink his past. He most likely put these thoughts out of his mind, for action rather than introspection had created the Samuel Colt of 1856. Through dogged determination, showmanship, and an uncanny understanding of popular tastes, desires, and symbols, he had created *his* empire.

The 1850s had been very good to Samuel Colt. In 1854, he was received in the Russian Court of Czar Nicholas I, among many other European monarchs. An international celebrity, he was one of the few American businessmen with worldwide contacts. By 1851, his Colt revolver had become a symbol of the fight for the West, and Colt was a household name. He was rich as well as famous. Colt seemed to be the exemplar of the self-made American man, an entrepreneur who became successful through hard work and ingenuity, overcoming many disappointments along the way. Colt saw himself in this manner, portraying his life as a rags-to-riches triumph through personal strength, a robust work ethic, and industrial genius. Some of this self-perception was accurate. His early life was marked by the death of his mother. The young Samuel Colt had led an arduous existence. After his experiences as "Dr. Coult," he had initially gone bankrupt in attempting to manufacture firearms in the early 1840s, and his attempts to convince the federal government of the practicality of his underground submarine land mines as safeguards for American harbors were unsuccessful. He had failed to enlist the support of the inventor Samuel F. B. Morse and his telegraph for other schemes.[3] In spite of these disappointments, he later reached the zenith of American society, ostensibly through his own prodigious efforts.

But, of course, success stories are seldom so individualistic and self-serving. Colt owed much of his accomplishment to moral and financial support from his father, Christopher Colt, his cousin, Elisha Colt, and especially his rich and shadowy first cousin, once removed, Roswell Colt. The latter not only supplied funds for many of Sam Colt's ventures but also served as a role model for a new type of speculative, risk-taking entrepreneur walking the line between legality and corruption, traits that characterized Sam Colt throughout his life.

Roswell Colt and Samuel Colt took advantage of a new capitalist society that began to arise by the middle of the nineteenth century. As the market gained a greater foothold in American life, more lenient attitudes toward the accumulation of debt arose. Bankruptcies multiplied and no longer retained the moral and financial stigma of failure.[4] New lands and new markets opened to Americans, and entrepreneurs increasingly speculated on Western economic opportunities. The early Republic also witnessed an expansion of scientific knowledge and invention, from Morse's telegraph to Cyrus McCormick's mechanical reaper. Emerging mass-production techniques allowed manufacturing entrepreneurs to become major forces in shaping the destiny of the United States; they began to overtake merchants as the primary sources of economic innovation. Small arms producers were central to this process. They pioneered new types of uniform production, which were then taken up by other manufacturers.[5] Further, the market for arms increased dramatically in the 1840s with Westward expansion.

Yet, despite these favorable trends, Colt was initially a failure. Ventures from his Patent Arms Manufacturing Company factory in the 1830s to his attempt to construct a submarine battery in the early 1840s proved to be unsuccessful. But these experiences provided Colt with a real-life education, teaching him the importance of contacts with family and politicians and giving him insight into the nature of a new American marketplace, lessons that would last a lifetime. He learned the moral values and business practices that would characterize his entire life. Most importantly, he came to recognize the symbols and images that would resonate deepest with the sentiments of the public as he developed an understanding of the American character as insightful in its own way as the more celebrated works of authors such as Tocqueville.

Colt was also shaped by the new populist and egalitarian social climate that was emerging in the United States in the 1830s, symbolized by Andrew Jackson, which influenced everything from popular culture to politics. Success for Colt would depend on navigating the new populist and democratic terrain of the Jacksonian era. For Colt, the age of Jackson proved to be the crucible that formed his personality, for he experienced defeat, triumph, and ultimately redemption.

Samuel Colt in the Age of Jackson

The 1830s was among the most tumultuous decades in American history. There was little certainty or stability in any aspect of national and personal life. In politics, the celebrated, flamboyant hero of the 1815 Battle of New Orleans, Andrew Jackson, sought to change Washington. Jackson's ascendancy to the presidency in 1828 marked a change in American democracy, as notions of a "natural aristocracy" of leaders shared by many of the founding fathers, from Thomas Jefferson to John Adams, gave way to a more egalitarian, populist, and raucous politics. Criticized by his opponents as a foolish, uncouth backwoodsman, Jackson reveled in these criticisms, eagerly embracing the mantle of a man of the people. He levied charges of corruption, fraud, and abuse of power against his "aristocratic" and "elitist" political opposition. He was particularly exorcised by the Second Bank of the United States (BUS). As a supporter of hard money, he believed that the paper money and easy lending policies of Nicholas Biddle, the President of the BUS, harmed the economic prospects of hard-working small farmers and wage earners while enriching a mercantile elite. The BUS became a symbol of aristocratic corruption for Jackson and his followers. He fought against the BUS throughout his Presidency and vetoed the bill that would have rechartered it.[6]

Jackson was not opposed to the Western expansion of the United States, however. During his terms in office, the growth of frontier towns and an increase in European immigration created a dynamic and unsettled populace. As many Americans moved west, Jackson signed the Indian Removal Bill, which relocated Native Americans to lands west of the Mississippi River. The removal policy opened up vast amounts of territory to settlers and land speculators. Land companies, state legislatures, and individuals all tried to cash in on the former Indian territory. A scramble for the Oneida lands in New York and the Cherokee lands in Georgia and elsewhere ensued. Jackson himself speculated in Indian territories and earned much of his reputation by fighting Native Americans.[7]

The expansion of the West and the egalitarian mass politics inaugurated by Andrew Jackson overlapped with and influenced the rise of a new American popular culture. Samuel Colt immersed himself in this new world of deception, novelty, shock, and sensation. Colt would only reach the height of his fame after traveling throughout the country as young Dr. Coult, a learned "medical specialist" who had nothing to do with guns. These trips throughout the United States, from Cincinnati to New Orleans, convinced him of the importance of the West for the future of his weapons sales. During this time, he began to vaguely outline a plan to achieve such success. For Samuel Colt, this new popular culture was a veritable cauldron of ideas and experiences, brimming with opportunities for anyone willing to seize them. Yet, like any culture in formation, its contours were less than clear, and Samuel had to experience its diversity to harness its vitality for his own ends.

As a nineteen-year-old heading north from a trip to New Orleans on the Mississippi River, Samuel Colt undoubtedly knew that he had a talent for showmanship. He had successfully performed his act as Dr. Coult dispensing nitrous oxide in cities from Cincinnati to New Orleans. Yet he was still unsure about his future. He knew that gun manufacturing was his passion, but he had not quite realized how to achieve his dreams. Colt may have had an epiphany on the Mississippi, apprehending that his flair for the dramatic could translate into a profitable gun business. He was in New Orleans during one of the most devastating epidemics to hit that city, as cholera killed five thousand people. He boarded a riverboat leaving New Orleans and was immediately met by passengers who had succumbed to the cholera panic. They asked the only doctor on board to help them. Dr. Coult had but one solution for their illness: laughing gas. He gave all who seemed ill a dose of nitrous oxide. The "sick" recovered, and Dr. Coult's reputation grew even greater. After the riverboat docked, news of Coult's remarkable skills at curing cholera became public knowledge, and people came to him for healing, almost as if he was a Messianic figure. Colt quickly left the area, preferring the life of the inventor to that of the healer. While Samuel Colt recognized that in reality none of the passengers was seriously ill, he also may have come to other significant conclusions.[8] He understood that people were hungry for men and machines that could make them feel safe and secure in a frightening, unpredictable world, and they would pay handsomely for it. Colt also may have realized that people were thirsting for a man of genius who could provide solutions to their problems.

Other performers were also learning the tricks of the trade in this new world of deception and entertainment. While Samuel Colt's travails as "Dr. Coult" predate the exploits of P. T. Barnum, it is Barnum who is most closely associated with the birth of American popular culture. In 1835, he decided to market Joice Heth, an African American slave who was supposedly 161 years of age, as the oldest person in the world and the nursemaid of President George Washington (none of these claims were true).[9]

Unlike the elite culture of the upper classes of New York and Boston, this was a disorderly working-class culture, epitomized by the rise of the penny press, museums showcasing exotic wares, black-faced minstrel performances, and freak shows. Commercial and ubiquitous, this new culture was created by "hawkers and walkers."[10] Puppeteers, peep show exhibitors, and animal showmen, among many others, traveled throughout the urban centers of the east and the frontier west, performing in places from street corners to taverns. They carried the materials for their shows with them from town to town, as curious onlookers might see a man traveling with anything from an orangutan to a hot air balloon. These performers pioneered new types of publicity, taking out advertisements in the newly popular penny press, printing handbills and bulletins for public display, and attempting to expand their popularity through word of mouth. Even well-known lecturers such as Ralph Waldo Emerson and Washington Irving embraced some of these new techniques, as lines between elite and popular culture blurred. This was in many ways a magical culture where deception mingled with reality, the genuine with the artificial.[11]

Medicine men were part of this "itinerant culture," and Samuel Colt as "Dr. Coult" presented himself as a respectable man of science whose knowledge of nitrous oxide could enlighten people regarding the latest scientific discoveries. Beginning first on street corners, Colt eventually worked his way up to lecture halls giving addresses on natural philosophy to complement the laughing gas shows. On a trip to Albany, New York, a local newspaper covered his performance and reported, "We never beheld such an anxiety as there has been during the past week to witness the astonishing effects of Dr. Coult's gas. The Museum was crowded to excess every evening and so intense was the interest which was manifested, that the doctor has been compelled to give two exhibitions almost every evening."[12] Dr. Coult played with these illusions quite self-consciously, confusing trickery and reality. Like P. T. Barnum, he practiced a kind of "artful deception" as a purveyor of laughing gas, tying his showmanship to a pseudoscientific discussion of nitrous oxide's history and benefits.

Dr. Coult also learned that people were attracted to sensational and dramatic portrayals of danger and redemption. The successful businessman required not only ingenuity and showmanship but also the subtle qualities of the artist who was able to reach the inner emotional depths of his audience. While visiting his brother John C. Colt in Cincinnati in 1833, Samuel teamed up with the sculptor Hiram Powers to put on a show that combined his expertise as a doctor in tune with the mysteries of the body with Powers's vision of the mysteries of hell that awaited the sinful. Cincinnati museum owner Joseph Dourfeuille turned to this combination of Dr. Coult's laughing gas demonstrations and Powers's "Infernal Regions" in 1833 after attempts to provide "serious" artifacts to museum goers failed to generate a profit. The show would begin with Dr. Coult's exhibition of the wonders of nitrous oxide and his learned discourse on the topic. But ticket buyers were treated to more than Dr. Coult's orations and experiments. They were presented with a vivid portrayal of a hell that still struck fear in an America that had only recently distanced itself from its Puritan past; yet this was a hell that was also entertaining. Drawing on Dante, Powers created a vision of the netherworld with wax figures, paintings, and mummies. An advertisement for the show described it as "The World to come . . . and comprising, Hell, Purgatory, and Paradise." A graphic depiction of Dante's *Inferno* was the centerpiece: "In the centre is seen a grand colossal figure of Minos, the Judge of Hell. He is seated at the entrance of the INFERNAL REGIONS. His right hand is raised as in the act to pronounce sentence, his left holding a two-pronged scepter. Above his head is a scroll on which are written the concluding words of Dante's celebrated inscription, 'Abandon hope, all ye who enter here!'" The advertisement goes on to state, "Birds and animals of hideous form and evil omen are fluttering over the heads and tormenting the sufferers. Large icicles hang from the rocks that form the Gate of Hell, and reflect on their bright surface the red glare of the fires within." Powers also developed a device that gave anyone touching the wax figures an electronic shock, provoking among the customers "astonishment, terror, and subsequently . . . fun."[13]

Colt had been intimately involved in the construction of the "Infernal Regions," supplying Powers with fireworks that heightened the emotional intensity of the exhibition. He not only recognized the appeal of danger linked with entertainment in the show but also used imagery from this display. Colt was fascinated especially by the centaur, the Greek mythological half-horse, half-man figure who represented the boundary between nature and culture. The centaur figured prominently in Dante's seventh stage of hell, but Colt managed to turn the monster into a civilizing hero whose human form became the pioneer or soldier merged with his horse. When Colt began producing his guns in 1836, carved representations of centaurs killing Indians were often prominently displayed on his pistols' handles. Colt's attraction to symbols like the centaur was not simply a passing fancy but went to the core of his identity. The popularity of the "Infernal Regions" and his acquaintance with Powers convinced him that artists best understood the needs and desires of the people. In Sam's words, "There is virtue in every heart, however depraved, which can be reached by a penetrating artist."[14] His experiences as Dr. Coult, while demonstrating the importance of showmanship, cemented his emerging sense of himself as an artist with the public as his canvass.

Colt also discovered the importance of the new penny press at this time, and his later success in firearms was due in no small part to his newspaper advertisements and favorable press coverage. Most nineteenth-century newspapers supplied business information, a scattering of international news, and a discussion of local, state, and national issues. Many had a clear political bias and were often supported by political groups. Their wealthy subscribers and sponsors ensured that these newspapers, often costing six cents, would remain elite representatives of opinion. By the mid-1830s a new penny press arose, led by Benjamin Day of the *New York Sun* and James Gordon Bennett of the *New York Herald*. They quickly became powerful organs of public opinion. These inexpensive papers relied on advertising and sales to the working class and frequently attacked the respectable press. They emphasized sensational stories of crime, scandal, and corruption that the elite press would not touch, often displaying headlines in bold type.[15] These papers appealed to workers, presenting a view in their own language of the world governed by chance, hoaxes, and self-interest and presenting their journalism as a means to ferret out truth from falsity. For example, in the spring of 1841, patrons of the penny press eagerly read the lurid stories, descriptions, and commentaries about the death of Mary Rogers, the "Beautiful Segar Girl." Seduction, abortion, licentious behavior, crime, and mysterious violent death claimed the New York City headlines for weeks.[16]

Samuel Colt utilized this new sensationalistic press for his own devices, befriending and sometimes paying reporters to write stories that publicized his arms ventures. Of course, he was thrown into the maelstrom of the New York penny press because of the murder trial of his brother John C. Colt. As Samuel became engaged in this tragic event, he not only supported his brother but, as was his custom, looked for opportunities to promote his revolvers. At one point during the trial, the prosecutor charged that John had used a pistol to kill the man. Samuel Colt, realizing the potential publicity bonanza for his guns, gave a demonstration of the accuracy and speed of his revolver. He actually shot at a target in the courtroom, showing that a revolver could not have been used in committing the crime.[17]

During this ordeal, Samuel Colt contacted his relatives in an attempt to raise finances to support his brother's defense. Colt's cousin, the rich merchant and speculator Roswell Colt, contributed a sizable sum to Samuel for the defense but requested that his name be kept out of the public eye.[18] This was characteristic of Roswell Colt, who shunned the limelight as much as his cousin Sam craved it. It was also typical that Roswell lent Sam money for various ventures. Sam borrowed money from Roswell twice in 1835 when he left the lecture circuit for the manufacture of firearms.[19] Samuel set up his initial factory in Paterson, New Jersey, under the tutelage of Roswell. Roswell also wrote letters of introduction for Samuel to the secretary of the navy and to members of Congress, among others, who helped Samuel receive a patent for his revolver in 1836.[20]

ROSWELL COLT: THE ORIGINS OF CASINO CAPITALISM

Samuel Colt's initiation into the political culture of Jacksonian America was guided by his cousin Roswell. In many ways, Roswell Colt served as Sam's benefactor and entrepreneurial prototype. But Roswell was not necessarily a wholesome role model. An innovative entrepreneur, speculator, investor, and friend to politicians, businessmen, and bankers, he also was known as a scoundrel and swindler who was deeply in debt and managed to just stay one step ahead of his creditors. Roswell was among the first entrepreneurs in the New Republic to see that money and reputations could be made by working on a national stage, and taking advantage of the opportunities offered by this new government. He was adept at using his friends and family to secure money, position, and power for himself. Samuel Colt learned several valuable lessons under Roswell's guidance: he learned to use friends and government officials for his own purposes; he adopted Roswell's very loose interpretation concerning the legality of bribing government officials; and he mastered the art of living in a grand style that was important for the image of a successful entrepreneur, even if it meant great personal debt. Finally, like Roswell, Samuel discovered that his enormous personal charm could be put to profitable use. If Samuel Colt was similar to today's publicity seeking CEOs, Roswell Colt exemplified the consummate insider, such as today's insider trader, using his exclusive contacts in government and business to enhance his fortune.

Roswell Colt made his initial wealth through his ownership and management of the Society for the Establishment of Useful Manufactures (SUM) in Paterson, New Jersey. Imagined by Alexander Hamilton as a blueprint for American industrial development in 1791, the SUM raised capital for the construction of a textile mill and mill village along the Passaic River. The project failed, and the stock appeared worthless. It was at this point that Roswell Colt was persuaded by his father to acquire as much of the so-called useless stock as possible. He did, and he turned his investment into a very profitable business to promote large-scale industrial development. Especially during and after the War of 1812, the SUM was reorganized, and Roswell Colt took advantage of economic opportunities offered by the conflict. During the war, Americans were deprived of British goods, and American manufacturers scrambled to construct factories to satisfy the domestic market for yarn and cloth. Colt had little interest in manufacturing goods himself, unlike many New England businessmen including the Boston Associates and the Slater family. Roswell Colt's SUM would develop along a different path than the newly built textile mills of New England. Colt abandoned all plans to construct and operate factories or workshops himself. Instead he decided to lease land and water privilege sites to prospective manufacturers. He engaged in stock speculation, derived incomes from leases, set the terms and pace of industrial settlement on the Passaic River, and guided the development of a new city, Paterson.[21]

He also cultivated personal ties that brought him fortune and recognition. An advantageous marriage increased his wealth and guaranteed him entry into the best homes in Baltimore and New York. He married Margaret Oliver, daughter of the wealthy Baltimore merchant Robert Oliver, who "was one of the greatest merchants in America at the time, and this connection advanced Roswell immeasurably."[22] The Colts lived lavishly first in Baltimore, then New York, and finally Paterson. After his marriage, Robert Oliver persuaded Roswell to move to Baltimore. Roswell confided to a friend, "Mr. Oliver insisted I should give up business, remove to Baltimore & live with him, saying he would make up to me for any losses."[23] Oliver kept his word and advanced his son-in-law $100,000 to construct a house that he built but never occupied and another $277,000 that Roswell promptly invested in shares of BUS stock and in business schemes owned or organized by his family.[24]

Roswell Colt, however, preferred the society of New York and New Jersey to that of Baltimore. Around 1830 he built a four-story mansion in Paterson costing one hundred thousand dollars, and there he and his wife raised their ten children and entertained leading politicians, businessmen, and celebrities.[25] He also kept accommodations in New York City where he regularly dined with wealthy and prominent officials and residents. In both New York and New Jersey he entered into friendships that would prove useful to his family and his business. He was well acquainted with New Jersey officials, members of both the Jackson and the Van Buren administrations, congressmen, businessmen, and bankers.

Playing both sides of the political field, he befriended Jacksonian Democrats and their Whig opponents, though his sympathies surely were with the latter group. He was a friend, confidant, and provider of funds to Whig politicians and businessmen such as Senator Daniel Webster, and Nicholas Biddle, head of the BUS and foe of Presidents Jackson and Van Buren. Biddle took over the presidency of a languishing Second Bank of the United States in 1823, reviving it through careful control of the money supply that restored financial stability. Roswell handled Biddle's personal business transactions, buying and selling stocks and securities, speculating in land, and serving to advance the interests of the BUS. In April 1837 Biddle confided to Colt, "The times are bad and must soon be better. My great ambition is now and has been to prevent a breaking up of confidence. . . . So cheer up and be ready to begin a fresh career."[26] Though Biddle would eventually leave the bank, it was not before Roswell Colt managed to profit from his friendship with the president of the BUS.

Roswell also nurtured other important contacts. New York was a bustling city in the early nineteenth century, displacing Boston as the financial capital of the nation. Its free spirited, entrepreneurial ethos fit Roswell's personality. He belonged to the Hone Club of New York, which was made up of like-minded entrepreneurs and politicians and was one of the most influential and prestigious political, economic, and social associations of the day. Only twelve men drawn from New York City and the surrounding states were asked to join this exclusive club in 1838. Members included Moses Grinnell, who owned a large shipping business and headed the firm of Grinnell, Minturn and Company, Richard Blatchford, a lawyer and agent of the Bank of England, and Philip Hone, after whom the club was named. Elected mayor of New York in 1825 as a Whig, Hone served only one year but remained at the center of local politics and society. He was counselor and agent to such powerful senators as Webster and Henry Clay. The former frequently dined at his home, was a guest of the Hone Club, and became an "intimate companion."[27] But Hone did not limit his friends to businessmen and politicians. His interests were broad, and he entertained authors, scientists, educators, and actors, including Samuel F. B. Morse, James Fennimore Cooper, and Fanny Kemble.

The money, position, political connections, and business acumen accumulated by Roswell Colt over the years were used to support his immediate and extended family. On the board of directors of the SUM sat his brother John O. Colt and several of his cousins. Family members looked to Roswell for funding, advice, and political contacts. In addition to helping Samuel Colt, Roswell assisted his own brother John in operating the Paterson Manufacturing Company, which produced cotton duck. Roswell endorsed several notes for him including one held by the BUS for fifty thousand dollars and another held by the American Life Insurance and Trust Company for an undisclosed amount.[28]

Roswell Colt's life seems like a success story, as he appears to be a generous and farsighted businessman who helped his family while entertaining powerful and important political and economic figures. But Roswell's methods were not always so pure. He used his relationship with Biddle to procure inside information on stock prices and other business ventures. Aware of the illegality of their transactions, Biddle and Roswell engaged in some bizarre interchanges. To avoid detection, Biddle sometimes communicated with Colt in code: "I mentioned Mr. Webster—His natural and proper ambition is 455—0662—096370—that will soon Y708—perhaps the 49470 of 570070037 except the 4Y94264 if they are very 557," wrote Biddle to Colt. Translated, the correspondence read, "buy—good—stocks—rise—banks of Mississippi—abandon—low."[29] Colt took this advice and acquired almost fifty-seven thousand dollars worth of stock in a Yazoo, Mississippi bank.[30] In May 1838, Biddle informed Colt that "to night my advices are from Washn that the virtual repeal of the Specie Circular which has passed the Senate will pass the house in a day or two. This will satisfy us and I will make an immediate move for a general resumption in conjunction with the South and West. . . . this will give an opportunity of repairing the losses of your friends which I have often heard you deplore." He urged Colt to "act promptly" and purchase local depressed stocks together with some of the stocks in specific New Orleans and Natchez banks.[31]

Roswell also received sizable loans from the BUS secured by Biddle. Although the exact amount of the debt owed to the BUS is not known, it appears that he borrowed over $300,000 to meet obligations.[32] In one letter, Biddle notes that $259,000 was lent to Colt, and he states to Roswell in another, "I can only say that you may rely with perfect certainty on getting the $20,000. How, when, or where you must say but have it you shall."[33]

Roswell's shady attempts to secure wealth could not keep up with his appetite for spending it. He accumulated enormous debt as his attempt to "keep up with the Hones's" required more and more cash. His lavish spending, speculation, investments, and loans to family and friends overwhelmed his ability to pay off his obligations. To one of his New York brokers in 1835, he was committed for over fifty-five thousand dollars, and his fortunes continued to decline. With the onset of the Depression of 1837, his stocks lost ground, and several of his investments in Paterson ran in the red.

Yet Roswell always managed to outsmart his creditors. For example, it is doubtful that Colt ever repaid the bank loans that he had secured during Biddle's tenure. Following Biddle's retirement from the Bank, Herman Cope, a bank official, began to press Roswell for funds. Negotiations dragged on for years, and as late as April 1842, the loans remained outstanding. However, no hint of impropriety was attached to the relationship between Biddle and Colt. As president of the Bank under both national and state charters, Biddle effectively brushed aside accusations that involved any abuse of power. Investigations of loans granted to newspaper editors, federal employees, and relatives during the 1830s found little wrong with the administrators of the Bank. No one investigated the Colt connection.[34]

Roswell's disreputable dealings extended into his personal life. His wife left him in the 1830s, convinced he was a liar and a scoundrel. The event that finally precipitated the split occurred over the construction of a new home in Paterson. After Roswell disregarded her opinion and put his personal plans for the house into place, she left him, taking six of her ten children with her. They failed to reconcile, and her family had little respect for Roswell Colt and his business acumen.

Her family even took him to court over Robert Oliver's will regarding the $300,000 he had advanced Roswell over his lifetime. They won a judgment, and Colt was under an obligation to repay $277,000 to the estate of his father-in-law.[35] To pay this debt, Colt conveyed a bond and mortgage on the SUM plus additional company leases to the Oliver family. This transaction, however, came to the attention of the SUM board of directors and stockholders complained charging Colt with fraud, duplicity, stealing and mismanagement. This was not the first time that Roswell had been caught using SUM assets for his personal use. This was a well tested maneuver, one that he had employed earlier to pay other commitments.

While his financial situation was precarious, his personal life also was floundering. Roswell's qualities as a businessman were not well suited for fatherhood. His sons turned out to be drunkards and failures.[36] Their lack of ambition and persistence clearly distressed Roswell. But what his children lacked, his cousin, Samuel, manifested in abundance. He became a surrogate son to Roswell, and he proved an excellent student of the business practices and ethical beliefs of Roswell Colt. Under him, Samuel learned to trust his own instincts, to outmaneuver company trustees and directors, to obtain lucrative government contracts, to use and often abuse contacts, family and friends, and to make and spend money. Colt opened his first fire arms factory in Roswell's home town of Paterson, New Jersey.

Samuel Colt's Paterson Factory

As Samuel Colt gazed upon his Paterson, New Jersey factory in 1836, his sense of joy and accomplishment must have been enormous. Freed from his alternative persona as Dr. Coult, he could devote himself to the manufacture of his weapons. The architecture of the mill reflected his emerging sense of greatness and his vision of an American Empire. In appearance, the mill looked unlike any other weapons manufacturing establishment. Four stories high, containing an attic and a bell tower, the factory melded firearms into its very design, integrating form and function. One commentator noted, "On the spire which surmounted the bell tower was a vane very elaborately made in the design of a finished gun and in front of the mill was a fence, each picket being a wooden gun."[37] Replicas of guns were everywhere. The factory represented a homage to Colt's fascination with his invention and his early recognition that symbols would be of central importance in the marketing of firearms.

Yet Colt was not simply a dreamer, for no detail of his production of guns was unimportant to him. He organized his workers into teams laboring side by side as Colt attempted to transform the artisan production of guns into a more standardized, uniform process. He undoubtedly felt proud that workers made guns of his invention and design—and for Samuel design meant more than mere function. As he viewed the elaborate artistic displays of his weapons, his thoughts may have drifted back to his time as Dr. Coult in the West. He had found an engraver, Gustave Young, who could translate his artistic ideas into reality through a special roller die that "impress[ed] a picture on the round cylinders" of his firearms. The handle of his pistols portrayed the centaur of the "Infernal Regions" fighting with wild

Indians. The handle of one of his first weapons, a ring-lever rifle, pictured a hunter proudly brandishing the weapon over a fallen lion and angry men using this firearm to fight for their freedom against tyranny. Images of the American eagle were also prominently displayed on the weapons.[38]

Though Samuel may have looked upon the mill with pleasure and saw himself as an artist as much as a businessman, the factory's financial problems and manufacturing difficulties would test his perseverance and self-respect. From its very founding, the Patent Arms Company demanded much of Samuel Colt. The procuring of funding for the enterprise had not been an easy task. Samuel approached Roswell Colt in Baltimore in 1832 mapping out preliminary arrangements for the manufacture of firearms. But Roswell was still a bit leery of Samuel's intentions, and this is when Samuel took to the road as Dr. Coult to raise funds for his manufacturing establishment. Nevertheless, Samuel Colt did not hesitate to ask his uncle for money early in his career. Moreover, like Roswell, Samuel quickly learned not to fear debt. In February 1834, for example, Samuel Colt was notified by his New York bank that he was overdrawn upwards of $5,000. In a note of explanation to his benefactor Roswell, he tried to explain the situation: "I am not quite certain that I adopted the most prudent course, but I thought that as we had funds in Bank to the amt of near half of the note which fell due yesterday it was better to overdraw than to suffer your note to be returned to Philadelphia, which would have undoubtedly been done before or by the next morning, as they are now so much on the alert during the present excitement that I had the notice of the overdrawing in less than one hour."[39] He also admitted that within the coming week, he owed another $7,685 and was without funds. This did not bother Roswell, as he allowed Samuel to continue to draw upon him for several more years.[40]

Samuel's accumulation of debt increased in proportion to his determination to manufacture and market firearms. The firearms industry was in its infancy in the United States. While the government attempted to manufacture arms itself, it also looked to private contractors in the weapons trade for innovation. The principle of the revolving breech had been known for many years, but Samuel perfected it, making it practical for ordinary operation. He began to pursue a patent for his revolving firearm. Patents were much easier to secure in Great Britain than in the United States, for the process of acquiring a patent was still in its initial stages in the early Republic. To finance a trip to Europe, he signed an agreement with Joseph Selden, a friend of the Colt family, to convey to him partial ownership (one-eighth) of his patents.[41]

Already recognizing the potential of a global marketplace, he left for Great Britain in August 1835. He soon received patent rights for his guns in England and in Scotland. He decided against disposing of any more of his patents until they had been approved by the U.S. Ordnance Office and reported to Congress.[42] Once Colt returned to the United States, the Colt family began a campaign to secure the exclusive patent rights for his firearms. Roswell Colt and Samuel's father Christopher Colt wrote letters to their friend Henry Ellsworth, head of the Patent Office, on September 22, 1835; Ellsworth had just taken up his appointment, and he was persuaded that Samuel could get the necessary patent.[43] Another sector of the government was also approached. Roswell wrote letters of introduction for Samuel to P. Dickinson, secretary of the navy, and to members of Congress.[44] Samuel's desire for a patent was successful, and he received it on February 26, 1836.[45] He was now ready to begin construction of a factory to manufacture his weapons.

The gun factory was to be located in Paterson, New Jersey, the residence and business location of Roswell Colt. New Jersey had to charter the new enterprise, and Samuel turned to Roswell and Dudley Selden for assistance. Selden was an attorney, a cousin of the Colts, friend of Roswell, and a former congressman whose family already had invested money in the Colt scheme. He would play a significant role in the newly formed company. With Roswell's aid, Selden secured a charter in March 1836 from the New Jersey state legislature for the new concern.[46] Money had to be raised for this venture. While Selden became the first treasurer and assumed initial control of the business activities of the firm, much of the fund-raising success belonged to Samuel Colt. Though Selden demonstrated the revolver to prospective subscribers and Roswell spoke of the enterprise to his friends, Samuel Colt's charm was a key to persuading wealthy individuals to invest in his firm. Samuel was a young man of twenty-two with very little experience in the manufacture of guns and no capital. Yet he not only convinced members of his extended family, such as Roswell Colt and Dudley Selden, to invest in his projects, but he also induced investors from prominent New York and Philadelphia families to subscribe to the stock of his company. Thomas Emmet, a well-known New York financier and lawyer, took one hundred shares and served as president of the enterprise; he and Samuel persuaded other family members, William and Robert Emmet, to pledge funds as well. William Edgar, a founder of the New York Yacht Club, took another one hundred shares, while Jacob Randolph, New Jersey hardware merchant and gun dealer, held one hundred shares. William LeRoy, brother-in-law of Daniel Webster and navy agent for New York, held one hundred shares. Herman LeRoy, Webster's father-in-law and a founder of LeRoy, Bayard and Company, once the largest shipping house in New York, and a former employer of Roswell Colt, acquired one hundred shares. Later he would become chief executive of the Bank of New York, which issued short-term loans to merchants using their merchandise as collateral. The largest number of shares, however, was held by Selden and Samuel Colt: 200 and 250 shares respectively.[47] The firm was capitalized at $230,000.[48]

An unusual business arrangement was made: the Patent Arms Manufacturing Company was separate from the ownership of the patent. While Dudley Selden was elected to the board of directors and became treasurer of the firm, Colt continued to perfect his guns and hired Pliny Lawton to set up the Paterson works. Colt and the firm's investors had expected to begin production with nine months, but they did not realize "what it meant to take handmade models and make reliable production pieces out of them, especially when the inventor was constantly making changes in design."[49] Moreover, problems between Colt and Selden were just beginning. Eventually the business arrangements would contribute to a rupture in the company and in the relationship among the shareholders.

The running of the factory and the production of weapons required amounts of cash beyond the initial capital investment, which Samuel Colt did not have. Always short of funds and continuing the itinerant ways that he had begun as Dr. Coult, he constantly took to the road trying to sell his guns and find bargains for machinery. Samuel traveled to Springfield, Massachusetts, and to Harpers Ferry, Virginia, to secure the best equipment available at the cheapest price after the firm was founded.[50] He set his sights on the U.S. Government, journeying from West Point to Florida to promote his firearms. The federal government believed that a viable armaments industry was essential to the defense and protection of the United States and that the country must be independent of foreign manufacturers. The government supported the establishment of two armories, one at Harpers Ferry and a second at Springfield. It also encouraged private entrepreneurs to manufacture firearms and issued contracts to various businessmen and gunsmiths.

Samuel Colt eagerly pursued the riches promised by government contracts. But he only found disappointment and failure in his attempts to secure them. One example of his frustration occurred at West Point in 1837. While still perfecting his guns, Colt fiercely competed with other firearms manufacturers. Rival inventors John Cochran and Baron Hackett also sought government contracts, and they tried to persuade the Ordnance Department to conduct trials to see which gun would be most useful to the army.[51] West Point was chosen as the site for the competition, scheduled for June 1837.

In a unanimous vote, Colt lost the competition. The Ordnance Department rejected Colt's weapon. They wrote that "this arm is entirely unsuited to the general purposes of the service." It was complicated and unreliable.[52] Colt had spent considerable time and money on the demonstration, and he had been led to believe that his weapons were favored by West Point cadets. He felt abused and deceived by the army. An angry Samuel Colt fired off a five-page, legal-size letter of complaint. He wrote, "I am confirmed in the opinion . . . that a large majority of the Officers of the board had previously determined either from prejudice or interest to condemn at all hazards all the new arms offered for their inspection." He then proceeded to refute every claim made by the board against his guns.[53]

This rejection not only helped solidify Colt's growing dissatisfaction with the government, but it also exposed the simmering conflict between Dudley Selden and Samuel Colt over management of the company. In April, Colt had told James Lawton, a blacksmith working for the firm, that he wanted a number of muskets and rifles produced for the West Point trials. But Selden interfered, scolding Colt: "I have told Mr. Lawton that I am unwilling to have more than one musket, one rifle, one large & one small pistol prepared for the purpose" of the trials.[54] Before the appointed examination period, Samuel Colt had gone to Washington, hosted a round of parties for officers and politicians, and tried to use his considerable charm to persuade them to support his weapons. Of course, the parties were paid for by the Patent Arms Manufacturing Company. Dudley Selden was furious at Colt for the expense. "You use money as if it were drawn from an inexhaustible mine," he wrote in February 1837. "I have no belief in undertaking to raise the character of your gun by old Madiera."[55]

Colt and Selden agreed on little regarding the management and direction of the firm. Colt thought that he could persuade the government to purchase his guns. This required long stays in Washington, holding exhibitions of his weapons, throwing parties and other galas for dignitaries, giving various "gifts" including specially made firearms to politicians and other important members of the government, and traveling to combat zones to persuade army officers to adopt his guns. He used his revolvers as collateral for loans. For example, Colt pledged firearm samples as security for a nine-hundred-dollar loan when entertaining potential clients in Washington, DC. When in New York, Samuel stayed at the Astor House, one of the most exclusive hotels in the city. All of this Samuel attempted to accomplish with little money. Much like Roswell Colt, Samuel turned to imaginative financial bookkeeping and massive debt to accomplish his goals. But because Samuel was not sole master of his financial house, he faced opposition from Selden, who questioned his tactics, ridiculed his skills as a salesman, and argued with him over money. Selden wanted to follow conservative business principles, while Samuel favored a more aggressive approach, going so far as to advocate bribing officials in Washington, DC. This horrified Selden.[56]

Samuel continued to demonstrate the quality of his guns to federal officials and tried to persuade them to purchase his weapons. But fortune evaded Colt. In February 1838, during the height of the Seminole Indian War, Samuel requested funds to travel to Florida to demonstrate and sell his guns to the army. Selden protested, so Roswell Colt agreed to back him. He journeyed to Fort Juniper on the Indian River in eastern Florida carrying one hundred rifles and revolvers to sell to the army. In March, Lieutenant Colonel William S. Harney tested the weapons and submitted an enthusiastic recommendation for their purchase to Major General Thomas S. Jesup. Writing to Colt the following month, he said, "I am still *more confident* that they are the only things that will *finish* the *infernal war.*"[57] Jesup bought fifty rifles and paid Samuel Colt $6,250 in draft form. An elated Colt began his return voyage home. However, Colt's boat capsized at the entrance to the harbor at St. Augustine. Samuel almost drowned, and he lost the $6,250. General Jesup refused to issue Colt another payment, for his previous draft was equivalent to cash. Selden, when he heard of Colt's adventures, was outraged. Dubious of the trip from the beginning, he doubted that Sam had lost the money and demanded "the amount of the draft without delay."[58]

Finally, an incident involving the personal safety of President Van Buren occurred and dashed all hope Colt might have had for an army contract. Colt had arranged to hold a demonstration of his weapons in front of the capitol building. Several men equipped with his pistols were set in a line, awaiting the order to fire. Colt and a group of military officers were intent on recording the precise time of the discharge, and they did not notice the arrival of the president's carriage. President Van Buren exited the carriage and stood on the steps of the capitol. Word to "fire" was given, shots rang out, and the loud noise made the president's horses bolt. The driver was thrown out of the carriage and impaled on an iron railing. Infuriated by the incident, Van Buren was forever prejudiced against Colt's arms.[59]

Given his failure to secure a government contract and beset by an atmosphere of intramural business feuding, Samuel turned to the general public as a market for his guns. News of his invention was widespread, and people began to ask about his guns and rifles. Some wanted them for military duty and others for hunting, defense, and security reasons.[60] By December 1837 the company began to advertise its guns for sale.[61] Within a couple of years, the firm had some success. Members of the armed forces of the Republic of Texas and the New Jersey militia requested weapons from Colt. In 1839, the firm manufactured and gave 300 rifles to members of Congress; the New Jersey militia received 120 carbines and 120 rifles; and the Republic of Texas Navy bought 180 carbines and 108 pistols, its army 100 rifles and 160 pistols.[62] Yet Colt was unable to market these guns to the population at large. Retail, the rifles cost from $125 to $150, an amount of money well beyond the financial means of the average person. The firm did not make a profit, and Samuel was always living on the edge of a financial precipice. He asked Roswell for loans "to save him from utter destitution" and kept his financial circumstances hidden from the Board of Directors.[63]

Samuel Colt's personal ordeal was shared by many others in the Panic of 1837 and its aftermath. The 1830s had been a decade of economic uncertainty. Economic turmoil in the firearms industry was symptomatic of declines in the manufacturing sector more generally. Factory owners in Lowell slashed wages, and the female workforce went on strike. Cut backs occurred around the state and spread to mills in Slatersville and Providence, Rhode Island and Jewett City and Putnam, Connecticut. Mills in Pennsylvania, New York, and New Jersey also faced economic ruin. Paper manufacturing mills in the Berkshires, shoe manufacturers in Lynn, and readymade clothing operations in the major seaport towns all felt the panic by 1837. These difficulties were not limited to manufacturing. Banking and financial institutions were hard hit, especially the nation's economic capital, New York City. The panic forced banks to suspend payment in specie, and many closed their doors. Other financial centers such as Baltimore, Boston, and Philadelphia experienced a decline of fortunes. Even the plantation south could not escape. Planters could not sell their cotton; banks faced closure; and internal improvement schemes were put on hold. This panic was the precursor of years of depression to follow.[64]

The Panic of 1837 precipitated changes in the Patent Arms Manufacturing Company. By 1839 Selden was out as treasurer. Samuel Colt had the firms books audited, and he found Selden had cheated the company. Selden was replaced by another shareholder, John Ehlers, yet Ehlers, like Selden, did not allow Samuel to pursue his freewheeling vision of capitalism. In January of 1840, Samuel was in Washington trying to lobby Congress to buy his guns, and his prospects appeared bright. As he wrote, "There can be but little difficulty in introducing them into the states service after we have obtained the desired results from Congress & this will soon enable me to be my Companies master in lieu of there controlling me as they have felt disposed to do the last year."[65] Now, however, John Ehlers became an impediment to the company's success. Ehlers failed to meet a contract to furnish the Texas government with guns; he did not respond to Samuel's letters for months at a time; and he did not advance Samuel money. Samuel Colt was frustrated. To his father he wrote, "The prospects for an early introduction of our arms into government service is britening [*sic*] under the new administration & if we had been able to substitute in Mr. Ehlers place a man who felt it his interest to promote harmony, our armory must prosper soon. As it is all is uncertain." Shortly thereafter, the firm went bankrupt, and Samuel was forced to look elsewhere for success. He was not alone, however. About 40 percent of all businesses failed during these years in the middle Atlantic states alone.[66]

THE COLT SUBMARINE BATTERY

Colt's passions and inventions went beyond firearms. After the Paterson experience, he turned to another interest that built on his childhood fascination with explosives. In the 1840s, Colt attempted to create a submarine battery for the protection of U.S. coastal fortifications. Disputes between the United States and England in 1841, particularly concerning the status of the state of Maine, made such issues pressing, as many in the United States were concerned about another English invasion like that of 1812.[67] Colt worked on his battery while living in New York City from 1841–46, renting a studio at New York University. There he studied chemistry and physics, making the acquaintance of scientists and inventors such as Samuel Morse who was teaching at the school and working on what would become the telegraph. Colt belonged to the National Institute for the

Promotion of Science, participating in its exhibitions. This also gave him access to other inventors and scientists.[68]

At this time, Colt invented an underwater mine that could be detonated from some distance away. Although the federal government gave him some encouragement, it was the private sector, as in Paterson, that provided monetary support. While the secretary of the navy procrastinated and then declined to fund "an experiment with the Submarine Battery at the public charge," a committee of the American Institute, chaired by Commodore George De Kay, offered to underwrite such an experiment. To Colt, De Kay wrote,

> Under a belief that the necessary aid would be granted the managers published in their circulars this among other objects calculated to draw together a large concourse of people. They are still willing & anxious to have an experiment tho [*sic*] necessarily on a smaller scale if at the expense of the Institute and to that end have empowered me to arrange the same, will you do me the favour to state as soon as possible what pecuniary aid you will require to enable you to blow up a vessel we will furnish of say Two hundred tons, she will be anchored off Castle Garden, and you are desired to blow her up on the 18th inst at 4 P.M. precisely.[69]

By 1842 Colt had signed up several investors in his Sub-Marine Battery Company. The secretary of the navy was notified of the offer and assured that the experiment would be conducted "without expense to the government or exposure of any secrets connected with my plans of defense." This test would afford Colt "an excellent opportunity to judge something of the amount of power required to be used when [he] make[s] the exhibition to test the questions propounded in the resolution of Congress."[70] Always the showman, Colt saw this as an opportunity not only to inform but also to entertain the public. "On Tuesday afternoon (18th inst) precisely at 4 o'clock," he wrote to his friend William Gibbs McNeill of Stonington, "I shall blow up a large barge (some 300 tons) of Castle Garden for the benefit of the American Institute, & the pleasure of many thousands that will assemble to witness the same."[71]

His demonstration on July 4, 1842, was successful, as his mine blew up a ship in a spectacular explosion, resembling a fireworks display. He also had three other successful demonstrations from 1842–44. However, the government did not fund Colt's invention, as it saw no urgent necessity for mining harbors on the East Coast after tensions with Great Britain abated. Colt also had powerful enemies in the

Congress, such as John Quincy Adams, who saw him as a publicity-seeking charlatan. Moreover, many scientists viewed the battery as an auxiliary to coastal defenses, not worth the investment that would be necessary for harbors to be thoroughly mined.[72]

Though his ventures in manufacturing and in developing a submarine battery were failures, Samuel's experiences before and after Paterson were a real life education for him. His time as Dr. Coult taught Samuel the values and predispositions of the average American. From Roswell Colt he learned and adopted a business ethos that accepted debt and corruption. Like Roswell, he came to appreciate the importance of cultivating personal friendships among powerful government officials, of lavishly entertaining guests, and of giving gifts to politicians when asking them for favors. Samuel also developed his approach to business during this time. Despite setbacks, he learned that promotional stunts were an important component of any successful marketing scheme. Failure had steeled Samuel; he seemed a living example of the philosopher Friedrich Nietzsche's dictum that "everything that does not kill me makes me stronger." He was determined to find a cost-effective method of manufacturing quality firearms. Moreover, Samuel learned that he could only truly depend on himself, that only he should run his business. His experiences with Selden and Ehlers had shown him that other businessmen did not approve of his gambling, dynamic, and risky version of capitalism.

But Colt's greatest insight extended beyond the confines of the economy into the cultural realm. Despite his failures, Samuel's greatest triumph during the Jacksonian era was to adopt, almost by osmosis, distinctive traits that he crafted into an inimitable persona, crystallizing an emerging American character. Colt incarnated the uniquely American traits of egalitarianism, restlessness, and a taste for novelty and change, described by Alexis de Tocqueville, the most perspicacious of observers of America.[73] In particular, Colt embodied a new American individualism that the famous author of *Democracy in America* saw as *the* distinctive quality of Americans.

Yet Tocqueville did not distinguish among types of individualism. There was certainly an economic individualism based on a desire to get rich through hard work and ambition, similar to the selfishness noted by Tocqueville. There was the individualism of the husband and father, the wife and mother, finding their mutual satisfactions in hearth and home. Yet there was also the individualism of the "American Renaissance," as authors from Ralph Waldo Emerson to Herman Melville attempted to craft a new American culture. Emerson, and later Walt Whitman, embraced an individualism that sought a life rich in experience and an inward feeling of joyous rapture, an appreciation of the multiformity of life. Emerson called for a "self-reliant" individual who defined himself not in terms of the past or in terms of borrowed European ideals but who heroically crafted a unique vision of the world. Melville, too, shared in this vision of American exceptionalism, as he opposed a new America to a corrupt and decadent Europe.[74]

Samuel Colt synthesized these different versions of individualism, personifying them in his iconic status as an original entrepreneur/inventor/artist. Sure of America's promise, he underscored his ideas about individualism in an 1844 letter to his half brother William, writing that "it is better to be at the head of a louse than the tail of a lion," and "if I can't be first, I won't be second in anything." Samuel advised William to think for himself. To follow another's dictates "is that of servitude and the soul that can do it is a slave." Furthermore, you must "select the object of your ambition . . . and reach its zenith of your hope, or die in the attempt. . . . Let your aim be high. . . . Think for yourself and act according to your own impulses. If you allow other people to govern you, you subscribe yourself inferior to them." Yet this ambition should aspire to originality and a life rich in meaning, rather than mere money making. According to Colt, "money is a trash I have always looked down upon. . . . Life is a thing to be enjoyed."[75]

Colt's fortunes would change with westward expansion and the proclamation of Manifest Destiny in Congress and the press. The Mexican War of 1846–48 followed by the California Gold Rush of 1849 required weapons for war and self-protection. Internationally, governments from Russia to England engaged in an unprecedented arms race as they prepared for war and the possibilities of civil strife in an uncertain European social context following the upheavals of 1848.[76] Sam Colt's genius was due in part in his Forrest Gump–like luck, as he seemed to appear at the center of almost every major social change of the antebellum period. More important was his ability to take advantage of these social changes that were shaping nineteenth-century America. He used his many experiences in different venues of American life and learned from the failures that had dogged his pursuit of wealth and fame to become the largest arms maker in the country by the late 1850s. Colt's vision of capitalism was to have a profound effect on American culture. The next chapter explores the mature Samuel Colt's economic practices and marketing practices in greater depth.

Chapter 3

Samuel Colt

From Industry to American Empire

The first World Exposition of the Works of Industry held at London's Crystal Palace in 1851 represented a salute to technology, invention, and progress. Reflecting the nineteenth-century belief in industrial development, the exhibition halls were filled with exciting displays from manufacturers. But none was more attractive than the one set up by Samuel Colt. Colt created a magnificent exhibit of his famous six-shooters, shaping five hundred of them into a shield, emblematic of their ability to protect the common man. But what struck the observer most were the beautiful hand-engraved barrels and handles of these pistols, for they resembled a work of art as much as a weapon. Europeans were astounded that such firearms could be produced so quickly in factories using standard parts rather than through the laborious work of individual craftsmen. Despite their aesthetic appeal and wondrous method of manufacture, an excerpt from a U.S. Senate Committee Report attached to Colt's presentation demonstrated the true worth of the revolvers. It read, "On the Texan frontier, and on the several routes to California, the Indian Tribes are renewing their murderous warfare, and a general Indian war is likely to ensue, unless bodies of mounted men, efficiently equipped for such service, are employed against them." [1]

The 1851 Crystal Palace showcased Colt's guns and other innovative American machines. The response to this exhibit was indicative of a burgeoning American gun culture tied to adventure and conquest that Colt helped to create and that endures to this day. Yet Colt was more than an arms maker; he was an early exponent of the American system of production that was a forerunner of mass production. In the nineteenth century, the United States began economically outperforming Great Britain. Colt's distinctive manufacturing process and marketing innovations became the envy of budding capitalists throughout the world. He was an early advocate of an aggressive global empire with American businessmen claiming world leadership through their technological innovations. This was an empire different from those of Europe. Colt and other proponents of empire believed America was not imperialist because it was not fighting other "civilized" countries but actually helping to bring its distinctive values to the world.[2]

Shortly after the Crystal Palace exhibition, on November 25, 1851, Colt gave a lecture to the prestigious British Institute of Civil Engineers that illustrated his vision of America. Colt enumerated several reasons for the success of his revolver on the Western frontier. He said, "Living in a country of most extensive frontier, still inhabited by hordes of aborigines, and knowing of the insulated position of the enterprising pioneer, and his dependence, sometimes alone, on his personal liability to protect himself and family, [I] had often meditated upon the inefficiency of the ordinary double-barreled gun and pistol." Soldiers too needed his weapons, for "the peculiar characteristic of the mode of attack by the mounted Indians, was to overwhelm small bodies of American soldiers by rushing down on them in greatly superior numbers."[3] Colt contended that his pistol was necessary for the protection of the pioneers of civilization in new countries and the preservation of peace in all nations. Colt in fact complained that his revolver had been too successful in the 1837 Florida Seminole War, "for by exterminating the Indians, and bringing the war rapidly to an end, the market for the arms was destroyed."[4]

Colt's straightforward words belie his gift as a cultural entrepreneur, manufacturing meanings as well as guns, and these meanings helped shape American history and made Samuel Colt an icon. Colt drew on and promoted symbols of America and the frontier that still color our understanding of the nineteenth-century frontier and have become a part of the nation's collective zeitgeist. He portrayed the West as a dangerous, warlike place, yet as the land that rightfully belonged to a young, adventurous, and expansive America. Brave individuals, whether soldiers or pioneers, had to summon the courage to confront dangers ranging from Indian assaults to attacks from wild animals. Through the ownership and use of Colt's pistols, settlers and soldiers could master this danger. The taming of the West depended on possession of superior technology, that is, the Colt revolver. Colt's genius was to merge images of his pistol, the self-sufficient individual, and empire into a seamless whole. These ideas fused in his self-created persona as a rugged, patriotic individualist, and the symbols of his business reinforced this image. The trademark for his enterprise, the rampant stallion—its wild eyes flashing, forcefully posed on its hind legs, an Indian arrow clenched between its teeth—represented a warrior mentality, the relentless drive and power of a culture headed West, literally devouring the Indians along the way.

Colt developed his revolver and his ideas in a new American social environment. By the mid-nineenth century a more relaxed attitude toward debt, a national rather than a local economy, and the sanctity of private property guaranteed by a nationally powerful Supreme Court defined this emerging economic and cultural world. Though the antebellum United States was still an agricultural society, it was swept up in the maelstrom of a rising capitalist economy. A new culture of constant change tied to industry and the market was remarked upon by commentators from Marx to Tocqueville. In Marx and Engels's famous phrase, "All that is solid melts into air, all that is holy is profaned."[5] In this context, Colt portrayed manufacturers as heroic figures. He personified the newly formed but now characteristically American fusion of rich businessman and democratic values, for he symbolized the egalitarian, plainspoken American who took on and economically defeated the Europeans in the manufacturing market. Colt was a new type of populist capitalist: while his egalitarian views and support of American imperialist ambitions in the West tied him to Democratic Party presidents from Andrew Jackson to James Polk, his vision exceeded that of almost all American politicians. He grasped the dominant role that America could play in the world. Like many Americans today, Colt saw the United States as an exceptional nation due in large part to its business culture, based on the entrepreneurial spirit of its business leaders. His supporters lauded him as a man who contributed much to his community, from philanthropy to job creation. The *Hartford Daily Times*, citing a birthday celebration for Colt, mentioned his "unmatched enterprise, his energy of industry, and the unstinted and hearty support which he has ever given to every scheme calculated to promote the growth and prosperity of our now flourishing city." In the *Times's* view, he was not selfish, for his enterprise contributed to the wealth and industry of Hartford. He created manufacturing establishments that allowed labor and capital to develop. On the thirteenth anniversary of the founding of Colt's armory, the *Hartford Daily Times* praised Colt for hiring hundreds of workers, including immigrants and women as well as men.[6]

Colt made use of the mania for genius and invention and combined it with a new kind of celebrity status. He was an inventor and adventurer, calling himself "ready for action," a poet "of wood and steel," in his lawyer Ned Dickerson's phrase.[7] Colt viewed himself as fighting against a bureaucratic state and faceless corporate gun makers and as someone who in his very person preserved American values of individualism in an age of rising conformity. He exemplified the inventor who, eschewing formal schooling, managed on his own effort and genius to make a fortune. A letter in the *Hartford Daily Times* from the "London correspondent of the *New York Spirit of the Times*" noted how Colt's weapons were superior to their imitators, lauding Colt as a "man of genius" who provided the opportunity for "heroic fame" in the Seminole and Mexican Wars and fights fought against Indians on the frontier.[8] In a July dispatch from the *London New Quarterly Review* reprinted in the *Hartford Daily Times*, Colt was characterized as "gallant," overcoming the "sneers" of military men to create a reliable, low cost pistol.[9]

Colt validated himself as an inventor through giving papers at conferences and meetings and joining many scientific organizations and competing for technical prizes. While the lecture at the prestigious British Institution of Civil Engineers in 1851 was among his most notable accomplishments, he received his first recognition for inventions at the American Institute in New York, winning awards not only for his guns but also for his submarine battery in 1836, 1837, 1841, 1844, 1850, and 1855. He helped to organize the Connecticut contingent to the Universal Exposition of Industry and Art in Paris in 1855 where he won three medals. He competed in local Hartford and Connecticut scientific contests, winning awards in 1852, 1853, 1856, and 1857. Colt was also involved in the Hartford Arts Union, which was dedicated to the development of the "arts," broadly defined, and in particular to industrial progress.[10]

Colt fought for patent rights and extensions for ten years, which not only validated his inventor/genius status but also prevented potential rivals from entering the marketplace. Patents became increasingly prominent in the United States during the midcentury, increasing from 995 in 1850 to almost 2,000 in 1854. Colt was often in court defending his patents and requesting extensions of them. Colt made use of his celebrity in these battles, for he tied his fight for patents to his genius and concern for the public good. He portrayed himself as the lonely inventor concerned with making his products available to the public while keeping others from stealing the fruits of his labor.[11]

THE MEXICAN WAR AND ECONOMIC SUCCESS

While patents were important to Colt's success, it was not until the Mexican War and the great demand for his revolvers in the wake of that struggle that his path to fortune was assured. Like many Northeastern industrialists, Colt had initially opposed the war, though not for well-grounded reasons. His views changed, however, after receiving a letter from one of the heroes of the war, the Texas Ranger Samuel Walker. Walker had been impressed with Colt's revolver, and he ordered 1,000 of them. Showing an amazing political flexibility, Colt became a war supporter on the spot and embraced the Democratic Party and its expansionist policies. Later in 1847, the army ordered a number of Colt's pistols. His pistols were also becoming popular outside of the military, as many settlers moving West began clamoring for his guns. The army order caught Colt by surprise. Without capital, factory, machines, or workers, Colt subcontracted his order to Eli Whitney Jr. He also paid Thomas Warner, formerly employed by the Springfield Armory, to construct his machine tools and to help him secure whatever equipment was necessary to complete the government contract. Whitney's armory was not as sophisticated as that of other firms, and although Colt had to secure machines and equipment for the Whitney armory from various companies including his own defunct Paterson works, he was able to produce 220 revolvers by June 1847. Little technological knowledge or innovation came out of this business venture. Because he lacked the best and most appropriate machine tools available, Colt had to rely on skilled workers to complete the contract. Labor costs averaged from 65 to 70 percent of the total cost for manufacturing a pistol. Such high costs could not be sustained if Colt wanted to compete successfully for future weapons contracts.[12]

Colt learned several important lessons from this endeavor: mechanization was crucial to achieving product uniformity and cutting costs, and the market for his arms extended well beyond the government. The general public wanted good, not perfect, weapons, and people were willing to pay a high price for them. They eagerly purchased the seconds from private arms manufacturers or the guns that failed in some way to meet government standards.[13] Fresh promotion strategies could target Western frontiersmen, hunters, farmers, and ranchers among others who needed good weapons to protect themselves, to secure food for their families, or to obtain hides for commercial sale. With increased urbanization, industrialization, and immigration and the rise in crime often associated with such developments, even city dwellers could be persuaded that they needed pistols for protection. Colt saw a viable market and was determined to tap into it. Beginning in 1848 and working out of a converted textile mill, Colt set up operations in Hartford.[14]

The product and not the process had guided his earlier attempts to manufacture guns. He came to realize that one required the other. While Colt was not the first man "to conceive of a multiple-shot pistol using a revolving cylinder magazine," he certainly perfected the production of the pistol and made it accessible to a wide market. While other manufacturers might prefer to produce the perfect, albeit expensive, weapon with interchangeable parts, he wanted to turn out a good, inexpensive weapon that would appeal to a mass market. The U.S. government was not the only customer. His concept of manufacturing emphasized mass production, low cost fabrication, and broad market appeal.

He was able to market his guns by taking advantage of the economic and cultural trends of his time. From 1820–45, American Western expansion stalled due to a lack of population growth, limited investment capital, and political disorganization. But by midcentury, not only the war with Mexico but also the acquisition of California, Oregon, and Texas, together with new modes of transportation, encouraged settlers and immigrants to move west.[15] The middle third of the nineteenth century saw an enormous increase in the technical sophistication of guns and other weapons technology, as wars were fought throughout Europe and the Americas. Colt embraced westward expansion justified by Manifest Destiny. For Colt, his weapons and manufacturing in general could help create a vast American empire. The emergence of guns was tied to this empire, as they became symbols of American expansion and power.

Colt's success was firmly in place by 1849. His lawyer, Dickerson, was able to renew the patent that allowed him to prevent competitors from infringing on his armaments. It was also the first year that he made a profit. In 1849, Colt created his pocket revolver, which became the most successful pistol of his lifetime. That year he made the first of several trips abroad to Europe and the Middle East to sell his guns, becoming a global arms merchant. By 1851, Colt employed about three hundred workers, producing forty thousand revolvers a year, increasing to five hundred men and fifty thousand revolvers a year by 1854. He built an armory in London in 1852 but had difficulties with British workers, finding them less pliable than those in America, and it closed in 1857. Yet by 1854, he had become so successful that he was able to build multifamily worker's tenements to house his labor force and to start construction of Armsmear, the Colt's future family home. In 1856 he adopted the persona of a more staid bourgeois and married Elizabeth Hart Jarvis, the daughter of an eminent, wealthy Episcopalian minister. She helped turn Colt in a philanthropic direction. They experienced their share of sorrow; they lost two children in infancy and another was stillborn shortly after Sam died in January of 1862.[16]

COLT AND THE CONNECTICUT VALLEY

When Samuel Colt established his first manufacturing venture in Hartford in 1847, the Connecticut River Valley resembled the Silicon Valley of 1990s California. It was an area of creative small businesses with a surfeit of technological innovation, inventors, and capital available for investment. The arms industry was just a small aspect of this manufacturing mecca. Yet the armament industry helped revolutionize the manufacturing process as industrialists of all kinds searched for more uniform and standard systems of production.

The federal government was especially concerned with weapons, and this history would shape not only the Connecticut Valley but also Colt's approach to firearms. National defense had been one of the first issues addressed by the new American president, George Washington, and the Congress. Experience in the Revolutionary War had demonstrated that the new nation could not depend solely on privately produced weapons or imported arms. Bills establishing national armories passed Congress in April 1794, and the American government began to develop a home-based weapons industry. Springfield and later Harpers Ferry were chosen as sites for the new mission. It was the War of 1812, however, that demonstrated the need to not only manufacture American weapons but to increase arms production and to manufacture a gun that could be easily repaired in the field. New production methods that emphasized the uniformity of parts appeared to be an answer. This was not a novel idea at the time. Some private manufacturers, including Simeon North of Middletown, Connecticut, had experimented with methods of making uniform gun parts. He carried out trials on barrel-turning lathes and developed one of the earliest milling machines.[17] In 1813, North contracted to supply the federal government with twenty thousand pistols with these specifications: "The component parts of the pistols are to correspond so exactly that any limb or part of one pistol may be fitted to any other pistol of the [twenty thousand]."[18]

Asa Waters of Millbury, Massachusetts also addressed the problem of turning musket barrels instead of grinding them. His answer revolutionized stockmaking, but much of the credit for his success belonged to an employee, Thomas Blanchard, a local mechanic who developed a lathe for turning irregular forms. While working with Waters on his grinding machines, Blanchard attracted the attention of Roswell Lee of Springfield who subsequently asked him to modify the armories' grinding machines. Thus began a long-lasting, on-again, off-again relationship with the federal government. Peripatetic, Blanchard moved back and forth between the Springfield and Harpers Ferry armories and between the public and the private sectors. According to Merritt Roe Smith, his new machine "represented one of the truly outstanding American contributions to nineteenth-century technology." The fourteen machines he made "completely mechanized the process of stocking and eliminated the need for skilled labor in one of the three major divisions of armory production."[19]

Governmental research and development programs continued at both armories. At Harpers Ferry, another prominent New England mechanic, John H. Hall, made his name. Much of the credit for interchangeability belongs to him. Originally from Portland, Maine, he too was spurred to action by the promise of government contracts following the War of 1812. By 1820 he was employed under special contract by the federal government to produce rifles at their Harpers Ferry armory. As a private contractor in a government factory, he was accountable to the government for costs and deadlines. Initially he ran over on both accounts. His attention was directed toward making his rifles using a new system of interchangeable parts. And in that, he was successful. Again, to quote Merritt Roe Smith, "John H. Hall stood foremost among those who combined inventiveness with entrepreneurial skill in blending men, machinery, and precision measurement methods into a workable system of production. The achievement formed the taproot of modern industrialism."[20] Interchangeability became an important feature of the American System of Manufactures.[21]

With the introduction or adaptation of Hall's ideas, the industrial production process changed, and the Connecticut River Valley in particular was transformed. Along the Connecticut River, a plethora of new industries associated with metalworking appeared in the nineteenth century. Several factors attracted mechanics, innovators, and dreamers to the region. Capital and a skilled, literate labor force were available. Boston had become a major capital market of the nation, and money flowed in from the textile industry, the China trade, and from British and European investors. Metalworking shops, foundries, and forges among other small businesses flourished. By the 1830s some of these mechanics had moved away from their traditional craft base and were experimenting with a division of labor, mechanization, and a new management style, all to increase production and expand markets. At midcentury, the region was world famous as the meeting place for new manufacturing technology and a testing ground for the American System of Manufactures.

Two hubs, Hartford and Springfield, led the way. The Hartford metalworking community became a center of technological innovation and industrial activity. Many of the leading manufacturers of the day set up operations there. Samuel Colt chose the South Meadow along the Connecticut River in Hartford to build his new armory. He was joined by the Vermont firm of Robbins and Lawrence, who moved their rifle subsidiary, Sharps Rifle Manufacturing Company, to the area around 1852. Shortly thereafter, Francis Pratt and Amos Whitney, whose backgrounds included apprenticeships in Lowell and Lawrence and employment at the Colt armory, set up their own shop to make gauges and machine tools in 1860. Charles Billings and Christopher Spencer followed a similar path before opening their metalworking shop later that decade.[22]

Further north along the Connecticut River, another technology district grew up around the Springfield armory. Firms included the Ames Manufacturing Company, who produced such items as textile machines, cutlery, statuary, and milling machines that it sold to both the wider public market and to manufacturers around the country, and American Machine Works, who manufactured stocking and milling machines. Both benefited from their close links and proximity to the Springfield Armory.[23] These hubs served as training centers for the scores of mechanics who subsequently disseminated precision and manufacturing technology throughout the United States. Many started their own shops, developed innovative machines, processes, and product, and served as teachers and mentors to a new generation of machine tool makers. The new technology was adapted to other industries including pins, screws, sewing machines, clocks, axes, swords, and barrels. A national market opened up for these mass-produced consumer goods.

Over time, as machines replaced men, operatives replaced craftsmen, and factories replaced workshops, men such as Samuel Colt began their careers and built upon the work begun by early mechanics and gun manufacturers. While Colt claimed to be the inventor of the repeating pistol, he drew on these men who came before him. He was able to dominate the market in part because of his advertising prowess and patent protection until 1857 but also because of his use of the engineering ability of Hall and others. Colt was a leader in utilizing cost control as an efficient way to protect market share and gain profits, as he encouraged constant technological innovation. Colt's armory in Hartford may have been the first establishment where all the different aspects of an incipient mass production converged.[24]

While Colt owed many of his ideas to those mechanics preceding him, little of Colt's success would have occurred without the contributions of one man, Elisha King Root. Colt hired Root as superintendent of his factory, and Root's engineering and organizational prowess contributed dramatically to Colt's wealth. Root perfected Colt's manufacturing system, guiding Colt's armory to new heights as it became the largest in the world by the Civil War. From his early days as a traveling showman to his business entanglements with Selden and his failed attempts to gain large government contracts, Colt had tried to find someone who had the knowledge, the determination, and the imagination to turn his concepts into an actual, working gun. Root did that and more. He made possible the production of Colt revolvers for the general market. Just as the Slaters and Lawrence supplied the public with fine and fancy goods and inexpensive sheeting and shirting, Root was able to provide them with inexpensive, well-constructed weapons. If Colt was the imaginative risk taker with novel ideas, his general superintendent, Elisha K. Root, was the artisan, the innovator, and an industrial pacesetter. Joseph W. Roe summarized the relationship between the two men: "The credit for the revolver belongs to Colt; for the way they were made, mainly to Root."[25]

Born in Ludlow, Massachusetts, Elisha Root learned his craft in the cotton mills and machine shops of New England. By the 1830s he found work at the Collins Company, a Connecticut factory that produced hatchets and axes. From 1832 to 1849 he supervised production, developed "machine based metal-forming processes," and introduced a sophisticated division of labor to increase the quality and output of edge tools. While at the Collins Company, he learned a great deal about metal cutting and metalworking methods. He developed duplicate die-forging techniques to solve production problems; he patented a number of machines; and he was one of the first, if not the first, to build special purpose machinery and apply it to the manufacture of a commercial product. His research on forging metal at the ax factory and his experiments on applying die forging to mass production made him a valuable asset to arms manufacturers.[26]

Colt needed a man like Root, and he was willing to pay whatever price was necessary to obtain his services. When he moved to Hartford and began to work for Colt, Root became the highest paid mechanic in New England and perhaps in the United States. Colt's business acumen proved correct. The blending of Root's technological knowledge and his entrepreneurial vision and marketing skills created one of the most significant advances in American business. As Paul Uselding argues, "Given the subsequent history of the Colt revolver, its creation and penetration of one of the first mass markets for a metal-fabricated article in the American experience with a relatively low selling price based on realizing significant production-cost economies, we are on reasonable firm ground in inferring that Elisha Root's work at the Hartford Armory was largely responsible for this successful 'commercialization' of the revolver." Their collaboration "demonstrates a convergence—perhaps the first in America—of essentially all the elements of modern mass production, even though complete interchangeability was not achieved."[27]

Root counseled Colt that uniformity and not the interchangeability of parts was the most economical and efficient way to manufacture guns. According to David Hounshell, "Like all New England arms makers at midcentury, Colt employed a gauging system to control uniformity during production. But the Colt gauging system was probably not as refined nor as rigidly maintained as that used at the Springfield Armory. Samuel Colt and Elisha Root believed that uniformity would be an effect, not an absolute goal, of mechanization. This conclusion is consistent with the overwhelming emphasis on mechanization rather than on the pursuit of precision manufacture at the Colt armory." [28] Both men realized that they had to adapt the available technology to meet their current needs. They operated in an increasingly competitive market for supplies, raw materials, and labor. Their business practices had to be streamlined; their technology had to be just sophisticated enough to manufacture a low cost, widely sought-after consumer product; and their marketing strategy had to be able to reach the widest possible audience. Root, who many believe was the model for "the boss" in Mark Twain's *A Connecticut Yankee in King Arthur's Court*, concentrated on the process, and Colt emphasized the product.[29]

Samuel Colt had finally found a mechanic he could work with and who was able to translate his vision into a real, workable gun. But Colt also was an innovative entrepreneur. He could take an idea and make it better. He utilized inside contractors, a system employed at Harpers Ferry by the federal government, at his Hartford armory. A plethora of subcontractors used his shop floor, machine tools, motive power, and materials to manufacture parts for his weapons; they were free to hire, pay, and supervise their own laborers. Moreover, Colt allowed them to accept business from other companies. Those in his employ included such innovators as rifle manufacturer Christopher Spencer and machine tool manufacturers Pratt and Whitney. Through these contractors, technical innovations were disseminated throughout the arms industry and also were applied to the manufacture of new products such as sewing machines, clocks, and agricultural equipment. But while Colt mechanized production, he was unable to achieve the precision demanded by mass production and the assembly line. Colt was never quite successful in completely implementing the uniformity of work that he desired, for his factories still required skilled labor.[30]

ADVERTISING

Technical changes were important to Colt's success, but marketing was just as central. Colt managed to capture the spirit of a new "democratic art" described by Tocqueville in *Democracy in America*. For Tocqueville, the culture of the market and a rough equality, most advanced in the United States, encouraged the creation of a social and cultural world of images that trumped reality. American businessmen attempted to give their products "attractive qualities which they do not in reality possess." This discussion of advertising *avant la lettre* could only appear in a society becoming obsessed with appearances, where people believed that social mobility was increasingly available to everyone. As Tocqueville stated, "In the confusion of all ranks everyone hopes to appear as what he is not, and makes great exertions to succeed in this object."[31] "Democratic arts" appeal to emotions, sensation, and adventure, all aspects of Colt's marketing schemes.

Colt imagined a new type of individualistic, emotional, and adventurous consumer who would be attracted to his guns, and he sought to appeal to them through his advertising and product development. From icons such as Davy Crockett to the novels of James Fennimore Cooper, the incipient American understanding of success was defined by constant movement in search of new opportunities and adventure, individual effort, and practical know-how.[32] Colt incorporated this sensibility into his advertising schemes. Rather than the thrifty, sober Puritan seeking solace in a sinful world, Colt drew on images of individualistic freemen and patriotic heroes. He envisioned a consumer who focused on his individual desires while seeking adventure and who believed that he could satisfy such urges through purchasing products. This new consumerism grounded in popular culture was linked to the capitalism that was arising in antebellum America. This confluence of populist belief and market activity would challenge the Puritan worldview in arenas from religion to the economy. Individuals increasingly lived in a world of emotions and half-truths and images, amenable to the appeals of advertising rather than to the secure truths of Puritan-inspired religion. For Colt, leisure time should not be a time for sobriety and study, but an occasion for adventure, invention, and expressive development.

Colt's innovative advertising techniques tied his weapons to narratives about the expansion of the West, which gave his guns a romantic and sensational patina that overshadowed their more utilitarian meanings. His revolver allowed white Americans to define themselves as technologically superior to and different from the alien other (the Indians), while providing them with a weapon to eliminate indigenous tribes. Colt drew on images of the strong-willed individual who created a new world after his own imagination yet whose weapon simultaneously promoted Americans' love of equality.[33] As the famous and anonymous quote put it, "God made man, Colonel Colt made them equal." Colt placed his guns within the context of a broad "republican technology," which was an integral part of the movement westward and which advanced American values of democracy and egalitarianism. Republicanism was tied to the idea of the public good and often had anticapitalist implications. But Colt managed to connect his guns and indirectly the market to the desire for American independence from foreign domination, contending that American manufacturing could be a crucial step in this autonomy. Like other inventors such as Franklin, Fulton, Morse, and Whitney, Colt linked American prosperity and moral advancement to the progress of technology.[34] Republican technology also fused beauty and utility; many of Colt's guns were so well crafted that they were stunningly attractive weapons. Moreover, he and other manufacturers contended that the arts and machinery drew on the same creative source and that the inventor's genius was similar to that of the artist.[35] Colt's talent was not only to utilize and exemplify these narratives of technology and progress but also to sell to Americans the spirit of adventure in language and images that they could understand.

Unlike other manufacturers, Colt brought new methods of marketing and advertising to the sale of guns, utilizing the techniques of allure and sensation that he had learned during his adventures as

Dr. Coult and that were associated with P. T. Barnum and the new popular culture of America. Colt's advertising campaigns embedded these promotional gambits into the heart of the manufacturing economy. When marketing his firearms, he used testimonials, accounts planted in newspapers, as well as many unusual, dramatic, and colorful ads to create a mythology about his guns, mixing science and fantasy together to create a powerful image about his six-shooter.

He had a knack for the slogan that could encapsulate an argument in a simple phrase. For example, in opposition to critics of his weapons, Colt referred to his revolver as a "peacemaker." He maintained that his pistols not only deterred violence from criminals who ostensibly feared a battle with a gun owner but also promoted the self-reliance of weapons-toting men who did not require government protection, especially in the West. In his view, well-armed nations were the best defense against war. When he donated a repeating pistol to the Connecticut Historical Society, he referred to his warlike weapon as integral to the peaceful organization of society.[36] Colt was constantly arguing that his gun would diminish wars. The *Hartford Daily Times* went so far as to quote a British clergymen who said that Colt's guns could bring universal peace by making war too destructive. If peace is to be had, "for every priest in a district, there should be 100 revolvers." His guns would make people think twice about using them. Again, quoting the *Hartford Daily Times*, "Place a revolver in the hands of a dwarf . . . and he is equal to a giant."[37]

Colt carefully cultivated relations with the emerging sensationalistic and mass circulation penny press. He benefited from sympathetic and exciting stories that depicted his protagonist, often a Texas Ranger, with peacemaker in hand, fighting wars, attacking Indians, chasing criminals, killing buffalo, or defending himself and his honor. Often he paid journalists to write such accounts or gave them expensive gift revolvers in lieu of direct cash payments.[38] The *Hartford Daily Times*, an avowedly Democratic newspaper, became a Colt supporter almost immediately after Colt's establishment began to produce arms. The newspaper printed dramatic adventure stories in which advertisements for Colt's weapons were intertwined with the heroic actions of two rangers, Samuel Walker and Dan Henrie. Walker, a hero of the Mexican War, had been one of Colt's strongest lobbyists in Washington and had cooperated with Colt in designing new, more effective weapons. However, Walker died in combat a scant two months after the founding of Colt's Hartford armory. What could have been tragedy for Colt's economic prospects, however, turned into a publicity bonanza for him. Colt persuaded the *Hartford Daily Times* to write stories that showcased Colt's weapons being used in romantic Western adventures. The heroic death of Walker was catalogued in the *Hartford Daily Times.* The story placed him in the pantheon of courageous American hero best symbolized by those who died at the Alamo. As the newspaper reported, "[Walker] had met danger in every form—had been wounded and pierced—but escaped from death, till he fell in the last of the fights, when the main force of the enemy had been dispersed."[39] Earlier, Walker together with Colonel Samuel Hays and a handful of Texas Rangers had attacked and defeated eighty Comanche Indians. As well, it was reported that Walker was among three hundred men involved in a fight with two thousand Mexicans. Although they captured and tortured him, he managed to escape and return to the American lines. After this daring escape, he joined the American forces marching into Mexico "armed with Colt's Patent Repeaters." Walker was an integral member in the charge that captured the Mexican general La Vega and was promoted to captain for his actions.[40]

Although a rugged frontier individualist, Walker nevertheless embraced the latest technologies in firearms, as "old customs and old fashioned arms, unwieldy and ineffective, found no favor with him." Rather, as the *Hartford Daily Times* reported, the men under "his command should depend upon Colt's Repeaters alone." This article on Walker's death was immediately followed by reprints of Walker and Colt's personal correspondence. In one letter from Walker to Colt, Walker stated that "the Texans who have learned their value by practical experience, have unbounded confidence" in your weapons. In another letter, he credited Colt with the success of the Rangers, for "without your pistols we should not have had the confidence to undertake such daring adventures."[41]

A later story in the *Hartford Daily Times* portrayed the exploits of Texas Ranger Dan Henrie who escaped from Indians by riding his trusty horse through a raging fire and fighting off a pack of wolves while managing to stagger back to civilization. His pistols were a key factor in his ability to stay alive. The story was followed by a report that Henrie was in Hartford "having traveled three thousand miles to procure some of Colt's Repeaters." The account ends with Colt gladly supplying Henrie with weapons, "though the orders that press upon Mr. Colt, for his pistols, are ten fold greater than he is able to supply."[42]

Colt would often expand upon the romance of the Texas Rangers. For example, a correspondent for the *Hartford Daily Times* stated that it would be a good idea for Colt to take command of the British troops in Southern Africa, arm them with Colt weapons, and teach them to fight like the Texas Rangers.[43] The barrels and handles of his revolvers were decorated with scenes from Ranger-Comanche warfare. Throughout the 1850s, he hosted visits by various Rangers to Hartford and used them to lobby Washington politicians. All of this helped to make him a rich man. Even Sam Houston lobbied on behalf of Colt's weapons, despite not personally knowing Colt. This changed, of course, as Colt tracked down Houston, thanked him, and began a friendship. These testimonials were more than just attempts to entice the government to buy Colt firearms, however. Colt did not neglect the wider public market. After the Mexican War, accounts began to portray adventure and danger on the frontier and how important it was for settlers to be well armed. This change was reflected in Colt's sales, as he sold many more guns to the public rather than to the military in the 1850s.[44]

These newspaper reports also tied the global use of his weapons to the progress of civilization and democracy, the defeat of indigenous savages, and the superiority of the white West. The *Hartford Daily Times* often printed "dispatches" from overseas correspondents who lauded Colt's weapons. One such correspondent argued that Colt pistols should be introduced into the British Army throughout the world. His pistol was said to be superior to British guns in all tests, and it was "a small weapon so simple and easy in its mechanism that a child might load and discharge" it. His guns had made British troops in South Africa into a superior force, for the revolver was "an extraordinary weapon." Its simple workmanship, low cost, and easy portability made it a "match for twelve ordinary guns." It allowed the white man to reestablish his superiority over the "savages" in the Kaffir War in South Africa.[45]

As if these heroic stories and testimonials were not enough to entice buyers, Colt also used exciting and dramatic pictorial displays of his weapons to sell them. He commissioned the artist George Caitlin to paint exotic scenes in which a Colt weapon was prominently displayed. Colt was aware of the artistic appeal of his guns, hiring engravers for the decoration of barrels and handles. He was able to produce a great number of these weapons because of a roll-die engraving machine that allowed for the reproduction of these adventurous scenes. But beauty came with an added cost. Those who wanted ornamental engravings on their pocket pistols could expect to pay an extra four dollars; add an ivory stock and the cost increased another five dollars.[46] Colt was constantly innovating and using new technologies for his guns, which allowed him to contain costs and increase production. The only major advance that Colt overlooked was the creation of metallic cartridges, which allowed Smith and Wesson and Winchester to gain some market share.[47]

Colt was one of the first to introduce direct advertising to consumers. He dispersed teams of sales representatives around the country, provided them with advertising brochures, and counseled them to create attractive displays and arrangements of his pistols wherever they were sold. Moreover, he was innovative in the design of brochures that advertised his guns. Most of his advertising broadsides stressed the low cost and reliability of his pistols, often defending them against criticisms. Sometimes he even grouped several different announcements together. In the May 1860 issue of the *Knickerbocker Magazine*, Colt placed eight different advertisements. They each presented a separate theme: reasons for preferring Colt firearms, price lists, new lines of military and sporting rifles, foreign testimonials, and directions on assembling and disassembling his pistols, rifles, and carbines. It appeared that he used this literary magazine to introduce his new shotgun for the field.[48]

Yet Colt also created very artistic broadsides unique for their time. In a particularly masterful 1854 advertisement, he placed a large picture of a disassembled gun at the center of the broadside, suggesting to the consumer how easy it was to assemble the weapon. The slogan "Colt Repeating Pistols" dominated the lower portion of this advertisement, underlined by Sam Colt's signature, thus playing on his celebrity to guarantee the performance of his weapon. The upper half demonstrated the romantic, adventuresome, and artistic nature of the revolvers, drawing largely on the United States' success in the Mexican War. Ornate borders encased scenes of heroic action involving Colt weapons. The upper portrait was taken from the Colt dragoon pistol, showing the Texas Ranger Hays and his compatriots killing Comanches in 1844. The middle frame featured Colt's navy pistol, showing a sea encounter between American and Mexican ships in 1843. The lower scene portrayed stagecoach passengers using Colt's pocket pistol to slay bandits who had held them up on their westward journey. These pictures were flanked by images of the famous 1759 Battle of Quebec during the French and Indian War and a hunter waving his Colt rifle over a dead buffalo. Such dramatic imagery shows Colt's vision of a new American empire based on military and industrial supremacy and the necessary role of his armaments in creating such an empire.[49]

Colt's promotional campaigns and production of aesthetically attractive guns helped to transform the firearm from a utilitarian object useful for hunting into a central symbol of American identity. Colt tied his products to American patriotism, asserting America's technological supremacy over Europe. Colt's pistols represented American values of freedom and individualism, that one was responsible for his own safety. Colt drew on and promoted the belief that America's push to the West owed much to technology, especially weapons and in particular Colt's pistol. He made sure that the *Hartford Daily Times* published reports of the use of his guns throughout the world, as reports of requests for his pistols from Calcutta to South Africa were duly noted in the paper.[50] As Colt embraced the global market, he and his pistols became an early version of the global brand, like Nike today. His name became synonymous with revolvers as he promoted and sold his guns to the general public and to governments throughout the world. Colt contributed to the militarization of the globe, supplying his guns to anyone who could afford them. Even today, American arms manufacturers are major producers and marketers of weapons throughout the world.

COLTSVILLE

While Colt was innovative in his manufacturing and especially in his advertising techniques, he also tried to design a novel factory village, one that he named after himself. Several notions informed his plans. First, it was financed completely out of his own pocket and reflected distrust and distain for Hartford's financial elite. Colt's animosity toward bankers and moneymen reflected his family's experiences with these power brokers. He had not forgotten the way his father had been treated during the economic downturn of 1819 and the hardships that followed. He labeled such moneymen as capitalists, men who produced nothing and sought to gain wealth at the expense of others. Second, Colt linked his interest with those of his workers to justify his manufacturing activity and to separate himself from the Hartford bankers.[51] Colt saw himself as a productive worker who, just like his employees, actually created a product. Bankers and moneymen, on the other hand, were simply greedy scoundrels. Just as the derogatory and insulting label "aristocrat" was tied to American politicians of all stripes, the Democrat Colt connected the term to capitalists, particularly bankers.[52]

Colt's relationship with his workers was not solely contractual but combined elements of tradition, especially paternalism, with market-oriented beliefs and practices. Unlike the nativist tendencies exhibited by the Slaters and Amos Adams Lawrence, Colt freely embraced European immigrants of all backgrounds, going so far as to build a replica of a German village in an attempt to entice workers to come to Hartford. Yet, like his contemporaries, he required a disciplined, docile workforce. To achieve this, he built a town around his factory and attempted to preserve social peace through a paternalistic culture. Although paternalism was common among employers in the early industrial era, he employed this cultural tradition in a novel way.

In creating an environment conducive to manufacturing, Colt realized that he had to build an attractive company town to offset the resistance to routine, time-oriented work so characteristic of factory employment. In doing so, he transformed Hartford. Already a thriving industrial city in the 1850s, Hartford's civic pride was demonstrated in institutions from a public high school to a modern asylum for the mentally ill.[53] But Colt was to have an impact on the future development of this up and coming town, and he quickly became its primary employer and manufacturer. Desiring access to water transportation, he bought land near the Connecticut River and constructed his factory, his home, and his industrial town there. But from the outset, he seemed torn by his desire to import European workers and make them feel part of this new, exciting experiment and the need to attract and placate a local, Yankee work force. It was unclear if both groups could get along with one another, and problems had arisen when manufacturers mixed Yankee and immigrant workers. The Lowell strikes of the 1840s, the threat by Protestant laborers to burn the Catholic church in Webster, Massachusetts, and the conflict between Irish and Yankee workers in Lawrence suggested that it would be a difficult task to accommodate native-born and foreign workers. But there were positive examples that Colt could draw upon for his new community. His company town was across the river from Cheneyville, a very successful silk manufacturing enterprise that was described as a "workers paradise." Close by was the Springfield armory, known as a well-organized, clean, aesthetically pleasing manufacturing establishment. Colt wished to emulate these towns and make "Coltsville" even more appealing to workers.

Within Coltsville, the Colt armory was the pinnacle of his achievement and encompassed the ideas of Colt and his supervisor Root. Together with architect H. A. G. Pomeroy, these men collaborated on the design of the new structure to be built in an area along the Connecticut River known as South Meadows. This location, however, was nearly a swamp open to flooding. To solve the problem, Colt constructed a two-mile-long dike and planted it with German osiers, a type of willow, which he believed would prevent flooding and hold the soil in place. Never one to miss an opportunity to turn a profit,

Colt built a factory to manufacture wicker furniture and baskets out of the willows. Besides turning a profit, this willow factory also promoted German immigration to Coltsville.[54]

The actual design of the armory was patterned after the Wauregan Mills, a textile company located near Plainfield, Connecticut. This factory was owned by a partnership that included Amos D. Lockwood, former superintendent of the Slatersville factory. Using this as a model, an H-shaped, three-story brick and sandstone armory was constructed on the South Meadows. Special care was taken for lighting and ventilation. Large windows, skylights, and gaslights provided illumination; hot air pipes heated the building; and special care was taken to prevent fires. A 250 horsepower engine supplied the power used in the armory.[55] The building's exterior was also special. The central pavilion was capped by an onion-domed cupola resting on an octagonal base. Designed by Colt, it was painted blue, studded with gold stars, and topped by a rampant bronze colt, the symbol for his company and representative of the Colt family's coat of arms.

Colt's new armory was extremely functional, and Colt was able to make quality weapons in the most economical way. The manufacture of pistols was broken down into a number of steps, and each process was located in a separate part of the building. Every section had managerial independence, and supervisors could meet quotas in their own particular way. About 80 percent of the pistol production process, however, was accomplished by machines. First, the cylinder, breech, and barrel were made using various gauges to insure uniformity, and then parts were sent for preliminary assembly. Colt's weapons required "final hand fitting in which the parts were filed to fit."[56] His armory turned out about 250 guns each day, and with the coming of the Civil War, business soared. His customary product line was supplemented with the introduction of "a new line of .31 caliber pistols, a .36 caliber Navy gun, and a .44 caliber Army revolver." By 1863 the factory had manufactured more than 300,000 revolvers making him the largest gun manufacturer in the world.[57]

While Colt paid his workers well and provided good working conditions for them, his benign treatment of his workers stopped at the factory door. He demanded military-type precision from his workforce with no leniency for tardiness or work that was not up to quality or speed.[58] Precision machines replaced hand labor; factories replaced workshops; and time labor replaced task-oriented work. Gone was the independent artisan who crafted an entire product from start to finish.

To compensate for his meticulous control over the workplace, Colt built an enormous complex around his factory, housing an estimated 145 families. He was especially interested in attracting artisans from Germany. Several Germans became his trusted aides. He sent one of them, Frederick Kunkle, to Prussia to find skilled workers for his factories, and Kunkle was successful in this endeavor. By 1860, German immigrants comprised about one-third of his workforce. To facilitate their assimilation into American life without destroying their sense of German culture, Colt designed homes and the surrounding grounds to resemble a village near Potsdam, the home of many of his workers. He created a village that featured duplexes designed as Swiss chalet cottages.[59] A tavern and boardinghouse mirrored those found in Germany; workers were encouraged to craft a Germania House where a German social club could function. He even went so far as to plant vineyards and allow livestock to be kept by his workers. This section of town, with its attention to such detail, attracted workers from nations beyond Germany.[60]

With all the attention given to this "little Potsdam," Colt had relatively little interest in his native-born workers. Colt designed multifamily tenements to house his Yankee workforce. On 1856, on Huyshope Avenue, five separate but similar style brick tenements were built. Three stories high, each building accommodated six families. On nearby Van Block Avenue, a similar set of units went up. This time the five separate tenements were four stories high, and each housed eight families. Unlike the little Potsdam enclave that was located several streets from the industrial site, these tenements were located in a block directly across from the armory. The little Potsdam houses were duplexes positioned several streets away from the industrial site.[61]

Unlike both John Fox Slater and Amos Adams Lawrence, Colt was not an absentee owner; he lived on the premises in his mansion known as Armsmear, designed in the Italianate style. Across from Armsmear lived Samuel's brother James B. Colt in an Italianate brick house less grand than Armsmear that was reportedly designed by Hartford architect Octavius Jordan. They both flanked the entry to a magnificent expanse, Colt Park. Part of the original grounds of Armsmear, this space was filled with statuary, ornamental ponds and special gardens.[62]

Colt tried to meld these three worlds: Armsmear, little Potsdam, and the brick tenement district. His company town contained parks, fountains, gardens, museums, a church, and schools. The centerpiece of his vision was Charter Oak Hall, a four-story building dedicated to labor. He wanted to provide cultural programs for his workers but in a setting that was their own. Though never completed, the hall was to have murals on its walls depicting industrial progress, reading, lecture, and discussion rooms, as well as a museum and spaces for celebrations. Colt wanted to create a technical college there to rival Yale, but he died while it was only in its planning stages. Charter Oak Hall never lived up to its potential as a center for cultural study and was used instead for parties and as a rehearsal space for Colt's armory band.[63]

But Colt did encourage social organizations and leisure activities that would allow all workers to mingle together. Organized in 1856 and approved by Colt, an armory band was assembled, and it played martial music with much pageantry and gusto, all the while spreading Colt's name throughout the region. His armory guard also served that purpose. This guard became known for its precision and military-like drills and was invited to perform throughout Connecticut and New York. Additionally, he allocated space for baseball games and glee clubs.[64]

Colt believed that a sense of ethnic distinctiveness could be combined with a strong belief in American patriotism. Colt planned enormous and festive Fourth of July celebrations for his workers, which included giant firework displays, parties, and free beer, all subsidized by Colt. He also encouraged mechanics balls and working-class dances. But Colt's tolerance for diversity did not extend to politics. To be a Colt worker meant to follow Democratic Party principles and act accordingly. Colt attempted to control the votes of his workers. He not only encouraged them to vote Democratic but fired Republicans among his workforce. For example, an 1860 broadside entitled "Mechanics, Working Men of Conn. Read, Read, Read!" claimed that Colt dismissed Republican workers from his armory based on their political affiliations. It accused the populist Colt of being in the forefront of "the oppression of free labor by capital." The broadside charged him with violating a fundamental right of freemen to choose political leaders free of coercion. Colt's actions represented "a most oppressive and tyrannical exertion of the money-power, against which it is the duty of every freeman solemnly and earnestly to protest."[65]

Politics and the Civil War

Colt was indeed a convinced Democrat; originally an alien in the Yankee town of Hartford, he was determined to stir up the political pot and challenge the local elite. He embraced the platform and values of the Democratic party, including sympathy for immigrants and their cultures, a desire for manufacturing growth, western expansion, and relations with the South that would keep slavery in place and not damage the Union. Colt also was not averse to the patronage and spoils system that were part of the Jacksonian legacy. His views took hold in Hartford in large part because of the statewide Democratic victory of 1853, which launched Thomas Seymour as governor and secured large Democratic majorities in the state legislature.[66]

Governor Seymour was a friend and confidant of Colt, and he granted Colt many favors. Though never in the military and never firing a gun in battle, Colt received an honorary military rank of colonel from Seymour. In a manner reminiscent of contemporary politicians and political discourse, "Colonel" Colt cultivated an image of himself as a patriotic icon whose revolver reflected the emerging strength of the United States. Colt gave presentation pistols to many senators and other influential politicians and political figures. He was so blatant about his bribery that he became a target of a congressional investigation on corruption charges in 1854, as Colt attempted to influence politicians to grant him an extension of a patent. Though Colt was acquitted, many believed that he continued to try to influence favorable government actions through gifts and money to politicians. He also gave many presentation pistols to European monarchs, such as Czar Nicholas of Russia in 1854; this served as publicity for his weapons as he traveled throughout the world to increase his arms deals. Ever on the lookout for new global sales possibilities, he gave Commodore Perry dozens of presentation revolvers for his trips to Japan.[67]

Colt detested the politics of the Republican Party and in particular its stance toward slavery. To the extent that Colt confronted slavery, like most Democrats, he did not see it as a moral issue. Indeed, during the 1830s, he played on the fears of slave rebellion to sell guns to plantation owners. Colt even suggested that he had come up with the very idea of his repeating pistol in the wake of the Nat Turner Revolt. In the words of an article in the 1837 *Journal of the American Institute*, printed with Colt's permission, "Mr. Colt appeared to be near the scene of a sanguinary insurrection of Negro slaves, in the southern district of Virginia. He was startled to think against what fearful odds the white planter must ever contend, thus surrounded by a swarming population of slaves. What defense could there be in one shot, when opposed to multitudes, even though multitudes of the unarmed? The master and his family were certain to be massacred. Was there no way, thought Mr. Colt, of enabling the planter to repose in peace?"[68]

Colt worried that the fight over slavery would be bad for business. He believed that if left to its own devices, slavery would fade away, as it was an inefficient economic system. Colt's Democratic leanings informed his unfavorable view of abolitionists and initial ambivalence about the Civil War. Colt thought that John Brown's 1859 raid on Harpers Ferry was the work of a traitor and a madman. He reacted to Brown's act by attempting to sell even more weapons in the Deep South and, succeeding in this effort, he justified these sales with his familiar argument that more arms deterred war. Though trade with the South was not restricted until 1861, many newspapers in New England from the *New York Daily Tribune* to *the New York Times* to the *Hartford Daily Courant* suggested that Colt was a Southern sympathizer if not an outright traitor to the Union. Yet Colt, ever the capitalist, sold guns to radical abolitionists as well as Southerners.[69] However, with the outbreak of the war, Colt quickly offered to raise and arm a regiment for the North. Colt was granted a commission by the Republican governor William Buckingham to create a militia. Colt made a proposal to arm the troops, for "the value of the arms covered by it is $50,000 and is to be an out and out gift to the state and that men skilled in the use of the weapons will be selected to teach the rest of the regiment." Colt even became an adviser to the Governor regarding arms, clothing, equipment, and the like for the state militia.[70] Colt chose men from his factory and the adjoining Sharp's rifle establishment to man the unit. He wanted his troops to be an elite fighting corps, and he had height and fitness requirements for entry into his regiment. Though officially titled the First Connecticut Rifles, it soon became known as Colonel Colt's Rifle Regiment. Yet Colt's desire for self-promotion, even in war, turned out to be the regiment's undoing. Colt not only upset many people because of his rabid desire for publicity and exclusionary methods of recruitment but also disturbed many men because he made the regiment into a unit of the U.S. army, rather than maintaining its commitment to Connecticut. The governor of Connecticut quickly recalled Colt's commission, and the unit was dissolved, many of its members joining other Connecticut regiments.[71]

It is difficult to know how wholeheartedly Colt supported the Union cause. He would die of gout in 1862 in the early stages of the Civil War. In many ways, Colt's early death allowed him to remain a symbol of American patriotism for generations to come. But clearly his major legacy involved increasing the romantic appeal of firearms, helping to revolutionize manufacturing more generally, and transforming American culture.

Colt was a great American individualist whose rise to prominence was much more complicated than the rags-to-riches tale he liked to tell. Colt drew on a number of images that both reflected and shaped the American culture of individualism, combining an optimistic view of the future with a nostalgic vision of an America that was already fading. Colt's particularly American version of individualism overcame the traditional duality of head-and-hand work, placing manual labor on par with traditionally more highly esteemed mental labor, as the practical inventor became a new model of success. Yet the cult of the inventor in American life helped to camouflage trends that were making the Horatio Alger story of social mobility more difficult to attain. Colt combined in his very person mental and manual labor at a time when the two were splitting apart in economic life, as capitalists increasingly did little manual labor and wage laborers found it difficult to move out of the working class, their independence compromised by a market society that increased social inequality and an emerging industrial system that they could not avoid. Even Colt's manufacturing symbol of a fierce stallion (a colt) mythologized an era that was fading, as the railroad and canal began to replace the horse as a mode of transportation.

Colt's advertising techniques also drew on this combination of individualism, nostalgia, and optimism. Colt convinced many Americans that guns were not only utilitarian objects that could be used for hunting but, in the context of an increasingly urban society, they were necessary for self-protection. He promoted the idea that guns were symbols of individualism and adventure and helped place ownership of the gun at the core of American identity. As America became more industrial and complex, his guns reminded people of a simpler time when problems could be solved by individuals, and power resided in them and not in an incipient corporate economy and an increasingly large federal government.

In his very person he was a prototype of the entrepreneur that is still familiar to us. Colt believed that his invention was the harbinger of a new economy. The repeating pistol exemplified the new industrial age; Colt's pistol was a manufactured product that every man could own and use, much like the computer today. Just as Bill Gates helped make the complex machinery of the computer easy to use and relatively inexpensive, so did Colt with his pistol. Both inventors made their products comprehensible to the average person by providing step-by-step manuals that allowed easy use in everyday life. Colt, like Gates and other inventors from Benjamin Franklin to Thomas Edison, represented that particularly American combination of genius, practicality, and entrepreneurial skill.

Samuel Colt might not have quite realized that "image is everything," but like most farsighted businessmen today, he understood that the right symbols for one's product and the creation of a recognizable brand name translate into enormous profits. Indeed, through his self-promotion, his relentless pursuit of profits throughout the globe, his risk-taking, his litany of lawsuits and disregard of debt, and his boisterous cultural egalitarianism, Colt was a prototype for many CEOs today. He combined freewheeling "casino capitalism" based on lack of government regulation, high risk-taking activity, and enormous debt with "crony capitalism" as he tried, by legal and illegal means, to secure government contracts through inside deals. Following the practices of contemporary companies from Enron to Haliburton, he wined, dined, and even bribed politicians for political favors. Colt attempted to intimidate, control, and eliminate his opponents through constant litigation, paying off politicians to renew patents for his guns, and asking friends in government for political favors. His actions demonstrate how free enterprise and government policies have always been intertwined, and their marriage continues today. For Colt, such activities helped to promote his vision of a dynamic and expanding American empire, where technological and military superiority guaranteed that American values would be found throughout the world.

Colt's vision of America was not without opposition, even among manufacturers. His casino/crony-style capitalism and vision of an emerging American empire stood in contrast to the second generation New England textile manufactures who also came of age in the Jacksonian era. Amos Adams Lawrence, Horatio Nelson Slater, and John Fox Slater were still in their factories and board rooms when Samuel Colt pioneered a new style of entrepreneurial activity. Yet they, too, would develop distinctive ideas about the American industrial and cultural future. Unlike Colt, the Slaters formulated a community-oriented version of a manufacturing society, fearing that a rapacious American empire would threaten the civil, peaceable ethos of small-town America. Lawrence also advocated a moral vision of capitalism that preserved the power of manufacturing elites while limiting the unbridled expansion of capital. Lawrence and John Fox Slater in particular saw their duty as wealthy men not to promote an American empire but to end the scourge of slavery that was harming America and to establish philanthropic charities and educational institutions that could morally uplift the population. Unlike Colt, these men came from wealthy backgrounds, and they also drew on strong religious and Republican values derived in part from their family histories, beliefs that were absent in the Colt lineage. Ultimately, the Slaters and Lawrence, despite their paternalistic rhetoric and charitable activities, contributed to the creation of a new disciplinary factory system based on the rational and contractual control of the workforce. It is to their legacies that we now turn.

Part II

The Slaters

From Paternalism to Contract

CHAPTER 4

THE SLATERS OF ENGLAND AND NEW ENGLAND

Samuel Slater has been called the world's first industrial spy, the Arkwright of America, the Father of American manufacturers, and the architect of America's Industrial Revolution. He established the first successful spinning mill in America, the prototype for hundreds of factories later constructed throughout New England. His significance, however, was not limited to machine and mill construction. He instituted the family system of labor and the Sunday School, and his son Horatio Nelson Slater would take the family firm to a dominant position in the textile industry. Yet he did not work alone. Throughout most of his career in America, he was assisted by his younger brother John Slater who organized the first factory town in an attempt to merge Jeffersonian pastoral values and the new industrialism, introduced mule spinning to America, argued for the use of the power loom, and was the father of John Fox Slater, one of the most important philanthropists in the nineteenth century. Together the two brothers owned factories in four states and represented the first of several generations of Slaters who dramatically impacted the future of the new nation.

Born in Belper, England in 1768, Samuel Slater was apprenticed to a progressive factory master, Jedediah Strutt, to study the art and mystery of yarn spinning. Strutt's cotton factory used waterpower to operate yarn-spinning machines invented by Richard Arkwright. During his six years in the factory, Slater learned almost every aspect of yarn production from the construction, operation, and repair of machinery to the supervision of hands. He realized that he could put this knowledge to profitable use but not in England's highly concentrated and competitive textile industry. Britain was also fiercely protective of its textile manufacturing industry. It banned the export of textile-related technology, going so far as to prevent anyone with advanced knowledge of the industry from leaving the country. Punishment for breaking these laws included fines, imprisonment, or even death. Recognizing the risk, he nevertheless decided to take a chance. Disguising himself as a "farm boy," he boarded a ship bound for America. He was determined to set up a spinning mill based on the Arkwright patents in the United States and to make a handsome profit from this venture. Slater's ambition was allegedly recognized by the British crown. Rumors persisted throughout Slater's lifetime that the British government had employed an assassin (albeit unsuccessfully) to kill Slater.[1]

In America, Slater was soon presented with job offers, one in New York and another in Providence. When the New York opportunity proved disappointing, he accepted an invitation from a wealthy Providence merchant, Moses Brown, to visit his enterprise in Rhode Island and to inspect the equipment that he had on hand to produce yarn. The machines were imperfect, but Slater could cannibalize them for parts and construct machinery based on the Arkwright models. Brown agreed and tried to hire Slater to build the machines and construct and run a factory. Since knowledge of the British patents was so scarce, Slater refused to be a hired hand and instead bartered his knowledge of cotton manufacturing into a half interest in the new textile firm. Two of the Brown relations, William Almy and Smith Brown, entered into a partnership with Slater and the cotton spinning firm of Almy, Brown and Slater was formed. Together the three men set up the first successful spinning mill in America in Pawtucket, Rhode Island. After Pawtucket, Slater never looked back and never expressed guilt about his early form of industrial espionage. Allegedly, when questioned by President Andrew Jackson about stealing secrets from the British, Slater replied, "I suppose that I gave out the psalm, and they have been singing the tune ever since."[2]

Not only did Samuel Slater launch the textile industry in the United States, he was partially responsible, although unwillingly, for initiating the machine-building trade. In their original contract with Slater, Almy and Brown inserted a clause that allowed them to "put in apprentices to the business." Scores of workmen passed through the mill, learned how to build and repair the machines, and then left to set up their own business. Initially many of them were itinerant mechanics. At the request of a budding factory owner, for example, they would travel to a village, work with local machine shop and foundry owners to construct Arkwright-style equipment, and then set it in motion. Some of these mechanics subsequently settled in the Providence area, and soon specialized firms engaged in the construction and repair of textile machines were established. Providence became a center for innovation, creativity, and the interchange of ideas for the manufacture of textile machines.[3]

Samuel Slater was the archetype of the American immigrant. Ambitious, risk taking, and flexible in business, he quickly adapted to the American economic scene while tailoring the British industrial system to the U.S. context. His alliance with Almy and Brown began to disintegrate as Slater became more comfortable with U.S. business practices; he also believed that his partners did not respect his abilities or business savvy. Slater then asked his younger brother John to join him in Rhode Island in the early nineteenth century. Subsequently, blood and marriage ties characterized much of their business. Ownership and management of factories were tied to kin, and families were employed in their factories. The Slater brothers also created company towns around their factories providing additional jobs, housing, churches, schools, shops, and gardens for their workers.

Samuel and John Slater were cultural entrepreneurs as well as manufacturers. Unlike the Colt family's orientation to a type of casino/crony capitalism, they developed a version of small-town and paternalistic manufacturing capitalism, which also addressed the democratic sentiments sweeping the United States. They helped to define the meaning of the factory system in republican and agricultural America. In their view, the factory should not be a place of worker degradation. Employers had a responsibility to workers that limited an excessive obsession with profits. "This firmness and uniformity of low profits is much preferred, by prudent manufacturers, to an uncertain and speculating business, liable to fluctuation between every high and very low prices," wrote Samuel Slater in 1832.[4]

Samuel and John Slater constructed their factories and their burgeoning textile empire during a time of enormous change in the United States. In the post revolutionary era, a crisis of authority engrossed the nation as the fledgling republic attempted to find its moorings amid new democratic pressures and institutions. Manufacturers like the Slaters searched for profitable ways to organize their early factories in this novel context. They faced a new republican polity and an emerging market economy in a predominantly agricultural society and confronted a culture in flux where the meanings of freedom and social responsibility were far from clear, and differences between public and private domains were not clearly marked. Democratic themes were part of this emerging culture, from the promise of individual social mobility, to an emphasis on the sanctity of the independent farmer and artisan, to the sovereignty of the people. These democratic and republican tendencies intersected with paternalism and liberalism, two other master themes of this era. The tensions and combinations of these traditions dramatically influenced the countenance of antebellum America.[5]

As the Slaters confronted an expanding textile market that spread from New England to the American West and eventually to the entire Western Hemisphere, they employed these traditions in various ways. The Slaters did not simply and unquestionably take traditions for granted but consciously utilized them to increase their economic output. Because there was no fully established pattern for textile manufacturing, they experimented with all aspects of the factory structure, from its technical organization to its system of labor.

Tradition for Samuel and John Slater often meant looking to the British experience when they erected their mills. But in attempting to replicate the British system, they helped to create a distinctively American orientation to manufacturing, as the conditions of the United States demanded technical and social innovations. Contractual, paternal, and democratic themes all appeared in the factory system developed by the Slaters. Differences from Great Britain included more attention to company towns to avoid the destructive aspects of British industrialization. American republican and Christian principles required that more dignity be accorded to labor. There was a greater role for religion among both entrepreneurs and workers and a respect for the family and the independence and paternal control of the adult male worker. As yeoman farmers and common laborers were transformed into factory workers, the Slaters had to hand over partial recruitment, discipline, and control of their workforce to factory families.

In sum, the Slaters did not simply adopt either a paternalistic, democratic, or contractual approach to manufacturing but combined them as conditions warranted. Indeed, for the Slaters, paternalism and the market were often not in conflict but reinforced one another. When they experimented with different forms of labor organizations, for example, they found that paternalistic schemes based on the family system of labor were most profitable. They also entrusted the ownership and often the management of their mills to their sons and other relatives. Family was an organizing principle for the Slaters as it was for many Americans. Of course, the Slaters were not benevolent father figures in some idyllic American pastoral past, but they found that labor discipline could be guaranteed by a patriarchal system that encouraged obedience to authority.

As the Slaters grew in prominence, they became more interested in the political and cultural fate of the nation. They faced three major tasks: how to organize their factory and labor force, how to deal with new politics of their communities and the nation as a whole, and how to promote the character that they believed would serve their workers, themselves, and the nation. They brought tradition onto the factory floor; they looked to unite manufacturers together in an association that would lobby government officials; and they preferred to enter and win local elections rather than solicit favors from politicians and officials. They believed that Christian beliefs and practices were necessary for a virtuous workforce and republic. Although they began to develop a national and even international consciousness as their industries expanded, they remained tied to the local values of the small towns in which they lived.

SAMUEL SLATER AND THE PAWTUCKET MILL

The story of Samuel Slater and the American textile industry begins in Pawtucket, Rhode Island in April 1790 with the formation of a partnership between American merchants William Almy, Smith Brown, and Samuel Slater. The merchants provided the funds, bought the cotton, sold the goods, and paid hands while Slater supplied practical know-how. At the site in Pawtucket, Slater recreated the machines with which he was most familiar. A water frame of twenty-four spindles and another of forty-eight spindles, two carding machines, plus drawing and roping frames comprised the initial equipment. It took the assistance of fourteen mechanics to build the machines and twelve months before Slater was able to produce an acceptable warp of cotton. Although Slater was a partner in the new enterprise, he was often referred to as "an English workman from Arkwright's works." Considered a mechanic and an outsider by the Brown family, Slater was never able to overcome those labels. Throughout their association, Almy and Brown attempted to limit Slater's influence and treated him merely as a hired hand.[6]

But Slater had day-to-day control of the Pawtucket mill and faced challenges that allowed him to develop a distinctively American approach to manufacturing. For example, he was very aware of the social environment in which he worked. The new factory that he oversaw fit in well with the townscape. Constructed of wood, some observers said it resembled a large eighteenth-century farmhouse, while others compared it to a country meeting house.[7] Slater and his partners were concerned with avoiding the "dark, satanic mills" that had so stained British industrialization. Republican America still believed it could remain a pastoral utopia with the machine integrated into the garden, to paraphrase Leo Marx.

Factories demanded a labor force, and Slater experimented with various schemes to attract and retain workers. In England, children had been hired to operate the machinery, and Samuel Slater carried this idea to America. He initially advertised for child apprentices and encouraged overseers of the poor to send their charges to the factory. Neither poor nor orphaned children worked out well. Costs for boarding, medical care, and supervision were high. Children also objected to the labor conditions and discipline exacted by Slater. Some ran away, and others resisted the regularity imposed by the factory process. Slater then decided to hire children from poor families in the Pawtucket area who were available after the Revolutionary War. Many parents were eager to send their children to the factory, but they were not at all comfortable with Almy, Brown, and Slater's treatment of them or their children.[8]

That paternal authority extended beyond the confines of the family was not sufficiently appreciated, especially by Slater's partners. As merchants, Almy and Brown had a long-range view of business, particularly the payment of debts. Accustomed to between six and nine months' credit, they were not aware that mill hands required prompt and regular payment. But Slater knew better, and he objected to the slowness of payment and to the attitude that his partners exhibited toward the issue. Parents began to come around and demand money or goods. They stated that they had no corn, no shoes, no clothes, and they could no longer send their children to work unless they received prompt payment for their children's work.

The punishment of the children also became a major issue. Parents believed that they were the primary disciplinarians and resented Slater's attempt to control the children while in the factory. They repeatedly took the children out of the mill, had them run errands during the day, and demanded that Slater refrain from punishing their sons and daughters. Operations were disrupted, and Slater could no longer countenance their interference; another form of labor had to be found. Again, Slater turned to what he had known in England. Jedediah Strutt, his former employer, had hired entire families and devised a division of labor based on age and gender that operated in his factory and mill village. Slater borrowed this concept of family labor and molded it to meet the needs of both employer and employee. At Pawtucket, children worked in the mill while their fathers accepted jobs in and around the factory such as painting, watching the mill, setting stones, and carpentry work. These were traditional occupations that allowed fathers to retain their authority and position in their families. All wages were paid to him; he did not have to compete with his children for factory work, and he received compensation for his work commensurate with prevailing wages for that trade. His position as head of household and primary provider was left intact. Women often remained at home and accepted outwork such as weaving and, later, hat, button, or broom making. The entire family was brought together under the umbrella of the factory system; parents had an important incentive to seek jobs in factory towns and to work with rather than against the mill owner. Their jobs and those of their children depended on their compliance.[9]

This system introduced at the Pawtucket mill worked out well for Slater and his associates. By the end of the decade, the primary features associated with the new factory system were in place. The factories were small-scale, yarn-spinning mills organized as a single proprietorship or joint stock company, managed by one of the owners, and powered by water. Manufacturers employed family labor to operate the machines.

The family system of labor became a key characteristic of the new factory system in America. The introduction of the family system of labor demonstrated that authority could not be exercised at will by the owner or overseer but had to take into account the traditions of paternalism and republican independence in the very structure of the factory. The family system of labor showed that paternalism and the market, far from being in conflict, could complement and reinforce one another and that *homo economicus* and *pater familias* coexisted quite nicely on the factory floor. The demarcation of the public arena of the workplace from the private realm of the family, a division so taken for granted today, was far from settled in this era. If anything, Slater's system demonstrated that the workplace could be structured according to familial values, at least to some degree, and that the factory system could assist in the maintenance of the family rather than contributing to its demise. In any case, like the problem of authority, public and private realms were negotiated, contested, and combined. *Homo economicus* did not emerge full-blown as the market became increasingly important and autonomous.

Yet capitalism was fast becoming a force to be reckoned with, and the market created rifts in the partnership of Slater, Almy, and Brown. In 1799, Almy and Brown, without Slater, bought a mill in Warwick, Rhode Island. When they sent a mechanic to observe Slater and his equipment, Slater became angry and threatened to toss the man out the window. But Slater could not stop the spread of new technology.[10] Slater, too, decided to look for other investment opportunities. Normally a cautious man, he took to his business ventures with gusto, as he could see nothing but opportunity in America. These early years of the nineteenth century were ones of haphazard and rapid expansion. First with his inlaws, he erected the White mill in Rehoboth in 1799 and called it Samuel Slater and Company.[11] Between 1803 and 1805, he joined with his brother John Slater and his former partners Almy and Brown and constructed a mill in northern Rhode Island. He later purchased land and water privilege sites in Oxford South Gore, Massachusetts. With partner Bela Tiffany, he constructed a textile mill and began to build homes and facilities for his workers. By 1817 this site boasted a cotton and a woolen mill, a sawmill, a gristmill, and sixteen houses. This cluster of mills, homes, and shops later became the town of Webster and the site of Slater's most significant investment. At the time he owned about seven hundred acres in the area.[12]

By the 1820s Slater had invested heavily in mill property and new equipment, and his debts rose accordingly. In East Village (Webster), he constructed another factory in 1822 and went into partnership with his brother John Slater. They purchased the Jewett City mill in 1823. This was a fully integrated factory, the first to not only spin yarn but also to manufacture cloth. In 1824 he built the Phoenix Thread Company and acquired the Steam Cotton Manufacturing Company in Providence in 1828. Acquisition of the Steam Cotton Manufacturing Company was a bold and imaginative move, for it allowed manufacturers to locate near their distribution points and supplies of labor rather than remain tied to river dam sites.[13] Within a few years, Slater manufactured 370,000 yards of fine Sea Island shirting.[14] Other investments included the Amoskeag Manufacturing Company in New Hampshire and the Springfield Manufacturing Company in Ludlow, Massachusetts. Furthermore, in 1829 Slater acquired the Central Falls Mill in Smithfield, Rhode Island.[15] Throughout the decade, he also continued to speculate in land.[16]

During this period of expansion, Slater followed a pattern that emphasized personal or family ownership and management of each business. His firms were largely joint stock companies or single proprietorships. His commitment to his family made good business sense in his view. He continued to believe that the most successful manufacturers "furnish money for the business and superintended its operation in person. They employed their families in the labors of the business, and, to the extent of this saving of wages of superintendence and labor, realized the gross profits of manufacture." Furthermore, "least successful of all have been those who, themselves engaged in other pursuits, have invested the nett profits of their own business in manufacturing, and left the latter to the superintendence of others. A large portion of these investments has been wholly lost through the waste, profusion, unskilfulness [*sic*] and want of fidelity of agents, superintendents, and other servants, hired at large salaries, and having no interest in the ultimate prosperity of the concern." He preferred security to speculation.[17]

A concern with security did not necessarily translate into a conservative approach to business. Samuel Slater overextended himself and invested too heavily in various business adventures. His family ties also hampered as well as helped him, as he loaned money to or endorsed notes for family and friends that they could not repay. When the Panic of 1829 set in, and demand for his products diminished, he could not meet the $300,000 worth of obligations that came due. To his partner William Almy, he appealed for a loan but was rebuffed. Instead, Almy bought out Slater's interest in both the Pawtucket and Smithfield mills. A group of wealthy Providence residents came to his rescue and issued thirty notes totaling $215,000 to help cover his outstanding debts.[18] The Panic of 1829 shattered Samuel Slater's confidence and forced him to question his friendships and to evaluate whether or not it was time to retire from active participation in his various enterprises. Other manufacturers had not suffered as he had. To Almy and William Jenkins, another manufacturer, Samuel Slater sold two thirds of his interest in the Slatersville venture, and to his brother John he sold the other third. As Samuel's fortunes began to wane, the business role of his brother John increased. John would turn his enterprise in a direction that emphasized the manufacturing community to an even greater extent than did Samuel, as small-town values, religion, and paternalism mixed with industry to create a new type of company town.[19]

JOHN SLATER

During the period when Samuel Slater was disillusioned with his Pawtucket partners, he asked his brother John to join him in Rhode Island. John Slater arrived in America around the turn of the century at the age of twenty-seven. Like his brother over a decade earlier, he did not arrive empty handed. He possessed knowledge of the latest British technology including mule spinning, which he introduced into the business. Mule spinning had several advantages over traditional throstle spinning: it allowed a wider range of yarn from very fine to very course to be twisted, created a uniform product, and promoted higher spindle speeds. This process produced about 20 percent more yarn than the competing throstles.[20] Also like his brother, John parlayed his knowledge into a partnership—Almy, Brown, and the Slaters. Each of the four owners initially possessed one-fourth share of the business. Almy and Brown still supplied the funds, and the Slaters supervised the construction and operation of the factories and the mill towns that grew up around them. In 1805 approximately 122 acres of land was purchased along the Branch River in upstate Rhode Island, and by 1807 a yarn spinning mill was constructed and placed under the management of John Slater.[21] At the time of its completion, it had the largest production capacity in New England.[22] Yet it was still essentially a yarn-spinning mill; handloom weavers wove the yarn into cloth. But change and increased competition was coming to the industry, and the Slaters had to decide how they were going to approach the introduction of new technology.

The Slaters faced increasing competition in the textile industry, especially from the Boston Manufacturing Company that was experimenting with new technologies and forms of industrial organization. During the War of 1812, the Boston Manufacturing Company began operations in Waltham, Massachusetts. Capitalized at one hundred thousand dollars, its owners received an article of incorporation from the state. They constructed a four-story brick factory that measured ninety feet by forty-five feet. It was also an integrated mill that combined both spinning of yarn and weaving of cloth. Through this firm, Francis Cabot Lowell introduced the power loom to America. Cloth could be woven by machine, thus eliminating the need for a vast network of outworkers.[23]

If the Slaters and their partners were to keep pace with the new Boston Manufacturing Company, they would have to set up power looms in their factories. Contrary to some reports that labeled the Slaters, especially Samuel Slater, as "entrepreneurial conservatives," the brothers began to investigate the feasibility of doing just that as early as 1815. William Gilmore, a Scottish-born mechanic with knowledge of the power loom and dresser, was brought to Slatersville at the request of John Slater. The Slater brothers appeared very interested in his ideas, but for a variety of reasons—including the recalcitrance of his partners (most notably Almy and Brown) to integrate the factory, a downturn in the economy, and indebtedness—they did not contract with him for the power looms. They also were not convinced that Gilmore could produce his machinery to their satisfaction and in a timely manner. This did not deter the Slaters, however. They eventually installed power looms in a factory they acquired in Jewett City, Connecticut in 1823.[24]

While there is considerable controversy among historians over the brothers' view of power-loom weaving, there is little disagreement over their establishment of factory towns in America. John Slater was among the first American manufacturers to design a novel form of community, the industrial village or factory town. Slatersville became the center of his attention for the rest of his life. John Slater's vision of the contented factory worker living in a village setting became a prototype for other entrepreneurs. Fronting a linear road known as Green Street, Slater constructed mill houses or tenements between 1810 and 1820. Care was taken in their building and placement. From two to four tenements were grouped together and surrounded by open spaces, fences, shrubs, and trees. Each one possessed its own unique colonial design and housed four families. Most of them were two and a half stories high with a central chimney layout; entry was through the kitchen; the rear room was a sitting room; and the upstairs garret was divided into bedrooms.[25] Across the road stood a building that housed both the church and school. Along School Street another collection of houses was constructed. Between the two roads a town green was installed, and later in 1836, a Congregational church was built nearby. This community was one of the first planned textile villages in the United States.[26]

Slater, of course, did not construct this village simply out of the goodness of his heart, though his religious beliefs played an important role, as we will see. The houses and tenements, taverns, churches, schools, shops, and stores were constructed to attract and retain a labor force comprised primarily of families. The introduction of the spinning mule, a machine that required considerable expertise and strength, was one of the few skilled positions in the mill. Because of its requirements, men operated the mules with the assistance of child piecers.[27] This arrangement made the recruitment of entire families even more imperative. A division of labor based on age and gender characterized these mills. Children operated the textile machines, which required minimal skill or strength, or worked with the mule spinner. Men worked in and around the factory, and women and some men wove the yarn into cloth on handlooms. Large family units were recruited; for example, in 1814 Slater's business associate sent the following families to Slatersville: "I have engaged Mrs. Hyde with 8 children, Mrs. Snow with 8 or 11 and Mr. Harding, Wife and 8 children, all to go to your place and will expect as comfortable accommodations as you can spare. . . . There will be at least 28 in Number. . . . I thought, large Families would be more acceptable to you than Small, and what children they were deficient of their own, I got them to make up from their neighbours."[28]

Christianity comprised an important component of John Slater's vision of a peaceable village. A conservative Congregationalist, John Slater was a deeply religious man. He organized the Sunday School at Slatersville, welcomed local ministers to his home, regularly attended services, sent his children to religious schools, and supported the establishment of churches not only in Slatersville but also in Cumberland and Woonsocket Falls, Rhode Island and Jewett City, Connecticut. He was supported by his wife Ruth. A devout Congregationalist, "her heart was deeply interested in the great truths of revelation, and her home was ever open to welcome those who came to speak and labor for Christ."[29] She worked in the Sunday School, attended Divine Services that included three meetings, one at ten thirty, another at two o'clock, and again at six o'clock, and participated in prayer meetings during the week.[30]

In 1814 Reverend Daniel Waldo of the Massachusetts Home Mission Society conducted religious services in Slatersville, and within two years the Slatersville Congregational Church was formed. Among the first parishioners was Ruth Slater. In Slatersville, John Slater supplied the funds to construct the Congregational church to be located on or near the town green.[31] For five years, the company owned the church building, selected the minister, Reverend Timothy A. Taylor, and influenced the direction of religious exercises. In November 1838 Slater gave the church to the community on condition that the pews be let to obtain money for the support of a minister. Slater promised to insure the building, to repair it at the company's expense, and most importantly to prevent other churches or denominations from entering the village. The prevailing attitude was that "one Protestant church in a village like this is enough."[32] This remained the popular sentiment for several decades.

Slater's turn toward religion occurred for many reasons. He clearly wanted to control the religious sentiments and practices of this community. Slater saw the disciplining benefits of Christianity, for it promoted sobriety, a strong work ethic, and a uniform moral code of behavior among his workers. He was responding to the crisis of authority that pervaded American society in the early nineteenth century as a new society and nation were emerging and the contours of politics, culture, and economy were far from settled. Slater surely experienced this crisis at the level of the workplace, and he turned to religion to help restore his authority. Moreover, Christianity itself did not escape this problem. Many commentators noted the decline of religious attendance and conviction in the new United States, as Puritan religious beliefs lost their sway over the people. The Reverend Jotham Sewall, one of the earliest ministers retained by Slater around 1810, thought that the textile communities of Connecticut and Massachusetts were devoid of religion and morality. He was appalled that local residents engaged in trade, found enjoyment in entertainment such as playing ball and generally ignored the Sabbath.[33]

John Slater's hiring policies reflected his religious preferences: "He gathered around him a highly worthy class of laborers, many of them of a decidedly religious character, and by his regard for their interest, secured their hearty cooperation in promoting his."[34] One Slater employee, represented the beliefs of many when she wrote: "I have enjoyed some precious seasons, since I returned from camp meeting. Sometimes when I think of leaving Slatersville, it strikes a dread upon me. Can I ever leave this delightful spot, where I have enjoyed so many delightful seasons and privileges, it seems to be a place highly favoured by God."[35]

These evangelical "fanatical" and "boisterous" religious practices of his laborers reflected a change in Protestant beliefs occasioned by the crisis of American society in the early nineteenth century. As democratic and individualistic beliefs and practices swept the nation, a new religious sensibility emerged. Evangelical beliefs based on direct experience of God's grace that led to being born again emerged as a distinctively American form of Christianity. While founded on the experience of the individual, it had indirect democratic effects, for not only could anyone be touched by grace but also he or she could express it in manifold ways, often in the animated idiom of working-class and rural life. From Methodist circuit riders to Baptist revival meetings, a more emotional Christianity began to sweep America. Mainline Congregational, Presbyterian, and Episcopalian churches lost membership, as they were suspicious of this emotional emphasis and seemingly spurious conversions. The central role of the clergy in directing the church was threatened.[36]

John and Ruth Slater were touched by this born-again revivalism and walked a fine line between their conservative religious beliefs and the democratic impulse of this new evangelism. They maintained allegiance to Congregational beliefs and, like many others in the religious establishment, believed that the evangelical fervor could be domesticated by ministerial control of the conversion process. Indeed, the Slaters' views reflected in part the ideas of a Puritan era when visible saints ruled the church; this was demonstrated in the covenant penned by Reverend Daniel Waldo, the minister who established the church in Slatersville. He was sent out by the Massachusetts Home Mission Society circa 1814 to minister to the new village. Like the previous minister, he was a Revolutionary War veteran, a "soldier under the Lord Jesus Christ," carrying on "war against Satan's Kingdom." He wrote the *Confession of Faith and the Church Covenant.* His views harkened back to an epoch when some Congregational churches would only accept visible saints as parishioners. In part it read, "The former to be administered to visible believers and their children only, and the latter to none but visible believers."[37] Only those people who were born again and were certified as such by ministers or elders could join the church.

This unstable amalgam of conservative Puritanism and evangelical fervor was made more complex by an emphasis on good works that also accompanied the new religious ethos of the nineteenth century. Ruth Slater, like many other women denied an outlet for public actions, threw herself into religious practices of charity. She was described in the following terms:

> "Christianity exhibits no more perfect achievement, than in the completed character of a spiritual womanhood; for we find the united result of a life's discipline and a heavenly faith in the Christian woman's old age. Providence has not withheld that confirmation of the power and beauty of religion from our eyes. We have felt new confidence in truth, new love for goodness, new zeal for duty, new trust in God, new gratitude to Christ, as we have looked on the ripened holiness" of this departed mother in our Israel: and, "as her strength fainted before the power of decay, behold the crown of immortality descending almost visible upon her head! The thanksgivings of the poor that she had blessed, the tributes of the sick that she had visited, the perfume of the charities she had scattered thronging up, made the fading light of her evening beautiful to behold."[38]

Good works could be demonstrated in part by the teaching of scripture and virtue in Sunday School. John and Ruth Slater followed in the footsteps of Samuel Slater in establishing a Sunday School in their company towns, a concept that Samuel Slater had borrowed from the British manufacturer Jedidiah Strutt. Marrying Protestantism to capitalism in a Weberian mixture of discipline and scripture under Samuel's watchful eye, children worked six days in his factory, and on the seventh day they were initially allowed free time. But neighbors complained about the noise and trouble the youngsters were causing and asked Slater to do something about it. He instituted schools on Sunday, and children would once again come to the factory. Under the tutelage of a hired teacher, they would learn the rudiments of reading and writing; often the Bible served as their primary, if only, textbook.[39]

John and Ruth's Slatersville Sunday School was organized in 1808. Like Samuel's, discipline as well as religious doctrine were taught to factory operatives, a group composed largely of children.[40] As with Pawtucket and Webster, the Sunday School was sectarian in nature and only later came under the auspices of the church. In 1838 it boasted 168 pupils and 24 teachers. By 1847 there were 240 students attending the weekly meetings. The links between the school and the factory were reinforced as Amos D. Lockwood, hired as an assistant superintendent of the mills in 1832, became superintendent of the Sunday School and played the church organ by 1834. One of his pupils described his supervision thus: "The Slatersville Sunday School was an orderly one. How could it be otherwise with Mr. Taylor and Mr. Lockwood at the helm? When the service was over, Mr. Lockwood who was superintendent, used to stand in the front gallery and call the name of the teacher of each class to pass out and there was no crowding or noise." Young people were not only expected to attend Sunday School, they had other meetings as well. One boy mentioned that he had a six o'clock gathering one day, an eight o'clock meeting on Wednesday, a Bible class at Mr. Lockwood's on Friday, and a temperance lecture later in the week at the school house.[41]

Yet John Slater realized the constraints on his attempts to persuade his workers of Christian virtue and made allowances for the working class and rural culture of his employees. Evident in the boisterous religious practices of his laborers that could outstrip ministerial control, the limits of Slater's power was also demonstrated in his approach to temperance. While Slater was opposed to liquor in theory, in practice he accommodated the wishes of his workers. In the early days of operation in Slatersville, he supplied alcohol for his employees. In September 1808 John Slater asked Almy and Brown to "please send by Stephon Buffum three gallons of brandy for the use of the mill."[42] After purchasing property for a mill in Griswold, Connecticut, John Slater opened a store in the village that supplied the hands with goods and liquor. He secured a state license to "be a retailer of wines and distilled spiritous liquors . . . at his store in said town of Griswold."[43] As in Slatersville, John Slater had to comply with local customs and offer alcohol to his workers. However, he was aware that it could cause problems among his workers. In 1826 a triple murder occurred in Slatersville when Andrew Davis, while under the influence of brandy, killed his wife and child and then turned against a neighbor who came to their defense. Nevertheless, liquor continued to be available, and indeed there were three public taverns that catered to the local community.[44]

John Slater's commitment to keeping his workers contented displayed his overall excellent business sense. He expanded beyond the Slatersville partnership. He purchased mills in West Boylston, Massachusetts, Jewett City, Connecticut, and Hopeville, Connecticut. Yet he remained bound to the community of Slatersville. Unlike many of the factory owners in the area, John Slater decided to make his home in his factory village. He constructed a federal, two and one-half story, five-bay, central chimney house in 1810 on School Street. It differed little from the worker tenements nearby. Indeed insurance costs were only two hundred dollars more for the Slater home than for those of his workers. There he raised four children: John Fox, William Smith, Elizabeth, and Minerva.[45]

Slater's dedication to his community was also demonstrated by constructing a library, stocking it with books, and building a schoolhouse. Despite the quaint village atmosphere, the accommodations and the services provided by John Slater all would have been for naught if he could not provide full and constant employment for people. Just as 1829 had marked the decline of the fortunes of Samuel Slater, for the John Slater family the 1830s represented a time of stress. The economy was in turmoil. Bills fell due, business was slow, money was scarce, and managerial turnover was high. In January 1834 it was suggested that a mill be closed to save money. [46] But John Slater's response to this notion was to retain and pay his employees promptly and to build the Congregational church.[47] Slater did not, or perhaps during the trying times in the 1830s could not, invest much money in new housing construction. He confided to his son, John Fox Slater, "It will be a hard time to get through this summer [1838] harder than I have ever seen since I came to this country."[48]

With the Slatersville mill, John Slater introduced a new type of industrial village into the world of manufacturing. His vision of a small-town community no doubt reflected his economic interests in securing profits, and he made sure that his authority in the community was well protected. Yet Slater's concern for the character and well-being of his workers did not just flow from an economic impulse or the paternalism so widespread in antebellum America. Like his workers, he was a religious man touched by grace and saw it as his Christian responsibility to treat his workers well and live in a temperate and inauspicious manner. Thus, even in anxious economic times, John Slater tried to maintain employment and good living and working conditions for his laborers.

THE NEW REPUBLIC

The Slaters' small-town capitalism was not parochial, however. Samuel and John Slater realized that economic and political interests were intertwined, and the struggles of the 1820s and 1830s impelled the Slaters toward participation in local and national politics. Here Samuel Slater took the lead. Samuel became involved in political affairs that directly affected his business. Like many other Northeastern manufacturers, one of his long time concerns was tariff protection. Following the War of 1812, Britain dumped cotton goods on the American market and threatened to send the local industry into depression. In October 1815, local manufacturers sent a sharply worded petition to Congress demanding they act to prevent any further importation of British goods. Facing ruthless competition, they sought tariff protection. Passed in 1816, the tariff, however, proved a disappointment. On cotton goods and woolen products the tariff amounted to 25 percent and zero respectively.[49]

Samuel Slater was unsatisfied with this result, and he became a political leader among his fellow manufacturers. He organized Northeastern mill owners to press the government to recognize the interests of textile manufacturers. In 1820 Samuel Slater chaired a meeting comprised of the state's textile mill owners. They voted to send representatives to a general convention of manufacturers in New York and to establish a permanent statewide organization, the Rhode Island Society for the Encouragement of Domestic Industry, to promote their interests. Slater was one of three vice presidents of the association. Tariff protection or even an outright ban on imported textile goods was an object of the group.[50] The tariff issue dominated much of the discussion and action among manufacturers for the next decade. In 1832, justifying his perspective with a nationalistic fervor, Slater argued vehemently for protection, and "total prohibition of foreign cotton, wool, and iron, whether crude or manufactured, at as early a period as the wants of our population would permit." If tariff rates were reduced, it would decimate the textile industry, which in turn would invite "destruction of a vast amount of the national capital; the dislocation of its productive labor; universal bankruptcy and poverty; the utter extinction of the arts of civilized life; in time, a retrograde movement of the whole community to ignorance, weakness and barbarism." He warned Southerners who opposed the tariff that "for good and for evil, our lot must ever be theirs." And "if, then, we must taste the bitter cup, they will most assuredly be doomed to drain it to the dregs."[51] He called for protection, and his efforts were largely successful. While the Tariff of 1832 lowered most rates to 25 percent, it retained high rates on cottons, woolens, and iron.[52]

Slater's activism in organizing New England textile mill owners to influence government policy exemplified the American penchant for organizing associations that Tocqueville saw as central to democracy. Tocqueville, like many other commentators on democracy, recognized that republics were amenable to demagoguery and corruption by private interests. The Colt family's proclivity for bribing officials demonstrated this potential pitfall of democracy, while the Slater's approach represented the associational antidote to corruption. Organizing people of like-minded concerns epitomized the "enlightened self interest" that was as necessary for a successful democracy as the exercise of public virtue, in Tocqueville's view. Organizations such as the Rhode Island Society for the Encouragement of Domestic Industry not only kept the government honest but also taught citizens the skills of democracy, the "habits of the heart" necessary for a thriving republic. Slater and his family also began to develop a regional and national consciousness in part through these political activities.

Yet the issue of associations had troubled the founders who believed that they hampered the exercise of public spiritedness and republican virtue. The reelection of Thomas Jefferson in 1804 seemed to put a stop to this problem, as his presidency ushered in years of Jeffersonian Republican domination of the political process. James Madison and James Monroe easily captured the presidency with the latter beating his rival John Quincy Adams by 231 to 1 electoral votes. However, while two-party opposition waned, conflict did not. Numerous organizations emerged to represent the divergent views developing in the young country. These divisions became apparent in the contested election of John Quincy Adams over his two main rivals Henry Clay and Andrew Jackson. Groups coalesced around the National Republicans and then the Whigs on the one hand and the Jacksonian Democrats on the other.

While the Slaters believed in the efficacy of political parties and local governments, they thought that democracy and republican values faced considerable opposition. Associations, while contributing to democracy, were also potentially one of its worst enemies. They felt that not all political associations were created equally. Samuel Slater and his sons saw the Masons as an especially antidemocratic group that had to be reckoned with.

For Samuel Slater, the problem with associations was not their political character but whether or not they were "secret" and undemocratic. The Masons appeared to satisfy both of these criteria, and Slater became a strong anti-Mason. Masonry especially epitomized disturbing trends in society. It was a secret fraternal order that could be found in more than one thousand cities and towns throughout the North. Its doctrines "sought to promote human happiness by enlightening men about the paths to virtue."[53] They deemed God to be benevolent and sought to practice tolerance, charity, and fraternalism. "It brought people together on a common platform of 'science' and ethical belief and banished 'all those disputes, which embitter life, and sour the tempers of men.'" All who believed in God, whether Moslem, Jew, Deist, or Christian, could join. But the fees and dues required for membership and the time it took to learn the complicated rituals demanded of participants precluded many from joining the organization. According to Paul Goodman, "Masons saw themselves as among 'the better sort' in a social order marked by much uncertainty. In resisting powerful currents which tended to atomize individuals and impersonalize social relations, Masonry offered men an institution through which they might re-establish some sense of community based on social class and a shared set of values and cultural style."[54]

For those outside the organization, the Masons appeared to be an entrenched group of privileged elitists who practiced secret occult rituals and caballed together to control the country. They were determined to undermine "equal opportunity and personal independence in a republican society." Antimasonry emerged to counteract their power. Politically, Antimasons had first been Federalists and then National Republicans after 1825. They did not come from the upper strata of society but from the workingmen, mechanics, and farmers. They opposed special privileges such as incorporation and monopolies and the political candidates who supported the programs.[55]

While most New England entrepreneurs supported the Masons, there was one major exception—the Slater family. Samuel Slater had resisted incorporation and preferred family ownership and management of business, positions in opposition to the Masons' support of incorporation. He did not wish to open his business records to outside eyes. By limiting risk and allowing a number of people to own a company, Slater believed that incorporation inhibited both republican values of independence and responsibility and the central role of the family in the perpetuation and control of business. These lessons were transferred to his sons. Antimasonry flourished in their company town of Webster, Massachusetts. It was the only town among the industrial communities in southern Worcester county to cast a majority of votes for Antimason candidates, George B. Slater also signed Antimasonic petitions in 1831 and 1834.[56]

Family Matters

Politics for the Slaters was a family affair, as relatives rallied around tariff protection and Antimasonry. Indeed, Samuel and John Slater placed a premium on family, both within the factory and in their personal lives. Bonds of familial trust and affection transcended the textile industry in a sense while also reinforcing business ties. When the Slater brothers' attempted to cede some familial control to outside agents in the Jewett City mill, these efforts to extend beyond the circle of the family were unsuccessful, and John Slater's son John Fox Slater entered the business at age seventeen. As with the family system of labor, paternalism and reliance on family did not restrict profits but actually promoted a more efficient enterprise. While John Fox Slater would become enormously successful in expanding the influence of the Slater name, as would Samuel Slater's son Horatio Nelson Slater, other sons of the Samuel Slater clan would prove to be poor managers and drains on Samuel's finances and emotions. Far from being a haven in a heartless world, Samuel Slater's family sometimes resembled Max Weber's image of the iron cage, imprisoning everyone within its orbit.

In 1823 John and Samuel Slater bought a struggling textile company in Jewett City, Connecticut, and two years later, on his own account, John purchased a small mill at Hopeville several miles away. Since John Slater chose to remain at Slatersville, and Samuel Slater was absorbed in his Massachusetts enterprises, he hired Ezra W. Fletcher to supervise the Jewett City property. Work was begun to improve the enterprise. Fletcher insisted that it was "important to meet all demands when due—as there has recently been a number of failures in this vicinity," and creditors took note. Within five months new houses were under construction, and in June the Jewett City mill was running. John Slater and Samuel Slater visited the property from time to time and worked together to decide major issues, from the introduction of the power loom to the organization of the labor force. Now that the Slaters were free of Almy and Brown, they included power-loom weaving at their mill.[57] Samuel Slater decided issues about workers, but he was much less solicitous of their care than his brother John. Samuel told Fletcher that they should release the spinners "as soon as it can be legally done. All my spinners at Oxford tend four side of 128 spindles. . . . In regards to giving the tenants notice, I think the measure advisable especially to all those who have in any degree shown the cloven foot."[58]

The major issue faced by the Slaters concerned whether actual familial control over the Jewett City property was necessary to ensure its profitability. During the 1820s, supervision of that property passed back and forth through a number of different factory agents including John Bacon, Sanford Meech, Henry Carpenter, and William Clark, in addition to Ezra Fletcher.[59] In 1828 John Slater hired a personal clerk, Robert Foss, to handle his correspondence with the Jewett City enterprise. By then Bacon was gone, and Sanford Meech was in charge. But John Slater was not satisfied with his work. Slater "is not a little disappointed at not receiving a line once a week as requested from you stating the quantity of goods sent to market, amount of goods manufactured, cost, etc. etc."[60] Disappointed with Meech, Slater admonished him to pay close attention to every part of the business. Meech wasted time and money, something John Slater could not abide. Once Meech sent a team to pick up some materials, but he sent it to the wrong location. John Slater was furious: "I have not time to say one half what I feel at the disappointment & the extra expense that will attend your not abiding by what was agreed to."[61]

In 1831 John Slater acquired his brother Samuel's interest in this mill. By 1832 the Jewett City mill was capitalized at $70,000, contained 3,508 spindles and 86 looms. His Hopeville woolen factory was capitalized at $30,000.[62] He still preferred to live in Slatersville and continued to rely on agents for the Connecticut mills. First Charles Hyatt and then Henry Carpenter were employed, but neither one appeared able to handle the job. Slater admonished them for failing to supervise the hands and indulging workers and for poor accounting. To Henry Carpenter he wrote, "You will please have the goodness to forward account of weaving from 16th April with the expenses of each week distinct & in *future fail not* to have the account forwarded by *Tuesdays mail in each week*."[63] Operations appeared no better at the Hopeville factory under the supervision of Samuel Collier. To Mr. Collier, Slater wrote, "Have once more the painful duty to request you to forward a *correct statement* of the weekly expenses as follows which if I mistake not you promised faithfully to perform."[64] And Collier had a hard time recruiting all the necessary hands. In one instance, John Slater had to advise him to pay one man more than was given to others. He also admonished him, however, "to keep this from the help as it might perhaps cause a little uneasiness amongst them."[65] The following year, 1832, Slater instructed his seventeen-year-old son John Fox Slater to join Samuel Collier and manage the Hopeville woolen mill. Four years later, young Slater had charge of both the Hopeville mill and the Jewett City property.[66]

John Fox Slater would manage the mills well and help turn the Slater name into a dynasty. His management of the Jewett City and Hopeville properties signaled a generational shift in the running of the Slater mills, as John Slater and his wife faced deteriorating health in the late 1830s. Ruth Slater became ill in 1838. "Mother is quite unwell again," wrote William Slater to his brother John Fox Slater, and she remained in problematic health until her death in 1867 at the age of eighty-three. More dramatically, in May 1843, John Slater died at age sixty-seven.[67] With the death of its patriarch, the family business passed to his sons, John Fox Slater and William Smith Slater. Their partnership, J. & W. Slater, lasted until January 1873. John F. Slater assumed oversight of the Connecticut mills, and William Slater remained in Slatersville and managed that concern.

While John Slater's transition of his business enterprises to his sons ran relatively smoothly, Samuel Slater's reliance on his family often meant pain and trouble. If anything, Samuel's family life was as difficult and problematic as his business ventures. In October 1791 Samuel Slater had married Hannah Wilkinson. Although they delayed having children for several years, in 1796 they had the first of seven sons and two daughters. Hannah died around 1812 shortly after their last son, Thomas Graham Slater, was born. While Samuel Slater married an English widow from Philadelphia in 1817, this union did not produce familial stability, and his household was troubled. One son, Samuel Slater 2nd died in 1821 at the age of nineteen. Earlier he had been sent to Massachusetts to supervise the Oxford property and became sick. Samuel Slater beseeched him to "be very careful of your health, and spare no pains to get restored to your former health." Samuel Slater 2nd returned home, continued to decline, and died within months.[68] Slater's youngest son, Thomas, caused considerable aggravation. When he was thirteen, Thomas and a friend ran off to New York. Samuel Slater remarked, "It is very lamentable thing that two young boys should be so thoughtless to leave a good house for an uncertainty, but so it is—"[69] By the age of twenty-two he was a social butterfly moving from one extravagant party to another. An invitation issued by Samuel Shove Jr. to Thomas Slater read, "You are hereby warned to appear at the house of Abraham Windon Esq. In Northbridge on Thursday the 8th of May armed and equipped as the law directs for savouring oysters tripe &c. I shall expect you to be on hand; we shall have a fine time as the right ones will be on hand."[70] His fondness for expensive clothing, food, liquor, and games almost landed him in jail. In 1843 a debt collector "with positive instruction to commit him to jail in case the demands were not settled called upon Thomas Slater to pay off a debt for horse keeping, board, and clothing." But when he saw Thomas, he found him in "a feeble state." Rather than execute the instructions given to him by the plaintiff, he demurred out of respect to the distinguished family to which he belonged."[71] Thomas Slater died in 1843 at the age of thirty-one.

Three of Samuel Slater's other sons, George, John, and Horatio, caused few problems. They were sent away to complete their education at the Episcopal Academy in Cheshire, Connecticut. The boys were taken into the family business. To his son John who was sixteen at the time and in school, Samuel Slater wrote, "You will have to make your appearance at Oxford, or here in one of the stores as per conversation with you some time past. It is highly important that one or more of my sons was learning the business so as to in some measure relieve me from the close attention which I have to attend to."[72]

Samuel realized that he would need his sons to run the business, and the Panic of 1829 prompted Samuel Slater to reorganize his business and give management responsibilities to them. Some land, mills, and dwellings were sold, other factories were consolidated, and Slater placed his three sons, John, George, and Horatio, in charge. At the age of sixty-one, Slater turned over the business to his sons, and a new firm, Samuel Slater and Sons, was created.

But the patriarch had difficulty ceding control of the factory, especially to his son John Slater 2nd. John had been involved with the family business throughout much of the 1820s. With Samuel Slater in Providence, John Slater 2nd was initially placed in charge of the Webster enterprise. But he was not allowed a free hand. His father made all decisions, including those involved with the labor force and town affairs. He decided when to sign contracts with employees, what rates of pay should be given to hands, whether or not the town should support a pauper farm, and other community affairs.

John Slater 2nd chafed under the yoke of his father, but his business reign proved to be turbulent and short-lived. In 1835 when Samuel

Slater died, John 2nd's business was in chaos. Shortly thereafter, John died while on vacation in St. Croix in 1837. He was then thirty-two years of age.[73] The family business would eventually pass to Horatio Nelson Slater who would continue the firm's dominant role in the textile industry. Along with John Fox Slater, he would create a legacy of business innovation and philanthropy that would last throughout the nineteenth century.

Samuel and John Slater were pioneers in the development of the American textile industry and the factory system more generally. They created the factory system in an economic world where the market for manufactured products was just emerging, where there was no agreed upon method of recruiting workers or organizing the labor force, and where the future of the industry was wide open. In experimenting with different forms of labor and factory organization, Samuel and John Slater, despite being immigrants from England, imbibed the American republican spirit of independence and frugality. Their economic activities were influenced by this cultural context. They feared the accumulation of debt and relied primarily on their families for economic and emotional support.

Indeed, the idea of family pervaded their lives, from the ownership of the mills to the organization of the labor force and the layout of the factory village. Blood and marriage ties characterized both management and labor. Family values were tied closely to small-town communities. John Slater in particular attempted to merge manufacturing with small-town values and beliefs. By the early nineteenth century, some American politicians were justifying industrial growth as a benefit for the people and for democracy, advocating the opening of the West for economic development. The Slaters certainly agreed with this sentiment, but unlike the Hamiltonian large-scale vision of industry supported by many entrepreneurs, they viewed economic expansion in more human terms, in the context of local communities based on shared family ties. This vision of small-town capitalism, outlined in embryo in John Slater's industrial village, would achieve fruition in the economic, political, and philanthropic activities and beliefs of his son John Fox Slater and the business activities of Horatio Nelson Slater, son of Samuel Slater. Yet with the onset of the Civil War and massive immigration, their commitment to small-town values and decent working conditions for their workers would be severely tested and eventually jettisoned in the new economic world of the Gilded Age.

Chapter 5

John Fox and Horatio Nelson Slater

Paternalism, Philanthropy, and the Disciplinary Society

On the death of Samuel Slater, the acclaimed father of American manufactures, the local *Pawtucket Chronicle* made a less flattering assessment of him: "Mr. Slater was not exactly a generous man. He gave little to public institutions and regarded not the appeals of private individuals. His object was gold. No man was more indefatigable."[1] Yet Slater had his supporters who saw in him and other manufacturers the embodiment of a new type of American character who looked to combine wealth, virtue, and patriotism into a new procapitalist mix. After his death, some biographers tried to transform him into an American icon. George S. White published the *Memoir of Samuel Slater* in 1836, a year after Slater's death. White was "anxious to make the volume of some permanence and benefit to the cause of American manufacturers. "Furthermore," he wrote, "I think the work is calculated to promote a patriotic attention to the general enterprise and prosperity of the country."[2]

These life stories were part of a new genre of antebellum biographies that celebrated the self-made man. Earlier studies had examined the lives of Revolutionary War heroes including Benjamin Franklin, Patrick Henry, and George Washington. These books were meant to be instructive, to espouse republican virtues, to be nationalistic, and to concentrate on public affairs and not on the private, domestic lives of great men.[3] But those published between 1830 and 1860 had a different mission. Private virtue and public success intertwined, and these categories became increasingly blurred in the topsy-turvy economic and social world of early nineteenth-century America. These new biographies were also instructive, and they detailed the specific process of character formation that led to the self-made man, promoting a narrative of the economic success story. Youth "should study biography for examples of character and its formation, and for the inspiration provided by the lives of those who had risen from obscurity and poverty to fame and fortune." Moreover, "the character one cultivated in private life placed one on the permanent path to fortune or ruin. . . . Industry, persistence, and temperance kept young men out of the clutches of 'confidence men and painted women,' while indolence, gambling, and drink rendered them easy prey for these unscrupulous characters," especially in an urban society increasingly dominated by a market economy.[4]

Samuel Slater's son, Horatio Nelson Slater, and his nephew John Fox Slater seemed to be the embodiment of these values. Inheritors of their fathers' textile mills, their mix of entrepreneurship, moralistic religion, and praise of self-discipline exemplified this new type of manufacturing hero who began to take his place alongside the pantheon of the great Revolutionary War leaders. Interests in community, family, church, and school were entwined with their business activities. Both became extremely wealthy, though John Fox Slater, unlike his uncle Samuel Slater, devoted much time and treasure to philanthropy. Horatio Nelson and John Fox Slater, however, were not content to serve as mere models of virtue and character. They actively tried to shape the emerging American culture into a Christian and capitalist mode. Closer to home, they attempted to mold their workers into a virtuous community based on discipline, a strong work ethic, and sobriety.

These men seemed to personify the classical argument about religion and capitalism advanced by Max Weber in *The Protestant Ethic and the Spirit of Capitalism*. Weber analyzed the connections between ascetic Protestant beliefs concerning individual salvation and a commitment to a calling and their relation to rational capitalism and the work ethic. Weber argued that Protestantism, based on the beliefs of figures from Martin Luther to John Calvin and the Puritans, promoted an individualistic, systematically rational lifestyle grounded in the idea of labor as a moral duty and a mark of character, which provided the psychological and cultural resources necessary for the rise of capitalism. While Weber recognized that ascetic Protestantism supplied moral legitimacy for an unequal division of labor, theorists such as Michel Foucault have explored the more subtle types of power and discipline that arose with modern capitalism. For Foucault, knowledge and power were always interlinked, and modern power works most effectively through institutions from military barracks to prisons that rationally shape the very understandings of morality and virtue of its subjects. The Slaters' Protestant vision of company towns and factories exemplified Foucault's ideas of disciplinary institutions, for they allowed the Slaters to develop techniques, from contracts to surveillance to Sunday church services, which attempted to create a docile and predictable labor force that accepted the authority of the owners.[5]

This type of moralistic capitalism was not foreordained. It arose through fits and starts, and its contours changed over time. The Slaters experimented with different forms of factory organization and often faced opposition from the laborers who they were trying to control. John Fox Slater and Horatio Nelson Slater were not just passive receptacles of an inevitable march toward capitalism, but they were active agents in developing technical and cultural approaches to textile manufacturing and the treatment of their workforce that helped to shape the very definition of the American economy and culture. Like Samuel Colt, they faced a new competitive market situation where the distinct interests of manufacturers and workers were beginning to coalesce and were often at odds with one another. Unlike their fellow textile manufacturers associated with the Boston Manufacturing Company, the Slaters concentrated on fine and fancy products rather than the coarse, inexpensive products manufactured by Lowell-style mills. Like these Boston entrepreneurs, however, they confronted an agricultural environment that was resistant to industry and whose traditional, rural values influenced a range of behaviors and beliefs, from expectations about the experience of labor to the nature of worker housing. The Slaters had to address the difficulties surrounding their traditional workforce while also integrating immigrants into their factory system. Initially they adopted a small-town, Christian solution to the problems posed by a manufacturing society; this differed from Colt's desire for a new global American empire. However, both Slaters ultimately jettisoned that approach for a more impersonal owner/worker relationship when new economic circumstances cut into their profits and their workforce became dominated by immigrants rather than native-born Americans. Although their similarities outweighed their disparities, there were also differences between the two men. John Fox Slater was committed to moral reform and the abolition of slavery, while his cousin Horatio resembled his father Samuel Slater in putting profits first and philanthropy a distant second. Whereas John Fox Slater is remembered for his philanthropic endeavors, Horatio

Nelson Slater is known more for his pioneering innovations in cost accounting and advertising.

Reminiscent of Colt, the Slaters relied on family networks, social connections, and political ties in consolidating and expanding their manufacturing ventures. The centrality of the family in antebellum American society was reflected not only in business relationships but also in labor practices. But as the family and the home became the repository of women's sphere of privacy and intimacy, in opposition to the public life of male activity, the family's relationship to an incipient industrial capitalism also became more complex. As a centralizing state and market economy arose, the self-contained family unit characteristic of an agricultural society began to lose many of its functions, from education and moral instruction to occupational autonomy. Yet it was not inevitable that the rules of capitalism would supplant those of the family. The Slaters faced a situation where the rights and responsibilities of the employer and the family were not clearly delineated and differentiated. Both the householder and the factory owner attempted to assert control on the factory floor and in their communities; this struggle precipitated conflicts over the management of labor. Yet throughout this era, the question of whether the family was to be simply a private realm with little impact on the workplace or play a role in determining the conditions of labor was a process subject to negotiation and often created confusion over public and private boundaries. John Fox Slater and Horatio Nelson Slater responded to these issues by attempting to create a paternalistic, moral, and Protestant Christian culture within their industrial communities. For them, "helping" their workers meant turning them into responsible, sober, and obedient laborers. Eventually they came to believe that the traditional, patriarchal family unit stood in their way. Management saw the family as an impediment, even an obstacle that had to be overcome to achieve greater profitability and efficiency.

While the ends were the same for both John Fox Slater and his cousin—a docile, sober, industrious worker—the means to achieve that goal differed. John Fox Slater in particular, as a devout Congregationalist like his parents John and Ruth Slater, believed that Christianity required service and that the wealthy had an obligation to help the less fortunate. But for Slater, such financial and moral obligations often stopped at the factory door. While trying to adapt the family system of labor to his needs, he constantly attempted to undercut the householder and to replace paternal with contractual relations within his mills. This assault on the family extended beyond the factory walls. Through his Sunday Schools, John Fox Slater taught his young hands his version of Christianity, often disregarding the wishes of their parents. He tried to create allegiances to the employer apart from, and in many ways superior to, those of the family. Until the post–Civil War era, he was unable to do so completely because of the paternalistic context of the time and the continued employment of Yankee families who refused to cede full control over their children to him.

Horatio Nelson Slater had fewer qualms about using more coercive means to create a disciplined workforce. After his father's death when family labor no longer fit his economic needs, he promptly challenged traditional prerogatives by paying hands individually, readjusting work schedules to include Sunday hours, and forcing all family members to work in the factory. Hands could accept the new conditions or quit. Irish and then French Canadian workers were available to take their jobs. Well before the Civil War, his community of Webster became one of the first immigrant towns in southern New England.

The Slaters were dealing with laborers at a time when class distinctions were becoming more pronounced. American workers and capitalists began living in different experiential worlds, and both of the Slaters would eventually face strikes by their workforce. Yet they attempted to avoid these struggles. The cousins envisioned a distinctively American manufacturing society devoid of class conflict, labor strife, and abysmal working and living conditions. The "dark satanic mills" associated with the British industrial revolution repulsed them. They sought instead to tie workers and employers together with a Christian culture and moral sensibility of labor and discipline that all could share. This was not the same type of discipline used by the earlier Puritans, who stressed eternal damnation for those who were not one of the elect. Rather, their version of evangelical Protestantism posited a free subject who could choose sin or the moral path. Here John Fox Slater was prepared to lead laborers along the proper route. The key was to create conditions that would allow workers to do the right thing. That is why detailed contracts were so important to him, for they not only prescribed workers' responsibilities, but they also represented a choice that the laborer had to make to work diligently for himself, for the Slater family, and for God, all of which dovetailed with one another. He helped to implement the disciplinary society, in Foucault's sense, where power was exercised through discourse and persuasion rather than direct coercion.

Force, after all, was the tactic used by some owners, such as slaveholders, to control those who labored for them. The existence of slavery provided John Fox Slater with a free conscience regarding his own treatment of workers. For most Americans, chattel slavery was fundamentally different from wage labor. Wage workers were allowed to move freely from one job to another. Because slavery was the boundary experience of freedom, wage labor could be equated with liberty. But such an equation was not self-evident. The republican tradition, represented most forcefully by Jefferson, had tied wage labor to dependency. But as industry developed and slavery became more clearly a scar on the national conscience, wage labor appeared in a different light. Slater could ill-treat his workers because he believed that they were free men who could make their own decisions. Commands could not simply be imposed on workers, for that would make them slaves rather than free men. Despite the discourse that compared Northern wage workers to slaves, a perception often advanced by Southern apologists, this stark division between confinement and freedom allowed Slater and other employers to mistreat workers and to keep their dealings from public scrutiny. Slater could forcefully criticize slavery as immoral and sinful while often treating workers as mere commodities.[6] He could clear his conscience by contributing money to educate freed slaves in postbellum America while at the same time employing young children, many of them under the age of ten, in his Jewett City and Taftville factories.[7]

At their deaths in the 1880s, both manufacturers had embraced ideas and values espoused by the Gilded Age. Profits first and people second became their watchwords, and their workforce became an expense that had to be reduced. To this end they employed immigrant workers, especially Irish and French Canadian Catholics, who by choice or necessity turned to factory labor. Because of the prevalent nativism of the era, few members of the general public protested management's rights to regulate their workforce. In this context, both of the Slaters allowed the conditions of their labor force and the situations in their company towns to deteriorate.

JOHN FOX SLATER

John Fox Slater's path to industrial wealth drew on his experience in the actual management of textile mills. He attended Plainfield, Wrentham, and Wibraham Academies but left school in 1832 at age seventeen to work in his father's woolen mill in Hopeville, Connecticut. Working with Samuel Collier there, he became a knowledgeable, adroit manager and businessman. By 1836 he took control of this factory as well as another cotton mill in Jewett City, Connecticut.[8] He learned the intricacies of the textile trade, developing a prudent business sense that translated into a great fortune during the Civil

War. Early on he gained a reputation for producing quality goods. His cousin, Horatio Nelson Slater, even stated that the goods produced by John Fox Slater were superior to those he manufactured at Oxford South Gore.[9] He was determined to retain that reputation; he inspected the cloth produced by his factories and threw out thin and problem pieces rather than sell them and tarnish his reputation. To one of his factory agents, he remarked, "Our goods once had a reputation for being almost perfect that is they were most always one thickness and well woven." The agent was to see that that quality was maintained.[10] A leader in textile production, Slater also became a powerful force in the transportation industry. He was the director of the extensive Midwest Chicago to Alton Railroad as well as the Joliet and Chicago line. But even as a young man, he realized that business entailed more than simply profit. He contributed generously to his Congregational church, expanding his philanthropic offerings to educational institutions and other "benevolent societies" as he accumulated more wealth, culminating in his one-million-dollar John F. Slater Fund for African American education and enterprise in 1884. At the time of his death in 1884, in addition to this trust, he had begun construction on a library in Jewett City, the site of one of his first successful enterprises.

The Jewett City Manufacturing Company was among John Fox Slater's most extensive industrial investments; it was located in a small, rural, agricultural Connecticut hamlet within the township of Griswold and first settled around the Revolutionary War era. From the outset, many village farmers realized that the swiftly flowing rivers in the area would be ideal locations for ancillary commercial projects. Utilizing the power afforded by the Pachaug River, they built saw, grist, and fulling mills. Later, at the turn of the century, cotton factories appeared, and the largest of these was the Jewett City Cotton Manufacturing Company, a partnership formed in 1809.[11] Like so many of the early factories, this mill carried all the earmarks of a Slater-style enterprise: small-scale production, yarn spinning, waterpower, a partnership form of ownership, personal management, and family labor. Yarn was put out to local handloom weavers who turned it into cloth.

This early two-story wooden factory employed about sixty men, adolescents, and children. The family system of labor predominated in a social world still defined by rural, agricultural values. As was common throughout the burgeoning industry that utilized the family as the source of employment, there was a division of labor based on age and gender. Men worked in traditional jobs such as teamster, watchman, field hand or common laborer, or in supervisory and skilled positions including superintendent, overseers, dyers, and mule spinners. Each earned the prevailing daily wages paid to adult males in the region: overseers earned about $1.25; mule spinners averaged $1.42; while common laborers received between $.50 and $1.17. The factory operatives, a group comprised largely of children, some as young as six or seven, earned the least at $.08 to $.34 per day.[12] Women remained in the home, sometimes taking in boarders and other times participating in various forms of outwork including handloom weaving.

The original factory owners, however, did not succeed financially, and the mill was acquired by Samuel and John Slater in 1823 for $17,100. They augmented their investment, and by 1829 an inventory of the property listed one new stone mill, an old wood mill, a store, a die house, and various houses, gristmills, sawmills, smithy, and about twenty-six acres of land. The houses, about nine in all, were scattered about town. Additionally, Samuel and John Slater acquired the Partridge farm, a 164-acre plot with a farmhouse, cattle, steers, heifers, a cow, and an old gray horse. Another house and fourteen acres of land were also included in the inventory of their Jewett City property.[13] Although from the outset John Slater had charge of the facility, he was basically an absentee landlord. He remained in Slatersville where he focused on that enterprise while Samuel Slater devoted his attention to his Rhode Island and Webster, Massachusetts mills. While the senior Slater brothers occasionally met to discuss business, they more often corresponded with one another about the future of the mill and its day-to-day operations. The Jewett City factory was run by a succession of hired agents until John Fox Slater assumed its management in 1836. At the age of twenty-one, this young man turned the factory into one of the most prosperous enterprises in the state. Upon the death of his father John Slater in 1843, the property went to his two sons, John Fox Slater and William Slater. They shared ownership of the Jewett City mills with their cousins. It was another six years before the brothers were able to purchase the outstanding shares from the heirs of Samuel Slater. They then formed a partnership, J. & W. Slater, and divided the administration of their property into two geographic entities: Jewett City and Slatersville. Their joint venture ended in 1873, and each brother assumed ownership of the mill he had previously managed.[14]

John Fox Slater was the true innovator in business affairs compared to his brother William. For much of his life, the Jewett City property remained at the heart of John Fox Slater's business activity. While this factory complex was modeled after those built by his father and uncle in Slatersville and Webster, it deviated from their enterprises in a significant way. John Fox Slater had not been given a blank page on which to plan an industrial community. His property was situated in an established hamlet that contained between eight and nine hundred people, five mercantile stores, a bank, and a Congregational church.[15] He had to adapt to the town's existing agricultural way of life, as farming still predominated among the people with farmers growing rye, Indian corn, oats, wheat, and barley for local consumption. They raised their own cattle, hogs, sheep, and horses. While most remained self-sufficient farmers, a few with state encouragement experimented with flax cultivation, and when the silk industry emerged, some of them planted mulberry trees and raised silk worms for the commercial market. However, there was little entrepreneurial energy among town citizens; as veterans of the Revolutionary War and the War of 1812, they valued church, school, work, and family.[16] Until the coming of the railroad in the 1830s, this community remained somewhat isolated with transportation confined largely to dirt roads.

Jewett City only slowly changed from an agricultural village to a commercial and industrial town. This unhurried growth continued from one generation to another. For John Fox Slater, technically operating the mill proved easy, but integrating it and the growing labor force into this environment required finesse.

Ownership of the mill made the Slaters the largest employers in town, and their mill workers constituted a growing market for housing, food, fuel, and clothing. Lodging was one central issue and demonstrated the restraints upon industry occasioned by an agricultural milieu. As manager of the mill, John Fox Slater had to find homes for his workers. He realized that those who worked in the factory and the families of children who labored for the mill had a right to company accommodations. If none were provided, he would not be able to recruit enough dependable workers. But the scant number of small, old houses he had on hand in 1829 could not supply his requirements. But he could not afford immediately to construct new factory tenements and relied instead on existing, dispersed housing. Purchasing some houses and renting others, he was able to meet most of their needs. Later he also promised to find a house "on the premises" for one family and "a good and suitable boarding place at the said Slater expense" for another family. Not only did he have to supply accommodations for his families, but they also expected to have access to fields, gardens, and barns where they could board their animals and raise part of their own food. When possible, housing carried with it a garden plot with barn privileges, providing that the family kept a cow in the winter months.[17]

While all members of the family were brought under the influence of the factory, householders retained many traditional prerogatives. Adult males refused to work as unskilled operatives and instead demanded that the manufacturer provide him with the type of labor appropriate to his position as householder. Such acceptable work included mule spinning, night watchman, painter, mason, teamster, and field hand. Wages were to be comparable to those currently paid in the region. Furthermore, the householder's patriarchal rights influenced the following: family work contracts, housing arrangements, wage payments, stipulations for education and training, factory discipline, and in some cases factory closures. His children worked in the factory. Married women or widows usually remained at home and often took in weaving, straw-bonnet making, or some other form of outwork. A patriarchal society buttressed that view. Heman Humphrey, conservative Congregationalist author of *Domestic Education* and president of Amherst College, wrote, "Every father is the constituted head and ruler of his household. God has made him the supreme earthly legislator over his children, accountable, of course, to Himself, for the manner in which he executes his trust; but amenable to no other power, except in the most extreme cases of neglect or abuse. The will of the parent is the law to which the child is bound in all cases to submit, unless it plainly contravenes the law of God."[18] While this view was compatible to the needs of Slater early on in his business career, the position of the householder later would prove an impediment to the efficient, profitable administration of his business.

Slater recognized that a new capitalist workforce demanded new types of behaviors. He began to transform this unspoken culture of mutual rights and responsibilities by instituting contracts, many seemingly trivial, that required particular behaviors on the part of his workers; he was gradually moving away from the traditional patriarchal system. His tenants agreed to pay rent, to take care that no ashes were to be kept in "any combustible vessel," to only house immediate family members in their dwellings, and to be responsible for all damages caused by their neglect. Furthermore, the company required that no hens could be kept on the property "inasmuch as they are a prolific cause of neighborhood difficulty" and that a hand had to "keep his cow yarded nights." In the 1830s annual rents ranged from $18.00 to $26.50.[19] Slater also recognized that not all of his employees would be householders, and he signed agreements with local residents to take in boarders. For example, David Terry was to take in six to eight boarders recommended to him by the company and was to receive the going rate for their room and board.[20] Still some families were left to find their own accommodations.

In the 1830s, factory houses consisted primarily of duplexes or single-family homes, places designed for family labor. John Fox Slater hired large families and required them to sign contracts binding householders and their children to work diligently for the company and to adhere to company rules and regulations. Although common throughout the industry and used by Samuel Slater at his Slater and Kimball mill and Smith Wilkinson at his Pomfret Manufacturing Company, the Jewett City contracts were more detailed than those of other manufacturers. Slater utilized the contract to begin paying workers individually rather than as a family unit.[21] He posted handbills around the mill complex specifying the general regulations to be observed by his employees. All absences required a written report giving reasons for nonattendance; smoking and drinking ardent spirits were strictly forbidden; and four weeks notice was to be given before quitting. Slater also expressed his "wishes" regarding the moral and general education of his employees. "It is the wish of the said Slater, that all persons pay a proper regard to the observance of the Sabbath, and attend public worship. Also, that parents and heads of families send their children to the Sabbath schools and week day school, so far as is consistent."[22]

The contracts devised by Slater for his workers demonstrated that forms of disciplinary power based on the surveillance of laborers and the inculcation of a morality of personal responsibility were beginning to take hold. Slater tried to fashion a diligent, obedient industrial worker who accepted a strong work ethic. Although spurred by the depression of the 1830s and 1840s, which induced many manufacturers to replace family labor with more malleable individual workers, such a form of labor discipline was indicative of new sources of control throughout the entire society, as traditional agricultural values gave way to commercial ones. Slater attempted to shape his workers' cultural beliefs and behaviors outside of the workplace as well. For him, the America of his imaginings was a Christian nation inhabited by hardworking, disciplined, Protestant people. The evils of sin, especially drink, were to be eradicated and a new, more gleaming "city on the hill" created. This vision of a Christian, benevolent, and sin-free America appealed to many businessmen such as Slater who saw it as their duty to use their wealth to advance this agenda. John Fox

Slater encouraged his workers to avoid liquor and regularly attend church services and provided scientific and moral instruction for them. Despite his ostensible commitment to family values, Slater was attempting to separate workers from their family commitments and to create a new allegiance to the factory and business values.

John Fox Slater's Sunday schools epitomized this new approach. They followed a similar path as those of Samuel Slater, who had introduced the first American Sunday School at Pawtucket, Rhode Island. As Samuel Slater's system of manufacturing spread throughout southern New England, so too did the Sunday Sabbath Schools. Based on British models, these schools were under the leadership of the factory master and were designed to keep children out of trouble on Sundays, to teach them rudimentary reading and writing skills, and to discipline them. Lessons learned in the schools were taken from the Bible, and emphasis was placed on obedience, honesty, and deference. The Sunday Schools established at Slatersville and Webster were among the largest in New England and a prototype for others. One feature of the Webster school was its "Constitution." Children pledged "to be regular in attendance, and punctually present at the hour appointed to open school. To pay a strict and respectful attention to whatever the teacher or Superintendent shall say or request. To avoid whispering, laughing and any other improper conduct."[23]

These rules and regulations were just as appropriate for the factory floor as they were for the Sunday School, and it was not surprising that such schools were found in Jewett City. But the Sunday School had to conform to existing community values, and the Slaters could not just do as they pleased. Before the Slaters took over the Jewett City mill, there were no Sunday Schools in the village. Local Congregationalists strictly adhered to Sabbath Day laws that banned working, conducting business, transporting mails, traveling, socializing, and attending amusements or shows on the Sabbath. Depending on the offense, fines of three dollars to seven dollars were exacted for each violation. From sunset on Saturday to sunset on Sunday, families were expected to obey these regulations. Attendance at schools on Sundays, even those designed to inculcate moral lessons, was discouraged by local ministers who regarded them "as a profanation of the Sabbath."[24] But after the Slater family took charge of the Jewett City mill, and by 1830, 163 pupils attended Sunday school classes. First John Slater and then John Fox Slater openly encouraged mill parents to send their children to the school. As well, funds were provided for the school's support.[25]

Slater also carefully developed a housing model that avoided class segregation. No distinctive working-class culture that could confront business values arose within his company towns. As Slater's success grew, more housing was needed. Enlarged in 1859 his factory now provided jobs to hundreds of people, and John Fox Slater soon began a housing project to accommodate the additional hands. That year, thirteen new tenements were built in an area later called Lincoln Square, named after the new president, Abraham Lincoln. These wood-frame, two-family homes were one and one-half stories high with gable roofs; they featured two offset chimneys and full-width porches supported either by square or Tuscan-style columns. Each home had a separate entry.[26]

Such comfortable housing reinforced Slater's reputation as a good employer. Having in 1846 replaced the original Jewett City wood factory with a large and safer brick structure, he tried to provide decent working conditions as well as good homes and educational and religious opportunities for his workers; he adhered to the laws of the state regarding employment procedures and regulations. By the 1840s Connecticut restricted the use of children under the age of fifteen in manufacturing establishments. The statute stipulated that if a child were to be employed under that age, he or she must have attended school at least three of the twelve months during the year of employment. Children under fourteen could not work more than ten hours per day. It was not until 1886, however, that the state legislature passed a law prohibiting the employment of children under thirteen from working in the mills under any circumstances. Slater more than complied with the rules. By 1860 no one under fifteen worked for his company.[27]

For much of the antebellum period, the population of the town continued to be largely native born, and the proportion of those engaged in agriculture and those in manufacturing was about the same. In 1860 the federal population census counted 351 farmers and 295 mill hands.[28] Workers born in Rhode Island or Connecticut comprised the largest part of Slater's labor force, and many of them remained in his employ for years and even decades. By the time of Slater's death in the 1880s, it was noted that the mill's superintendent had served grandfather, father, and son; the bookkeeper and four of the seven department overseers had worked with him for at least forty-seven years. Slater's son William claimed that he "maintained uninterruptedly the good-will of those whom he employed." He was determined to keep the mill running throughout the years despite economic downturns, war, or interruption of supplies. Again his son noted, "When business was dull and all seemed blue, it was still his desire to run as long as possible, because of his dread of throwing his employees out of work. He was one of the first in his neighborhood to insist on the shortening of the hours of labor by one hour per day, when this subject was agitated some ten or twelve years ago."[29]

THE CIVIL WAR AND ITS AFTERMATH

The 1860s was a pivotal decade for Slater. His fortunes were transformed by the war. A Republican supporter of Abraham Lincoln, he was also a friend and long-time neighbor of the first Republican governor of Connecticut, William Buckingham. Slater and Buckingham shared a common interest in education, and both served as trustees for the Norwich Free Academy, supported Sunday Schools, and led Norwich in its preparation for and participation in the Civil War. A second friend, Moses Pierce, president of the Ashland Cotton Company of Jewett City, abolitionist, former Free-Soil advocate turned Republican, and philanthropist, worked with Slater on many local and national issues including African American education, the Norwich Free Academy, temperance, and concerns associated with the health and well being of children. The two men also participated in several business ventures together including the Norwich Bleaching and Callendering Company and later the Ponemah Mills.[30]

The first "war meeting" held in Norwich represented a gathering of the town's leading citizens including Governor Buckingham and John Fox Slater. Slater was appointed to a committee to recruit soldiers, form military companies, and fit them for service. Again and again, Governor Buckingham turned to his Norwich friends for help. He pleaded, "Close your manufactories and workshops, turn aside from your farms and your business, leave for a while your families and your homes, and meet face to face the enemies of your liberties!" Slater was appointed chairman of the Norwich Patriotic Fund Committee to collect and appropriate funds for the war effort.[31] Slater became involved in war preparation programs. As chairman of the Patriotic Fund Committee, he took the lead in recruiting soldiers for the Union cause and was among those who suggested offering a bounty to anyone who agreed to enlist.[32]

John Fox Slater prospered during the war. Slater and his cousin Horatio Nelson Slater sold cloth to the Union that was used for uniforms. In 1860 his worth was estimated at $50,000, but within a decade his real estate was valued at $50,000 and his personal estate at a whopping $1,718,000.[33] He was in a position to invest in other ventures, such as the massive Ponemah Mills of Taftville. This mill complex, which was to become one of the largest in the world, was constructed in Taftville, a small village near Norwich. The original owners could not complete the project, and several years later it passed to wealthy Connecticut and Rhode Island investors including John Fox Slater, William Slater, and Moses Pierce, among others. They paid about one and a half million dollars for it. It was among the first American mills to utilize Egyptian cotton for the manufacture of fine fabrics. When operating at full capacity, the mill employed about 1,500 workers and produced several million yards of cloth annually.[34] Like other industrial sites, housing and amenities were provided. Workers rented company houses and shopped at the local store.[35] In 1871 John Fox Slater was named the first president of the firm and remained in that position until his death.

Though Slater's service in the Civil War had conveniently contributed to his fortune, as he had a secure market in the Union Army, the postbellum business climate, however, was quite volatile. Slater's commitment to his workers waned. By the 1870s, the nation was entering its first major postwar depression. Some factories shut down completely; others went on shortened schedules; and most tried to cut costs and increase output. The Ponemah Mills suffered as well. As the vicissitudes of capital and the market influenced more and more of daily life, labor and management relations deteriorated. Ethnic and class differences between management and labor became pronounced, replacing the shared culture that Slater had tried to create before the war. To overcome the depressed market, the owners changed the type of goods they produced from fine and fancy to coarse and cheap cloth. In January 1873, the company also reduced wages about 12 percent and ten months later again reduced workers' pay by a similar amount. Although hands initially absorbed the wage cuts, by 1875 many found that they could not adequately live under these new conditions. Operatives earned between $8.25 to $9.00 for a sixty-seven hour week, about 16 percent less that some of the other mills in the region.[36]

Such low wages did not go far at the local store owned by the company: "The men complained that they did not handle the money they earned, and that their bills were settled for, not by, them." Deductions for rent and store goods were taken directly out of their wages, and oftentimes workers received very little in their pay envelopes. One worker complained that he and his daughter received nothing for three months of work, while another stated that for the same period he received a mere $.71. The company also kept back one month and three days pay just in case workers quit suddenly or tried to abscond without paying their bills. "There was a very general impression among the men that the company were determined to have all their earnings, whether a large or small bill was incurred at the store."[37] They complained to Slater; he offered "to raise the wages of some of the operatives but not of all." The situation escalated, and workers formed a union. Incensed, management refused to negotiate with the union and threatened to fire union members. The company did, however, increase the pay of some of its workers by about 5 percent. But it was too late. On April 7, 1875, workers went out on strike; the mill was closed, and when it reopened a week later Slater and his management team had turned to scab laborers. Their former hands were given thirty days notice to vacate their tenements, and many left the village to seek work elsewhere.[38]

At the Jewett City mill, changes also occurred, especially in the composition of the labor force. A significant number of immigrants began to move into the town. By 1860, it was estimated that one in six residents was foreign born, with the Irish comprising the largest percentage of that group. Irishmen first arrived with the building of the railroads in the 1830s and 1840s. Soon some of them found their way into the Slater mills, and by 1860 they constituted about 40 percent of the workforce.[39] Although New Englanders still predominated and constituted over 50 percent of the workers in 1870, Irish and especially French Canadian workers filled more and more jobs. But change was not restricted to the ethnic makeup of the workers. A new feature of the evolving workforce was an increase in child labor. Once almost eliminated at the Slater mills, by 1870 about 23 percent of the workforce was composed of children from eight to fourteen years of age.[40] As paternalism faded, the laws of the market took its place. Whether native or foreign born, more and more parents put their young children to work in the mills. They cited hard times, low wages, intermittent unemployment, and the death of a spouse as reasons for sending their children out to work. Child labor laws and compulsory school attendance acts were either ignored or circumvented. Management complied, as cheaper labor meant larger profits. They also claimed that parents threatened to quit if the superintendent failed to hire their young children; in their view, they were merely complying with parental wishes so that the best help would remain in their employ. Whether or not these assertions were true, child labor became an integral part of Slater's operations. For example, John Brown of

Rhode Island worked in the Slater mill alongside three of his children, Mary, Ervina, and Charles, fifteen, twelve, and ten, respectively. James Caliman, an Irishman, placed two of his young children, ages twelve and eight, in the factory while John Tetrault of Canada had three young children, ages eight, ten, and thirteen working there.[41]

Housing patterns also changed. Additional duplexes, multifamily tenements, and boarding houses were built. Constructed between 1868 and 1880, these homes were spaced tightly together, exhibited "barracks-like qualities," and lacked porches or extensive exterior detailing.[42] These new barracks-like structures represented harbingers of the Foucauldian disciplinary society, as predictability, uniformity, and rationality ruled within and outside of the factory floor. Utilitarian structures, they resembled mill housing found elsewhere throughout New England.[43]

Slater came to resemble more and more a stereotypical business tycoon, concerned with profits rather than the situation of his workers. In 1842 after he moved his residence from Jewett City to Norwich, he conducted all of his business from home and had little contact with workers.[44] By the 1870s, his interests had expanded beyond the textile industry, and he served as a director of the following concerns: the Norwich and New London Steamboat Company, three railroad companies including two that ran through Chicago, the Norwich Fire Insurance Company, and Norwich City Gas Company. Furthermore he sat on the board of directors for the Worcester-based Washburn and Moen Manufacturing Company.[45] Slater's notion of a beneficent employer was always double-edged. In addition to providing good working conditions for his workers, he expected their obedience, compliance, and practice of Christian virtue. As his sense of responsibility for his workers faded in the competitive textile industry and the money mania of an incipient Gilded Age, Slater increasingly resembled the capitalist who had no tie to his workers other than "naked self-interest," in Marx and Engels's famous phrase.[46] But Slater did not simply retreat from any sense of public responsibility. Rather, he channeled his efforts into philanthropy, the abolition of slavery, and the moral uplift of African Americans. Challenging slavery eased his conscience regarding the treatment of his own workers and allowed him to exercise the service and stewardship of wealth demanded by his understanding of Christianity. He was able to compartmentalize the worlds of work, education, and slavery, seeing them as different spheres based on different principles of action, which had little to do with one another.

SERVICE AND RESPONSIBILITY

Slater always had an interest in philanthropy, which came to fruition with his move to Norwich in 1842. He married in 1844, took advantage of the town's economic growth, became involved in church and local affairs, and began his philanthropic undertakings. Situated at the headwaters of the Thames River, Norwich was one of the leading commercial towns in Connecticut by the American Revolution, and the war only strengthened its economic position. Town merchants imported a wide variety of goods including such luxury items as jewelry, silver, clothes, books, and drugs, which they sold to an increasingly prosperous population of merchants, artisans, local shop owners, and country shopkeepers. With the onset of the war and with New London, its chief local rival under threat from possible British invasion, Norwich took the lead in establishing new enterprises including shipbuilding, privateering, and provisioning. The state designated Norwich a commissary depot, a central receiving and dispatching center supplying the Continental Army and French forces in Rhode Island with goods.[47]

In the post–Revolutionary War period, Norwich continued to expand, and its merchants became active in West India trade. Horses, cattle, and country produce were exchanged for salt, molasses, rum, sugar, coffee, and tea. Manufacturing also flourished with iron works, cutlery and pottery workshops, and paper, clock, cotton, and even chocolate mills established in town. Norwich Falls became the center for much of this activity. It was there that Amos H. Hubbard, future father-in-law of John Fox Slater, established his paper manufacturing business. Begun in 1818, he first produced hand laid paper, but by 1830 paper making had become mechanized. Amos formed a partnership with his brother Russell, and they built two mills at the falls complete with lots and tenements. By 1850 his real estate was worth fifty thousand dollars. The in-laws to be of John Fox Slater were one of the most prominent families in Norwich.[48]

It was not Norwich's manufacturing history nor the Hubbard family's wealth but the town's antislavery climate that would have the most influence on John Fox Slater. Norwich was a hotbed of abolitionist sentiment; it was a station on the underground railroad, and home to a sizeable group of African Americans who resided on Jail Hill. Several of the local residents even served as agents for the Boston based newspaper, the *Liberator*, and were linked to some explosive antislavery issues including the famous Prudence Crandall affair. In 1831 Prudence Crandall, a young Quaker school teacher, was asked by local residents in the rural town of Canterbury, Connecticut to open and operate a school for girls. Among the girls who sought to matriculate at the school was an African American, Sarah Harris of Norwich. Crandall agreed to let her join the classes. All white at the time, local parents protested her enrollment and withdrew their daughters from school; rather than acquiesce to their demands or close her school, Crandall reopened it with black pupils. She enlisted the aid of William Lloyd Garrison, publisher of the *Liberator*, and the Reverend Samuel May, pastor of the nearby Unitarian church in Brooklyn, Connecticut. By 1833 enrollment stood at about twenty girls. Canterbury residents disapproved and harassed both Crandall and her students. Sentiment around the state also worked against Crandall. The State Assembly passed a law stating that if African Americans from outside the state wanted to attend private schools and academies, they had to first obtain permission from the town to matriculate. Even under these threats, Crandall continued her work, but eventually she was arrested for violating this act and was sent to jail in Brooklyn and in due course left the state. Sarah Harris later married a blacksmith and moved to Rhode Island where she raised her family. Two brothers, Charles and William, resided in Norwich and continued to work as agents for the abolitionist William Lloyd Garrison.[49]

This atmosphere of heated debate and activity around abolition and black/white relations pervaded all of Norwich, including its religious institutions. The Second Congregational church, which Slater joined after his advantageous marriage to wealthy, prominent Marianna Hubbard in 1844, was renowned for its support of a Sunday School for black and white children. Entry into the Hubbard family brought Slater into contact with community leaders and activists, especially those concerned with the plight of slaves. The Hubbards were involved in the Norwich Sunday School movement, which began in 1815 when a few African American boys were brought together and taught to read and write. The following year another school for indigent white boys was organized, and shortly thereafter, the two groups merged. The instructors sought to inculcate good manners, right living, and basic reading and writing skills. The teachers were expected to "use their utmost endeavor that they [the pupils] may be gathered into the fold of the Great and Good Shepherd." A school for girls also was started, and because of space shortages, the boys' and the girls' schools were held in the same building, although each occupied a different room. By 1817 white pupils numbered forty-seven girls, forty-eight boys, and forty-one African Americans: the latter ranged in age from six to fifty-six years. A formal merger of the schools later took place, and the school came under the supervision of the Second Congregational Church with William C. Gilman as superintendent.[50]

This service-oriented Congregationalism represented a new form of Christianity different from its Puritan ancestor. Ministers such as Lyman Beecher and Charles G. Finney argued for a useful religion that emphasized helping one's fellow man, for holiness was tied to benevolence, not selfishness. These liberal sentiments often translated into support of the abolitionist cause, which was taken up by many in Norwich with great zeal.

Members of Slater's congregation epitomized these new religious values. The congregation was comprised of both rich and poor, black and white. Parishioners including merchants and industrialists such as Amos Hubbard, Russell Hubbard, William Gilman, Hamlin Buckingham, and William Williams, joined in communion with the families of William M. Harris, Joseph Guy, and Fitch Pelham, who were African American worshippers. This church was among the first institutions in town to support the immediate abolition of slavery. As early as 1834, Rev. James T. Dickinson preached a sermon outlining his support for the abolitionist cause and called for the establishment of a local anti-slavery society. Slavery was a sin, he said, and "every person whose sentiments in regard to slavery are correct, but who does not exert his influence to extend those sentiments, is also chargeable with sin. There is need, then of an anti-slavery society among us. We need such a society to correct and embody public sentiment, and cause it to bear against this sin."[51]

Many in this congregation championed a number of causes designed to assist blacks. Several of the same families that supported the Second Congregational Church Sabbath School for indigent black and white children and who joined the local Abolitionist Society also provided for the building of Norwich Academy, a racially integrated secondary school. This institution would be open to all the children of Norwich regardless of color, gender, family name, or income. The academy was "to stand between the common school and the university, reaching with one hand to the humblest child of poverty, and with the other opening before him the door of honor and usefulness."[52] A privately endowed institution, it would be supported by wealthy Norwich businessmen who "wanted to secure a course of instruction in the higher branches, so that young persons might here be prepared to enter upon the different callings of life, as mechanics, merchants, navigators, scholars, agriculturists, or professional men, but as the grand result, the Academy was expected to become the means and instrument of elevating the standard of the common schools."[53]

The original donor list included such familiar family names as Hubbard, Williams, Coit, and Buckingham.[54] Also on that list was John Fox Slater, who had developed a keen interest in education. Together with Russell Hubbard, Slater donated the scientific apparatus for the school. Throughout his life, Slater continued to contribute his time and money to the academy that lived up to its mission by educating rich and poor, black and white, and male and female students. The school became synonymous with the Slater family when in 1884 William A. Slater built Slater Memorial Hall on its campus. Named in honor of his father, this grand building hosted lectures and music programs and housed a special-collections library and a museum devoted to the fine arts.[55]

Slater's philanthropic work had just begun. Together with Judge Lafayette Foster, he acquired a ten-room house on a three-acre lot in Norwich and turned it over to the United Workers, a charitable organization. This building, the "Shelter Arms," served as the primary hospital in Norwich until the William Backus facility was built in the 1890s. Slater continued to support the activities of this organization, which included the establishment of an employment bureau, sewing schools for girls, and a Christian home for children. Like many other similar associations of the era, the United Workers was designed to assist destitute women and children and to encourage their moral development. Presaging the combination of female leadership, moral reform, and Protestant piety that would characterize the Progressive Era, its membership was confined largely to Protestant, middle- and upper-class women who were considered among the leading ladies of Norwich.[56]

Many of Slater's gifts grew from his association with the Congregational church, and he helped to organize and support a new church to be built in his neighborhood. The Chelsea area to which the Slater family moved in the 1860s continued to grow and attract new residents. They soon tired of commuting downtown to attend services at the Second Congregational Church and decided to organize their own society. Appointed a member of the building committee and elected an officer in the Park Ecclesiastical Society, he solicited funds for the new structure. Total costs for the church amounted to one hundred thousand dollars, of which Slater contributed thirty-three thousand. Beautiful stain glass windows can still be seen in the church. Designed in part by Louis Tiffany, the east group windows facing Crescent Street were donated by Slater to memorialize his daughter Marianna who died at the age of twenty-eight.[57] Another ten thousand dollars was contributed to keep the church in repair.[58]

But John Fox Slater was not defined by his family life or even his business career. He is best remembered as the patron for the education of former Southern slaves. At the time of his death, his support of education, religion, and racial justice all intertwined to define his most generous public gift, the John F. Slater Fund. In 1882 Slater set up a one-million-dollar charitable foundation for the education of former Southern slaves. He was definite about the purpose of this fund:

> The general object which I desire to have exclusively pursued is the uplifting of the lately emancipated population of the Southern States, and their posterity, by conferring on them the blessings of Christian education. The disabilities formerly suffered by these people, and their singular patience and fidelity in the great crisis of the nation, establish a just claim on the sympathy and good-will of humane and patriotic men. I cannot but feel the compassion that is due in view of their prevailing ignorance which exists by no fault of their own.
>
> But it is not only for their own sake, but also for the safety of our common country, in which they have been invested with equal political rights, that I am desirous to aid in providing them with the means of such education as shall tend to make them good men and good citizens—education in which the instruction of the mind in the common branches of secular learning shall be associated with training in just notions of duty toward God and man, in the light of the Holy Scriptures.[59]

Administrators of the fund included Daniel Coit Gilman, president of Johns Hopkins University; Dwight Woolsey, president of Yale; and the Reverend Leonard Bacon, minister of Slater's church. Former president Rutherford B. Hayes was designated president of the trust.

This fund capped Slater's philanthropic efforts. It demonstrated that widespread philanthropic endeavors by businessmen did not begin with figures such as Rockefeller and Carnegie. Indeed, Slater was part of a larger culture of philanthropy that expanded during the antebellum years. The economic ascendancy of antebellum manufacturers was soon matched by their cultural impact. Charitable giving often went to religious and intellectual institutions that tended to perpetuate or defend the positions of elites in their communities. Among the Boston manufacturing elite, Abbott Lawrence gave generously to Harvard University, while his brother spread his largess more broadly, giving about half of a million dollars to various charitable projects between 1841 and 1852. John Lowell Jr. founded the Lowell Institute, and Nathan Appleton patronized the Boston Athenaeum, the Museum of Fine Arts, and the public library, among other concerns.[60]

Many also recognized that their money could be used to encourage discipline, respect for property, punctuality, temperance, and deference among the lower orders. They coupled their beneficence to elite institutions with their giving to various community organizations such as Sunday Schools, city missions, Bible tract societies, evening schools, libraries, and lecture programs. While Slater's gifts also went to both strengthen his social and economic position and control the behavior of the poor, the immigrant, and the industrial worker, he was distinctive among philanthropists in his concern for the newly freed African slave. At the time of his death, he ranked among the leading philanthropists in the country and was compared to Stephen Girard, Peter Cooper, Johns Hopkins, and George Peabody. In *American Philanthropists*, published in 1887, Slater was described as "an active helper in all that tended to promote the cause of Christianity, among nations, as the spiritual progress among individuals." And "the light and happiness resulting from Mr. Slater's beneficence will make his name and memory dear to the American people, and will add to the fame of Connecticut thrift one more example of New England liberality."[61]

John Fox Slater had made a fortune during the Civil War and was among the wealthiest men in Connecticut. In the antebellum years, he grew his business, participated in local affairs, became a major philanthropist, married, and began to raise a family. He was considered a model citizen and businessman; his reputation was pristine, and amity could be observed in his home, factory, and community relations. Later, this changed and indeed was turned on its head. Not only did relations with his employers deteriorate, but Slater had a very difficult personal life that belied his public reputation. His daughter Marianna died young. She left behind two young daughters, Carolina and Elizabeth. Soon thereafter his son William left for Harvard. To further complicate matters, he separated from his wife, leaving Slater alone and depressed. For a man who valued family above most other institutions, tried to live up to the values and expectations of his parents, and had supported the family system of labor in his factory communities, the disintegration of his own family was devastating. Yet Slater was in many ways suffering the personal consequences of larger social changes, including those that he had helped to implement within his workforce. In postbellum America, the family felt the impact of the new economic order with its emphasis on individualism, social Darwinism, and materialism. Moreover, among Slater's employees, his actions had undermined the family by challenging the prerogatives of the householders, forcing some family members to work on the Sabbath, paying each laborer for his work, and ignoring educational and child labor laws. It was ironic that his own family crumbled as well under the new economic and social system that he helped to create and sustain. Slater lived until 1884 and was survived by his estranged wife, a son, and several grandchildren, leaving behind a complicated legacy.[62]

Horatio Nelson Slater, His Father's Son

While John Fox Slater turned his father John Slater's mills into a fortune, the fate of Samuel Slater's burgeoning business empire fell to his sons, in particular Horatio Nelson Slater. Samuel Slater, sixty-one years of age, rheumatic, with an outstanding debt of $215,000 and facing strong competition from both foreign and domestic producers, decided that changes had to be made if his business was to continue. He formally took three of his sons into the business and created Samuel Slater and Sons in 1829. At the time George, John, and Horatio Nelson were twenty-five, twenty-four, and twenty-one years of age respectively. A fourth son, Thomas, only seventeen at the time, was excluded from the partnership.[63]

The creation of the company merely legalized the relationship that had long existed between Samuel Slater and his sons. Slater groomed his sons to manage the family business. The boys received their early education at the Cheshire Episcopal Academy in Cheshire, Connecticut. They studied the classics including Latin, and George even evinced a desire to prepare for entry into Brown University. Throughout their several years at the Academy, Slater kept in close contact with his boys, offered them advice, and monitored their progress. He admonished Horatio Nelson not to waste his time but to prepare for the future. In response, his young son showed a bit of defiance and wrote, "I do not, however, spend all my leisure time idly. I read considerable and play some for play is necessary in order to keep Nelson from being a dull boy."[64] Their education was cut short in 1821 when Samuel Slater called the boys home and reminded them, "It is highly important that one or more of my sons was learning the business so as to in some measure relieve me from the close attention which I have to attend to." John had a choice of the Webster mills or one of the local Slater stores, while his brother Horatio Nelson began to serve his apprenticeship first at one of his father's stores, then a machine shop, and finally the mills. George B. Slater worked in Webster and later in Sutton, Massachusetts. By 1829 all three boys were brought into Samuel Slater and Sons.[65]

Samuel Slater tried to keep his sons close to him, and indeed it appeared that he succeeded. When in his sixties, his health failed, and by 1833 he sometimes was confined to his bed.[66] Slater lingered another two years, and after he died, John, George, and Horatio reorganized the business selling off some property, fixing Providence as headquarters for their firm, introducing hired, specially trained men to actually manage day-to-day operations of the factories, instituting cost-accounting features, and reorganizing the labor force.

Of the original three brothers in Samuel Slater and Sons, two of them died early: John Slater in 1838 at the age of thirty-three and George B. Slater in 1843, then thirty-nine years of age.[67] To Horatio Nelson Slater fell the tasks of not only running the Slater businesses but also caring for the families of his two deceased brothers. Lydia, the wife of George Slater, was left with two young children, William and Elizabeth, ages nine and twelve respectively. They continued to reside in Webster, but William turned to farming and not manufacturing. John Slater's widow, Sarah, assumed guardianship of her children—including Horatio Nelson, named after his uncle—and left town for Rhode Island.[68] Later, young Horatio would be adopted by his uncle Horatio and would become primary heir to the Slater fortune. Thomas Slater, the rebellious black sheep of the family, remained largely outside the Slater business ventures.

Until he retired in 1888, Horatio Nelson Slater guided the family enterprise. Throughout his lifetime, he tried to measure up to his father's reputation. Horatio was a practical businessman concerned with controlling all aspects of the family business from production to distribution. He implemented innovations in cost accounting and advertising and adopted a hard-line approach to labor discipline and order. Horatio carried on his father's vision for their company town in Webster, Massachusetts. He confronted an agricultural world that did not automatically produce disciplined factory workers; he utilized a version of Christianity to instill obedience in workers and hired immigrant workers to displace native laborers as economic conditions changed.[69]

WEBSTER

Initially Horatio's business concerns were intertwined with those of his brothers, and they built a company town and factory in Webster, Massachusetts. Like the Jewett City community of John Fox Slater, the area of Oxford South Gore that later became Webster was an agricultural district that had to be transformed into a manufacturing center. When it was incorporated as a town in 1832, Webster already had been associated with the Slater family for more than twenty years. With partner Bela Tiffany, Samuel Slater purchased 270 acres of land in south central Massachusetts; he bought out his partner in 1818 and continually expanded his holdings thereafter. When incorporated, Webster consisted of four villages, North, South, East, and Depot, and encompassed about 14,000 acres of land, rivers, and Webster Lake, originally known as Lake Chaubunagungamaug.[70] This community of 1,170 people revolved around the textile industry. Factories and company farms dominated the landscape. Tenements, boarding houses, and a number of retail stores supplied the needs of laborers and operatives. In many respects, the village displayed the earmarks of the earlier Slatersville enterprise, a community that incorporated the needs of a new system of production with the values of a rural labor force comprised of families. Of the villages that formed Webster, East Village was the location of Slater's home, the "Hermitage." It was here that the family stayed when they were in town. But in terms of economic activity, South Village was predominant, and it is the district discussed below and will hereafter be referred to as Webster.

Webster exhibited the open-field village pattern found in Slatersville. Along Main Street stood general, grocery, and dry goods shops and a bakery, hotel, tavern, and churches. Nearby were the semidetached and detached homes of workers. Single-family dwellings were necessary to accommodate the family system of labor. These well-constructed, stone, two-story duplexes each included a kitchen, parlor, and bedroom on the first floor, two bedrooms on the second floor, and a basement. Set back from the road and containing an allotment of land large enough for families to grow spring and summer vegetables, the homes preserved the pastoral conditions so familiar to many of the laborers. Families kept farm animals such as cows, horses, and cattle, but they were put out to graze on one of the company's several farms. These services were not free, however, for cow keeping or plowing gardens, the company charged a fee. A monthly assessment of $.25 per animal was charged for grazing and $.26 for plowing gardens.

For the next generation of factory hands, amenities increased. An ice dealer commenced business in 1858, followed by an enlarged Slater Company store in 1867 and the Webster Five-cent Savings Bank years later. The store sold goods to both operatives and the general public. This two-story building contained four separate departments with "everything for personal use and adornment" and employed thirty-seven clerks. It was estimated that sales totaled one thousand dollars per day.[71] Beyond the stores and shops were the mills and company farms.

The entire township was dominated by the Slater family. From the outset, they attended to every aspect of community development. Enthusiastic Whigs, both John and George Slater took an interest in local and state politics. For example, in 1832, John was elected to represent Webster in the Bay State legislature.[72] At this time, the state was controlled by the Whig Party, many of whom were in league with the leading industrialists of the state. They were committed to economic expansion and forestalling the passage of egalitarian and populist reforms. With the exception of the common school movement that they supported, Whigs believed that private philanthropy guided by Christian moral values should provide for the poor, the unfortunate, and the infirm. For many Whigs, reform revolved around personal character building. They alleged that temperance, compulsory school attendance, and strict Sabbath Day observance, for example, would do more to uplift and assist the people than the ten-hour day movement, child labor legislation, or debt relief. To insure that they remained in power, the Whigs supported a poll tax, the open ballot, and a sunset law that effectively prevented laborers from going to the polls after work. The Slaters were jubilant when Whigs won in 1835. The Whigs "have triumphed over the Jackson and workingmen in our town meeting," and the following year the "Whig votes exceeded the Democratic about 50 percent."[73] John Slater had hoped to become a prominent party member, but he died on January 23, 1838. By this time, his brother George had become involved in local politics. Repeatedly elected to local office including selectman, highway surveyor, and fire warden, he served the town until he succumbed to tuberculosis in 1843.[74]

Even with the active participation of the Slater brothers before their early deaths, Whig control of Webster took some time to insure. Though the Slaters controlled several local and state offices, initially the town residents did not follow the Whig mold advocated by them. The first votes cast for the statewide offices of governor and lieutenant governor went to Antimasonic candidates. At the next election, Webster voters supported Samuel Allen on the Workingmen's Party ticket. Populist in orientation, antiaristocratic rather than anticapitalist, and with roots in the western counties, inland cities, and seaport towns, this movement was not strong enough to carry the state. John Davis on the National Republican ticket was elected governor, and the next election saw Edward Everett, a Whig, receive the support of Webster residents as the Slaters' wishes predominated.[75] The trend continued in the election of a representative to the General Court in 1836. Manufacturers throughout southern New England were determined to keep the Whigs in power. Agent Storrs of Union Mills in Webster told Horatio Nelson Slater that "one thing is very certain that the Whigs must carry out their principals in their business as they now will be successful, they have already begun in Connecticut. Many mills in Stafford Connecticut have discharged all that oppose Whig measures, Dea. Porter and the Stafford Mfg. Co., have none in their employ but Whigs."[76] The only anxiety Storrs expressed concerned the rise of the Liberty Party in town. "The liberty party has been very disgusting in this town, they are too mean to be called men," wrote Storrs.[77] The Whigs continued to predominate, and Slater's criteria for employment emphasized "our good Methodists," temperance advocates, and Whig supporters.

The Slaters' community interests went beyond politics. During the 1830s, the Slaters encouraged the construction of or paid for almost everything in Webster. In 1834 they offered land and funds to the Methodists if they would construct their new church in town. Residents used the basement of this new building to hold town meetings and to transact business. Two years later, the Slaters gave some land to the town for a public cemetery. Company stores supplied the hands with goods. Factory farms provided town residents with dairy and meat products and the firm allowed them to pasture their animals on company land. Fire prevention also fell to the Slaters, as did poor relief and public education.[78]

The Slaters were also attentive to the moral culture of the town and especially how education impacted such concerns.[79] As early as 1815, Samuel Slater organized his first Sunday School in Webster. Later responsibilities for these schools fell to the Methodist, Baptist, and Congregational churches. Teaching of basic skills was transferred to the local common schools. When the town was incorporated, the area was divided into four school districts, and they were supported at town expense, much of it provided by the Slaters. State Laws required that children be taught for six months in orthography, reading, writing, English grammar, geography, arithmetic, and good behavior. Further statutes required all children from six to fifteen years of age to attend school or be regularly employed. Children under twelve had to attend school from eleven to eighteen weeks annually.[80] While the Slaters supported education and inserted the same in worker contracts, their support had limits. There was a rift between what the town advocated and what the Slater's required.

After the deaths of his brothers, Horatio Nelson Slater was concerned to "keep the schools where they belong," so that formal education could be subordinated to the needs of the factory. In 1848 he asked his lawyers about his "liability for employing children in factory under 12 years of age, more than 10 hours a day."[81] Slater's approach did not sit well with many parents in Webster, for concern over the public education of the town's children became so heated that local residents passed an ordinance insisting that children attend school. In part it read:

> Whereas the Legislature in establishing free schools aimed to provide means whereby the young might become fitted, not only for the duties of private life, but also to become good citizens and useful members of society capable of . . . and sustaining and perpetuating the institutions of a free Religion and a liberal government and as these objects cannot be secured without a competent knowledge of the principles on which they are founded—therefore—Resolved—That the School Committee only as shall in there judgment be qualified to give instruction in relation to the natural rights of man in the fundamental principals of a sound and rational morality and of a free government and to see that such principles are taught in the various schools. . . . To see if all parents and guardians of children and youth are careful to give their children and wards the requisite amount of schooling each year and also if there be any cases of truancy or habitual absence from school contrary to laws and if all or any of the above specified irregularities shall be found to exist that the committee shall proceed to apply the remedies for such cases made and provided.[82]

One month later, they voted to build a high school.[83] The status of public education continued to be a contentious issue between the town and Horatio Slater throughout his lifetime.

The religious life of the community was also central to the Slaters' interests. As in Pawtucket and Slatersville, Webster supported a number of churches including the Baptists, Methodists, and Congregationalists. A small clapboard Baptist church was constructed in 1826 followed by the Methodists in 1828 and the Congregationalists ten years later. Of the three denominations, the Methodists predominated, and they received ample support from the Slater family. The Slaters took steps to see that the Methodists came to and remained in Webster. They provided the land for the church building, laid its foundation, purchased two-fifths of the church pews for the use of Slater employees, built the parsonage, maintained the property, and encouraged their hands to attend public worship and even tolerated ancillary programs such as camp meetings. In 1839 the Webster mills closed because "this being camp meeting with our Good Methodists, it will be rather a broken one with the Mills."[84] Revivals often followed a standard format. Four days in length, they often began on Friday and continued through noon on Monday. At daybreak each morning, those in attendance were "blasted up" by a trumpet call, and the day's activities were divided into four convocations; often emotional, accompanied by preaching, exhorting, and singing, these revivals proved an important recruitment tool for the Methodists. Once awakened and converted, the next step was baptism. A story was often told in Webster that during a revival, a number of men in the community were brought to the church and asked to be baptized by immersion. Since it was winter and the Methodist pastor was not in good health, an accommodation had to be made: "Bro. Dixon manufactured yarn at the East Village: he had a large tank in which he washed his yarn: the brethren utilized that for a batistry by building steps up then down into it, warmed the water, heated the water very warm." And then the minister, "standing outside the tank baptised the candidates." Throughout the area, revivals were held regularly.[85]

Regular attendance at worship services was expected, and people attended other church-sponsored functions such as Bible-reading classes, prayer meetings, and the all-important Sunday School. Webster boasted one of the most successful schools in Massachusetts. "The present state of the Sabbath School in the Webster station of the M. E. Church must be viewed as in a state of more than ordinary prosperity," noted members of the Webster Quarterly Conference in 1841. By 1848 there were 148 scholars and 22 teachers attached to the school. [86] Like John Fox Slater, Horatio Nelson tied the church to the workplace. The curriculum advocated obedience, deference, punctuality, temperance, and self-control. Many of those who ran the Sunday school were the same men who supervised factory operations. Both Charles Waite and William Kimball, Slater mill supervisors, were actively involved in Sunday School activities as well as department overseers, second hands, and mule spinners.

Adults were not exempt from church oversight. Moral lapses such as drinking, gaming, disputes with neighbors or kin, gossiping, indebtedness, Sabbath breaking, even adultery were subject to church discipline. And the reach of the church even extended to other towns and states. Mr. Brown, a local Webster resident, was observed on a spring day entering a billiard saloon in the Connecticut town of East Thompson; he was brought before the Church Board, questioned, failed to repent, and was discharged from the congregation.

If the church failed to persuade people to change their behavior, the community would take up the challenge. A question was placed before a town meeting in 1842 regarding liquor licenses, and the town voted not to grant "any person or persons for License as an inholder and seller of ardent spirits." A voice vote was taken so that everyone in town could see who supported and who opposed the sale and use of alcohol.[87] These churches also adopted abstinence pledges and supported the establishment of a temperance hotel. Apparently this suppression of alcohol was difficult to sustain. By 1849 a tavern was opened in town, and people were picked up and charged with intoxication. Sally Clough, for example, was "charged with being a common drunkard." It was noted that "Sally, is a tough specumen [sic] Irish lass, and has the reputation of being able to imbibe more rum, in a given time than any emigrant from Cork in town. She plead not guilty to the charge against her, boldly avowing she should strive for liberty till the last. However, she was sent up for thirty days."[88]

BUSINESS AND THE FACTORY SYSTEM

Though Horatio Nelson Slater and his brothers struggled to maintain a traditional Christian community outside of their mills, they proved to be industry innovators in several major fields including accounting and marketing. Throughout the Samuel Slater years, the business relied on double-entry bookkeeping. But with the reorganization of the businesses, the Slater brothers began to experiment with some new business ideas. Many of their initiatives were first undertaken with the Sutton Manufacturing Company, incorporated in 1836. Under the direction of George B. Slater, the firm manufactured, bleached, and printed a variety of textiles including cotton, wool, and silk. Additionally they had a machine shop for the construction and repair of their equipment. With real-estate values limited to $150,000 and the whole capital stock fixed at $300,000, this corporation represented a departure from the previous partnerships and sole proprietorships preferred by Samuel Slater.[89]

Accounting procedures deviated as well. The Slaters introduced an early form of cost accounting that predated other firms. The historian Alfred Chandler, for example, believed that the need for such methods developed with the railroads, and H. Thomas Johnson dated the earliest use of cost accounting to the Lyman Mills incorporated in 1854.[90] But the Slaters use of cost accounting dates to the late 1830s and early 1840s. By 1840 expenses for the Sutton mill were calculated monthly. The categories were broken down as follows: carding room, stretching, spinning, warping, spooling, mule room, dressing, and weaving. Within each category, products or items used and labor employed were listed with their costs. For the carding room in January 1840, fourteen entries were made on a day-by-day basis. Each entry usually included the cost for labor and for other items from glass lights, screws, and brooms to machine repairs and coal. Prices were tallied, and separate listings were made for the amount of cotton worked, funds transferred from Providence, and cost for the month's labor. Similar accounting was made for each room or department. Summaries of the various categories were then transferred to a separate page in the ledger.

For example, in the summary entry for January 1840, it cost slightly over 6 cents per yard to manufacture cloth. Labor and incidental expenses were almost 3.5 cents per yard. Over the next eleven months, the entries became more detailed, and by the end of the year, the cost per yard of cloth had dropped to 5.1 cents; of that, labor accounted for slightly less than 3 cents of the total cost per yard of cloth produced.[91] Though not as sophisticated as some other accounting methods, this scheme nevertheless proved to be invaluable to the firm.

Horatio Nelson Slater and the Expansion of Samuel Slater and Sons

At the time of the deaths of John and George Slater, Samuel Slater and Sons was a profitable firm, but under Horatio Nelson Slater's management, the company reached new economic heights. Samuel Slater and Sons remained a closed family enterprise with Horatio Nelson Slater as director and manager. He expanded the business, enhanced its public image, initiated new business and labor procedures, and formed its operational plans. As the credit reporting agency of Dunn and Bradstreet wrote in 1856, "H. N. is very intelligent and judicious in his business and has been very successful." From what they could judge since the firm was so guarded, they were estimated at between $250,000 and $500,000 and "steadily improving."[92]

One of Horatio Nelson Slater's innovations concerned marketing. Samuel Slater's partners had controlled the distribution of the yarn and wick manufactured at Pawtucket. As the market grew and expanded geographically, Horatio Nelson Slater turned to commission agents to handle sales. No longer would factory owners have to deal directly with a multitude of small retailers and country merchants; they could consign their products to commission agents located in the major cities of New York, Philadelphia, Boston, Providence, Baltimore, and Chicago, among other places, and then find the retailers.[93]

He was determined to maintain control of his products, however, and he made sure that his agents followed his directions. Slater calculated the cost per yard of cloth or yarn, the terms of payment, and the place of delivery. There was no discussion over price. One New York firm tried to negotiate a price for Slater sheeting and offered to sell the cloth for 7.25 cents, but Slater said, "We do not now allow them sold at less than 8 cts." The commission agent, T. N. Underhill of New York, agreed that if the Slaters would "protect us from decline on the bales unsold if the price should not be sustained." But the conversation did not end there. For over eight months Underhill argued for a lower price and better terms: "It is not always the case that this market will sustain the Boston price of every class of goods. I am impressed with a belief that we cannot sell your goods at a profit. . . . It is a dangerous argument to conclude the mass of good people who buy of you can be strained up to the highest point which the necessities of one may reach. I advise care in this thing."[94] Yet his entreaties went unheeded as Horatio refused to cede control over any aspect of the distribution process that he could command.

Slater recognized the importance of patriotism in advertising. By 1843 Slater offered to place the firm's own stamp on their goods and gave their customers a choice of the following: "Samuel Slater and Sons," "Webster Sheeting," or "Manf. Expressly for family use."[95] Thereafter, Slater marks varied with the changing economic and political conditions of the country. During the Mexican War, goods stamped with "Triumph of American Manufacturers" were extensively used. As the commission agent noted, "We expect to make a great display with the goods from the 'Sons of the first manufacturer in the United States.'" The "Triumph" stamp continued to be popular. One agent wanted goods but specified "as to the stamp for I should not care about them under any other stamp than the Triumph, having sold them for the last four years." Later the "Pride of the West" stamp was very popular. After all, "a great deal 'is in the name.'"[96] These stamps proved an excellent advertising tool, but they were not the only instruments used to generate business. Merchant's fairs, exhibitions, trade circulars, and catalogs all extolled the quality of Slater thread and cloth. Horatio Slater even had a booth at the famous Crystal Palace exhibition held in London in 1851. There Slater was able to assess his chief rivals, the spool cotton manufactured by Coates of Great Britain and the cloth produced by leading German firms, and he was determined to make inroads into their competitors' customer base.[97]

The volume of sales increased during the Civil War when the Slater company furnished uniform cloth to the Union Army, Navy, and Merchant Marines. At the war's end, Slater received contracts to provide uniform cloth for railroad conductors, porters, and the Pulman service together with hotel employees, coachmen, chauffeurs, and domestic servants. It was in the postwar years that Horatio Slater decided to abandon the commission house system and open his own sales department, Samuel Slater and Sons, Incorporated. In 1866 he began to sell his own goods out of New York. Several years later he opened a shop in Philadelphia, then other outlets in Chicago, Boston, St. Louis, and Baltimore followed.[98]

While Horatio Nelson Slater attempted to control the distribution of his cloth, his mania for power was even more evident in his management of the mills. Although he employed factory managers to conduct routine operations, he made all decisions regarding payment of hands, price and terms for sale of merchandise, reservoir water levels, fire protection, the speed of machines, and even whether to use gears or belts to drive the picker shaft. Repeatedly, agents told customers, retailers, commission agents, operatives, and villagers that they could not take any action without the express consent of Mr. Slater: "Our Mr. H. N. Slater will probably be here next week at which time we will write you as the writer is not authorized to take any action on the subject."[99] Like his father, he was familiar with all kinds of machines and made improvements to many of them; he even built his own looms. Following his father's lead, he was not above industrial spying. On a trip to England he visited several mills in part to examine their products: He was admonished "If you cannot gain access so as to examine into all those discover a part as you are hurried through the mill and by some manuvering obtain some information from some of their principle workmen by a few presents after their hours of labour are over. But it would be worth double to see yourself and judge of all those particulars." Because the British articles were known for their superior coloring procedures, Horatio Nelson Slater was urged to "gain access to some of their principal dye houses. Much may be learned particularly in the process of coloring Black."[100]

Horatio Nelson Slater also dramatically reorganized the labor system. During the Panic of 1829, Samuel Slater had almost gone bankrupt. The most alarming expense was labor. The family system of labor was costly and inefficient. Adult males refused to work alongside their children in the mills and had to be provided with traditional jobs in agriculture, construction, and transportation. They were paid the prevailing wages in the area for such work. Children and adolescents provided most of the labor required in the factory. Horatio Slater decided that it made no sense to employ men at substantially higher wages than those given to operatives. Times had changed; labor was no longer in short supply; the factory system had been in existence for over forty years and was a feature of the rural landscape. To cut costs meant to tamper with family labor.

Horatio Slater showed little remorse in jettisoning the family system of labor and its patriarchal culture. He dispensed with most family contracts and hired hands individually. This gave boys and girls an independent income for the first time. They, not their parents, received their wages, and parents had to negotiate with their children over the disposition of those wages. If disagreements arose or if the children wanted more freedom or independence, they could leave and obtain employment and lodging elsewhere. Further rules eroded the family system of labor. Men and adolescent boys were required to work on Sundays in some of Slater's factories, and this disrupted the traditional Sabbath routine practiced by many factory families. Mule spinners no longer had the prerogative to hire their own piecers. This task fell to the factory master. Previously, employment as a piecer was often given to the mule spinner's son, nephew, or family friend, and it proved a training program for future employment in this skilled occupation. Fines were introduced for shoddy work, tardiness, disorderly conduct, and absence without permission. Traditional morning and afternoon fifteen-minute breaks where operatives could slip out of the mills, play, or run errands or just chat with their friends were abolished. Agents complained that workers took advantage of the release time and often stopped the mills for almost an hour. Not only were breaks discontinued but also the factory agents lengthened the work day, increased the speed at which the machines were run, and introduced the stretch out, forcing hands to operate additional machines. Many families resented the new work rules and complained. Their only recourse was to leave the factory. Those who protested were let go, placed on a blacklist, and often were unable to find work anywhere else in the area. By 1860 native-born workers formed only 28 percent of the Slater textile labor force.[101]

Their departures did not disrupt factory operations. There was a ready supply of immigrant workers willing to work for the wages Slater paid and the conditions he set. Irish and French Canadian families were hired to replace many of the Yankee operatives. As of 1860 they represented about 60 percent of the labor force. Over the next decade, Webster would become a destination for immigrants, especially for the French Canadians. Of the thirty-four major factory towns in southern New England in 1860, only Woonsocket, Rhode Island, had more French Canadians than Webster.[102] Still, they did not replace other immigrant workers. The Irish continued to have a significant presence among the workforce in Webster, although their occupations were no longer confined to textile factory work. They became shoemakers, domestic servants, farm hands, and even merchants, as well as factory operatives.[103]

Migratory immigrant families and extended families filled the factory jobs. While some family units were large with as many as eleven or twelve children, more typical was the newly hired family of Francis Laboisiere. French speaking, Catholic, and unskilled, Laboisiere placed four children in the factory, promised Slater additional hands if asked, and agreed that both he and his wife would work as well.[104] These workers moved into the newly constructed tenements built by Samuel Slater and Sons. Located near the factory, constructed of wood, with few windows, these three- to four-room tenements were small. With limited open space between the tenements and with little or no backyard space behind them, operatives were not encouraged to grow their own vegetables or to keep their own farm animals. Living conditions deteriorated. Diseases such as typhus, cholera, and tuberculosis spread throughout the town. Dysentery, lung fever, stillbirth, and even teething were recorded as causes of death. Some families appeared especially unfortunate. William Hickey and his wife Anesthesia, both about twenty-two years old and born in Ireland, came to Webster in the 1850s. Their first child Mary Ann, age four months, died in July 1854 of cholera infantum; the next year, Anesthesia died of complications from childbirth, and her son James died one month later of dysentery. In 1856 William Hickey remarried. That year his new wife, Ellen Dwyer, died in childbirth.[105]

For these immigrants, life was precarious, and many of them turned to the Catholic church for support, which dramatically increased ethnic and religious tensions in Webster. Initially, Catholic services were held in Webster by itinerant priests. It was not until the 1850s that the Catholic community in Webster constructed St. Louis Roman Catholic Church. In 1853 Father Napoleon Mignault became the first resident priest in Webster. Born in Canada, he presided over the congregation during a period of tremendous religious tension in town. In fact, local Protestant residents even threatened to burn down the church.[106]

This incident coincided with the spread of nativism in New England, symbolized by the election in Webster of a Know Nothing candidate to the state legislature. The Know Nothing Party, also known as the American Party, swept the state in 1856. Best known for their anti-Catholic and anti-immigrant stance, they also supported a number of social reforms and immediately translated their agenda into laws. Temperance and public education were among the issues Know Nothings supported. In Webster, temperance laws had already been passed. The Massachusetts Liquor Authority was established to oversee the sale and distribution of spirits. Railroads such as the Norwich and Worcester lines notified Samuel Slater and Sons that "under the new liquor law of the state of Massachusetts this company will refuse to transport any liquor, under any circumstances. The requirements of the law you are probably familiar with and it will be useless for me to give any further directions in the matter or explain whys or wherefores."[107] Certainly temperance was one of the issues Samuel Slater and Sons supported, and now they had the help of both the town and the state. Many Catholics opposed the temperance movement and believed that the regulation of morals belonged to the church and not to the state.

Yet Catholics and immigrants were not alone in their discontent. Despite these ethnic and religious differences, class issues gradually became predominant among the workers of Webster. For many of the laborers, regardless of national origin, the 1850s proved a difficult time. Living conditions had declined: overcrowding, disease, crime, violence, xenophobia, and the morality police all made life difficult for all workers. Within the factory, the speed up, stretch out, long hours, and increasingly low wages created animosity toward management. A major recession in 1858 forced some mills to close, while others went on short shift, and operatives found it hard to find work or to be constantly employed. L. Briggs of Masonville wrote to a Webster agent,

> I have just had applications from parties living at your place for work. They inform me there is a report circulating in Webster to the affect that I was up there Saturday to hire family help, thinking you might be deceived by such games I take the liberty to contradict them. They are false in all respects. We are over run with help and any number of applications from out-siders. . . . We shall not pay any prices which will pay help to leave work if they are making a living, I advise you to stick

to low prices, as we are determined to, and what machinery we cannot run in this way we shall let stand.[108]

It was during these trying times that some of the workers in Webster decided to strike. In 1858, between twenty-five and thirty weavers walked off the job demanding an increase in their wages. But the turnout lasted less than three days, and Slater's agent reported, "We are pleased to observe that the weavers as Exp. [expected] have reconsidered their position and are now . . . at work."[109] Of course, the wages were not increased. Samuel Slater and Sons became committed to a policy that would "discharge part of the help and reduce production [when] goods do not sell very well."[110]

Relationships between labor and management remained strained thereafter. The idea of a caring, Christian community shattered on the shoals of economic change and profit. Though residing in Webster until his death in 1888, Horatio Slater was able to maintain a pliable workforce in the post–Civil War era, ruling through coercion and fear rather than developing any bonds of trust between labor and management. Not only was Horatio Nelson unconcerned about the conditions of his workers, he did not leave a legacy of charitable giving like John Fox Slater. His philanthropic contributions included donations to Chester Academy, the school of his youth, and about fifty thousand dollars to Brown University, although the latter money was given with numerous restrictions on when it could be spent. In all, his philanthropic aid was less than one hundred thousand dollars, a pittance of his wealth. For example, when he died, his adopted son inherited approximately nine million dollars.[111]

Borrowing from their respective fathers' paternalistic model of economic and social life, in their initial forays into the textile industry, Horatio Nelson Slater and John Fox Slater developed a version of a manufacturing society based on a commitment to small-town values of trust, care, and responsibility shared by all members of the community. John Fox Slater in particular, through his philanthropic giving to educational institutions and his establishment of the John F. Slater fund for African Americans, envisioned a manufacturing society based on local townships that were committed to providing instruction for deserving men and women of all races. But for the Slaters, patriarchy gave way to a disciplinary society, as contracts increasingly replaced informal rules of conduct within and outside of the factory. After the Civil War, the Slaters became more typical capitalists concerned with profits over the welfare of their workers, especially as Catholic immigrants increasingly supplanted native-born laborers.

Amos Adams Lawrence, too, was a textile manufacturer inspired by a strong Protestantism that informed his antislavery beliefs and nativist tendencies. Like John Fox Slater, Amos Adams Lawrence believed in the importance of education, but Amos Adams concentrated on institutions of higher education with the goal of creating an elite that could guide the country. Though his father, Amos Lawrence, and his uncle, Abbott Lawrence, were very successful businessmen, they did not place nearly as much emphasis on succeeding in business as did the patriarchs of the Slater clan. Having attended Harvard College and never serving an apprenticeship in a textile mill like the Slater brothers, Amos Adams Lawrence devoted much of his life to promulgating and attempting to implement a national vision of an urban, Protestant elite whose values of hard work, obedience, philanthropy, and nativism could enlighten the emerging manufacturing society.

Part III

The Lawrences

Manufacturing and the Moral Life of an Industrial Urban Elite

CHAPTER 6

AMOS AND ABBOTT LAWRENCE

PHILANTHROPY AND POLITICS IN ANTEBELLUM AMERICA

"Mr. Lawrence was a model man," wrote William M. Thayer in his book *The Poor Boy and Merchant Prince*. "Men like him are 'few and far between.' From childhood to old age, his career was adorned with the brightest virtues. His life disproves that oft-repeated sentiment, that the highest success in business cannot be achieved, while strict regard to morality and religion is observed."[1] Written just five years after the death of Amos Lawrence and designed as a handbook for young men and boys, Thayer outlined what it meant to be successful, the character traits that were needed to triumph in business and in life. He described the various steps necessary to succeed in business: hard work, sobriety, attention to detail, religious devotion, and self-control. Thayer writes, "If a man lays up a fortune in a series of busy years, while he has dwarfed his soul, and ignored every moral and religious obligation in the effort, he has been successful only in part. . . . If he has a million of dollars and no character, he is not worth much." Mr. Lawrence was the epitome of the successful man.[2] Thayer was not alone in that assessment. Reverend Theodore Parker eulogized Lawrence as "The Good Merchant" and a man who "knew the true use of riches."[3]

The father of the influential textile manufacturer, philanthropist, and political figure Amos Adams Lawrence, Amos Lawrence Sr. made sure that his son followed these principles. Because of their privileged background, Amos Lawrence feared that his sons would try to live off their inheritance rather than provide for themselves through industry, economy, and correct living. To Amos Adams he wrote in 1835,

> It is as certain that a man cannot bring into action, the powers he is endowed with, without labour, whatever his calling or profession, as it is that he cannot enjoy health and vigour, in an atmosphere of tainted air. How unwise then for any parent to wish to place his son in a situation of such ease as to tempt him to forgo the benefit that is certain to follow the central and systematic use of his body and mental powers and notwithstanding the folly of this, we see the thing done everyday, and young men are ruined because their fathers have been successful in their labours—and this is your danger, and it is what I want to impress upon you—no man comes to much here without hard work, which hard work is his best mode of enjoying life, and it is your real enjoyment that I am most anxious to promote.

Speculation and what he labeled adventure were to be avoided. Again his father continued, "I had rather see you make such progress as you can stand under, than to go on in that successful style of adventure, that would make you very rich, in a few years, or if unsuccessful, might leave you worse off than when you began."[4]

He warned his son not to be indolent just because his family had money: "You ought to feel that your duties and responsibilities are greatly increased by this start and to bring into use all your talents, if so, happy will it be for you. In all matters of deep concern to you I shall be ready to council and advise at all times, but the responsibility after all must rest on yourself-and this is a point you must never lose sight of."[5] Children should make their own way and not expect their parents to support them. "A young man who cannot get along without such aid will not be likely to get along with it," he confided to his diary.[6] Such tenets guided his life.

Born and educated in the small town of Groton, Massachusetts, Amos Lawrence came to Boston in 1807. Three of his brothers, Abbott, William, and Samuel joined him there. By midcentury, the Lawrence clan was numbered among the richest residents of that town and served as role models for those who believed that through industry, clean living, and religious devotion, any boy could rise in American society. The Lawrence brothers were touted as the poor boys who made good, even though their family backgrounds suggested otherwise.[7] Amos and Abbott joined forces, forming A & A Lawrence in 1814. In the following decades, this firm that first distributed British cloth and later domestic-made goods became one of the most prosperous enterprises in New England. But Amos and Abbott did not stop there. They invested directly in several Lowell projects before turning their attention to the development of the textile town that bears their name, Lawrence, Massachusetts. Amos Lawrence in particular became a major philanthropist, while Abbott Lawrence turned to politics as well as philanthropy in his bid to influence the economic and social direction of America. They were among the first Americans to connect manufacturing, philanthropy, finance, and politics. Amos Lawrence's son Amos Adams would extend this model that intertwined enterprise, culture, and politics, and through his activity, he ensured that the Lawrence name would be known throughout the nation.

AMOS LAWRENCE: VIRTUE AND CHARITY

Amos Lawrence loved New England and believed it offered "more virtue, & more of everything that constitutes the true greatness of a people than any other portion of our country."[8] Again and again, he would return to the town of his birth and to the values learned there. The Lawrence family had been residents of Groton, MA since 1660 and held a respected position in that town. Samuel Lawrence, father of Amos and Abbott Lawrence, served as an officer in the Revolutionary War, held local positions as a selectman, town clerk, assessor, and moderator, and was a church deacon. To support his large family of eight children, Samuel worked both as a farmer and a shoemaker. This declining agricultural village of about 1,800 people, however, offered limited occupational options for his sons. What it did offer the boys, though, was Groton Academy. Along with forty-two men from the village, Samuel Lawrence launched the school. Under headmaster Samuel Holyoke, a Harvard graduate, Groton offered a classical curriculum designed to prepare students for college. The oldest Lawrence boy, Luther, graduated from Harvard, became a lawyer, and practiced in Groton. For the Lawrence children, Groton gave them a degree of sophistication, learning, and gentility. These country boys also made important personal connections at the academy with some of the area's leading families that would serve them in business and politics for the rest of their lives.[9] A belief in the efficacy of education would inform the Lawrences's philanthropic work throughout their lives.

After the Groton experience, Amos Lawrence was determined to succeed economically. He began his business career as a country-store clerk but left that position in 1807 and traveled to Boston. His intention was to remain only long enough to network, establish his credit worth, and then return to Groton to open his own business. But he was offered a position in a mercantile house, accepted it, and began his merchant career.[10] Amos Lawrence became one of the most successful merchants in Boston. He seemed to embody to an almost stereotypical degree the characteristics that Weber ascribed to the successful merchant in *The Protestant Ethic and the Spirit of Capitalism*: "sobriety, frugality, a systematic ordering of his conduct, a calculating approach to his business practices, and a conviction that this morality was a prerequisite for economic success." In his early trading days, he practiced the maxim, "Business before friends," and he approached his dealings with tunnel vision. Strict rules governed his commercial affairs: never procrastinate, keep an exact accounting of all expenses and profits, be punctual if not early to the office and to meetings, be vigilant and prepared, observe carefully and "apply what is good & discard what is bad," avoid speculation, and be concerned that nothing "blemish" your good name. To this list, William Thayer added the qualities that made Lawrence a good man: industry, frugality, system, purpose, perseverance, integrity, politeness, Sabbath observance, benevolence, and optimism.[11] These rules guided his life, for such habits in Lawrence's words "have been the foundation of my good name, good fortune, and present happy condition."[12]

Economic Success

The firm A & A Lawrence was a selling house that initially handled British cloth, but later more lucrative opportunities opened when the company was chosen by the Boston Manufacturing Company and the Merrimac Company to distribute their American made cloth. They extended their markets to the West, the South, and then overseas to South America, Mexico, and China. By the 1830s both Amos and Abbott Lawrence had expanded their business interests to include textile production and financial institutions. By then they were joined by two of their brothers, William and Samuel. They too entered the textile commission business forming the firm W & S Lawrence. The siblings proved successful. In an 1833 survey of the wealthiest men in Boston, Amos and Abbott made the list with assets of $250,000 or more. Fifteen years later, both Abbott and William Lawrence were assessed at more than $500,000 each.[13]

While not as wealthy as his brother Abbott, Amos Lawrence nevertheless held an interest in many ventures besides A & A Lawrence, including the Tremont and York mills, the Suffolk Bank, the Boston Insurance Company, and the Massachusetts Hospital Life Insurance Company. He was not only successful in manufacturing but in finance and banking as well. He helped to make Boston one of the chief capital markets in the United States. Among the institutions he worked with was the Massachusetts Hospital Life Insurance Company, chartered in 1818. The name of the company, however, was misleading. While it was connected with Massachusetts General Hospital, its primary function was to serve as "the Savings bank of the wealthy." It was a testamentary trust, a vehicle used to circumvent partible inheritance laws by permitting families to keep their capital intact while allowing it to grow through the investments of a trustee. The trust's beneficiaries would share in the profits.[14] Within five years, its trust deposits totaled about five million dollars, and over time its depositors included Boston's elite families.

The Lawrences alone had eight separate trusts. Both Amos and Abbott Lawrence served as directors of the Committee of Finance for the Insurance company, the most significant agency in this concern because it advised the officers on investment policies. Money was invested in banking, real estate, and later manufacturing stock. From this institution, loans were made to individuals; while they had to provide collateral for the loan and pay interest, no repayment date was set. William Appleton, David Sears, and the Lawrence brothers carried large loans that they used to expand their textile holdings and other ventures. It was estimated that loans to the Lawrence family and to business ventures located in the town of Lawrence alone totaled about one million dollars. For Amos Lawrence, the Massachusetts Hospital Life Insurance Company allowed him access to capital but as importantly gave him an opportunity to try to insure the economic position of his family for generations. A moneyed aristocracy anchored in Boston thus emerged.[15]

Amos Lawrence invested in another financial-services institution, the Suffolk Bank. Chartered in 1818, this bank subsequently served as the clearinghouse for all banknotes that circulated in New England. In the first half of the nineteenth century, banks issued their own notes, and at one time, there could be thousands of notes in circulation. The actual worth of the note and the issuing bank were sometimes open to question, and bankers occasionally did not have the expertise or knowledge to adequately evaluate the myriad of banknotes they received. To solve the problem, note brokers became increasingly central to the enterprise. They bought notes at a discount then returned them to the issuing bank for full payment. At first the Suffolk Bank went into the note brokerage business, and later it became a regional note-clearing house. Members of the system were required to keep an interest-free deposit at Suffolk or at one of the other Boston member banks. Suffolk then accepted and net-cleared all the banknotes that its members deposited at par. By the early 1830s, most banks in New England had become members, and because of Suffolk's par-clearing policy, notes issued by members of the system were exchanged at par throughout the region.[16]

This system together with overdraft privileges among other services made the Suffolk Bank an especially profitable institution. By the 1840s dividends averaged 8 percent and in the next decade rose to 10 percent. Additionally from time to time surplus funds were distributed to stockholders. Amos Lawrence was among those who received these huge dividends.[17]

Abbott Lawrence, too, participated in this venture, and throughout these years, the bonds between the brothers strengthened. Their partnership in the commission firm of A & A Lawrence remained intact throughout their lifetime. They worked together on innumerable business projects including the Tremont, York, and Essex firms, the Suffolk Bank, and the Massachusetts Hospital Life Insurance Company. In addition, Abbot invested in the Boott and Massachusetts mills, pursued interests in railroads, including the Boston and Worcester line and the Western Railroad, and was associated with the Hamilton Bank and the Merchants Insurance Company.[18] Toward the end of his life, he was interested in the China trade, one of the most lucrative business ventures of the era. Writing to his good friend Nathan Appleton in April 1854, he reported that "money matters remain about the same. There is no distress nor apparent anxiety for the future." By August 1855, when Abbott Lawrence died, his family shared over one million dollars, not including real estate and moveable assets, while another $171,000 was split among friends, servants, and charities.[19]

ABBOTT LAWRENCE AND POLITICAL LIFE

Amos and Abbott Lawrence shared many business ventures but had different perspectives on the rough-and-tumble world of American politics. While Amos remained largely in the political background, due in part to his own personality as well as his ill health, and regarded politics as a seamy endeavor, Abbott Lawrence entered the public sphere as a politician and public servant and became quite politically successful. He began his political career because of economic questions. The 1828 tariff focused attention on northern manufacturers such as Abbott Lawrence who advocated a high tariff to protect and promote domestic industry. Such tariffs made it easier for timid investors to place their funds in what were still considered risky businesses.[20] Although the so-called "Tariff of Abominations" was passed and rates on manufactured goods and raw materials, including raw wool, rose, the issue would not go away. Southern opposition to the tariff continued, and Abbott Lawrence became alarmed and angry. Concerned that some of the provisions might be rolled back, he began a letter-writing campaign to preempt any change that the South might make. He argued that lowering the tariff on wool, for example, would stifle the development of stuff goods and interfere with the manufacture of broadcloth, both wool products: "Nothing but absolute necessity would induce me to agree to a reduction of duty on stuffs." He encouraged members of the House of Representatives to "hold fast to the Tariff of 1828 upon all the great branches of industry. I would not provoke unnecessarily our Southern brethren but I would tell them in the floor of the House some wholesome truth, which they richly merit."[21] Abbott emphasized the effects that low tariffs would have on other businesses such as carpet manufacturing. American manufacturing would be devastated, and this would have an impact throughout the country. Through a series of questions he asked,

> Will they bring down the laborers wages in this country to the standard of the pauper labor of Europe—Will this Government destroy the middle classes in this great Republic—The bone and sinew of this country and place the property of the many in the hands of the few. The monied men of the country have nothing to fear from the change, the rich will become richer and the poor poorer, our middling classes poorer—the property that is to be sold by the sheriff will of course fall into the hands of the overgrown rich, and the farmer is hereafter to be the slave of an aristocracy.

He concluded that "God forbid that I should advocate separation but I speak advisedly when I say that I am ready for separation in preference to surrendering a principle upon which all our property, our happiness depends."[22]

In 1834 he ran for the House of Representatives from the Suffolk district, won the election, and gained a seat on the Ways and Means Committee. After one term he decided not to seek reelection for health reasons but was persuaded in 1839 to run again. Again he won but only served a short time, resigning in March 1840 because of ill health. Notwithstanding his personal problems, he continued in politics serving as a federal commissioner to settle boundary disputes.

He actively supported Whig candidates such as William Henry Harrison, Henry Clay, and Zackary Taylor. He even forayed into national electoral politics. When some of his supporters asked him to join the Taylor ticket, he accepted the challenge but lost the nomination by about six votes.[23]

While Abbott Lawrence was attracted to politics, his brother Amos disdained it. Regarding Abbott's near election to vice president, Amos wrote, "If my vote would make my brother Vice-President, I would not give it, as I think it lowering his good name to accept office of any sort."[24] Despite such protestations, Amos Lawrence changed his mind when his brother was appointed representative to the Court of Great Britain stating this was "the only office that I would not advise against his accepting."[25] His friends shared that view, one of them equating Lawrence's diplomatic service to that of Benjamin Franklin.

Abbott Lawrence proved to be a role model for his young nephew Amos Adams Lawrence. Unlike his father Amos, the young Amos Adams came to embrace politics, following his uncle into the Whig Party and later taking a public stance on controversial issues from slavery to immigration, running for office, actively supporting candidates, and even organizing a third party. Just before Abbott Lawrence died, the two joined forces supporting the New England Emigrant Aid Company, an organization formed to combat any extension of slavery into the Kansas territory.

PHILANTHROPY

Though Amos Adams Lawrence was influenced by his uncle Abbott's political career, his father Amos left a legacy of charitable giving that also dramatically affected the young man. Amos Adams Lawrence grew up in a culture of philanthropy. While Amos Lawrence left a profitable inheritance to Amos Adams and his siblings, such investments returned more than money. The Massachusetts Hospital Life Insurance Company also supported charitable causes and institutions. Its early charter stipulated that it must share its profits with Massachusetts General Hospital. This it did, and the hospital in turn invested in the insurance company. A special category called "institutional deposits" was set aside for such organizations as Harvard College, the American Academy of Arts and Sciences, the Boston Athenaeum, and the Bunker Hill Monument. These organizations deposited money into an account, and the funds were treated in the same fashion as the personal trust funds of the Boston elite. These institutions were also among those favored by Amos Lawrence and he was partly responsible for the distribution of Massachusetts Hospital Life Insurance Company trust funds.

Amos and Abbott Lawrence became two of the leading philanthropists of the era. This was especially true of Amos Lawrence. The Protestant values of Amos Lawrence not only meant systematically controlling one's life but also engaging in good works. Like many members of Boston's elite, Lawrence tried to live by a strict code of conduct that valued family, friends, neighbors, business associates, community, and nation.[26] To be successful meant avoiding self-love and self-gratification and using wealth wisely. As Paul Goodman noted, "Believing in the gospel of progress, Boston's leading families saw themselves as agents of improvement. . . . His claim to superiority in a republic stemmed not from hereditary privilege but from personal achievement. Endowed with wealth, honor, virtue and wisdom, he was also a patron of culture and innumerable charities, an exemplar of republican simplicity, and a leader of the nation."[27]

During the last two decades of his life, Amos Lawrence lived each day as though it were his last. He had made his money in the textile business, and now he wanted to put it to work. He argued, "I am satisfied that we do better by being our own executors, than by hoarding large sums for our descendants." He was a steward of wealth, and he was determined to spend most of his money before he died. As he wrote, "I adopted the practice ten years ago, of spending my income. The more I give, the more I have; and do most devoutly and heartily pray God that I may be faithful in the use of the good things intrusted [sic] to me."[28] He supported the sentiments of others who believed that "it has always been the use made of wealth acquired in trade, which has been the object of commendation and honor, rather than the success in its accumulation." Amos planned his philanthropy like he ordered his business. He dispensed money, clothing, and goods to individuals and institutions. By the end of his life, it was estimated that he gave away about seven hundred thousand dollars. For individuals, he kept a ledger where he recorded the names, ages, number of children or dependents, and reasons of those who applied to him for assistance. Each day he handled approximately six requests and tried to answer them promptly. He evaluated these appeals, considering them either meritorious or frivolous.[29]

Amos just did not give money out of the goodness of his heart, for there was a proselytizing and evangelical strain to his Protestantism. With each gift of used clothing, cloth, hardware, shoes, or money came an assortment of books from the American Tract Society or the

Sunday School Union. These works were "scattered with a liberal hand . . . to many, who, otherwise might never have been reached." He also carried such religious tracts with him and gave them away as he traveled about town.[30] This was the usual way the American Tract Society employed to distribute these short, moral lessons. From four to sixteen pages, these tracts promoted Protestant godliness and morality. Titles included *Poor Sarah or the Benefits of Religion Exemplified in Life and Death of an Indian Woman* by Elias Boudinot, or Tract No. 512, *Murderers of Fathers, and Murderers of Mothers* by Rev. Edward Hitchcock, president of Amherst College, and *Beware of Bad Books, Tract No. 493*. In *Beware of Bad Books*, the author cautions readers to avoid books of fiction because "they are generally bad in their character and influence. Their authors are commonly bad men, and wicked men do not often write good books."[31] Lawrence also gave away the book *Letters on Tobacco, for American Lads; or Uncle Toby's Anti-Tobacco Advice to his Nephew Billy Bruce*, written by the Rev. George Trask. Much like the books distributed by the American Tract Society, it dealt with moral issues focusing on tobacco and its ally alcohol. According to Trask, these twin evils brought on poverty, vice, disease, delirium, and early death.[32]

But Amos Lawrence is best remembered for his gifts to institutions. Educational institutions were especially prominent on his list. Williams College received from thirty to forty thousand dollars; Kenyon College and Wabash College were granted funds, one an outright gift and the other funds to establish scholarships for Lawrence Academy graduates.[33] Lawrence was specifically interested in the Bunker Hill Monument, a project that became his personal mission. For over a decade, Lawrence tried to collect funds to build a monument and create a public space to honor those who fought at Bunker Hill. His father had served there, and the area became sacred to him. Through perseverance and pressure he solicited funds, and finally, after contributing ten thousand dollars himself and persuading Judah Touro of New Orleans to match that sum, he was able to raise the fifty thousand dollars needed to finance the project. At the dedication ceremony, the host honored both Lawrence and Touro through rhyme.

> Amos and Judah! Venerated names!
> Patriarch and prophet press their equal claims;
> Like generous coursers, running neck and neck,
> Each aids the work by giving it a check.
> Christian and Jew, they carry out a plan;
> For, though of different faith, each is in heart a man.[34]

Lawrence was also interested in the moral and social condition of the working class and the poor and financed charities to assist them. He purchased a large building on Mason Street in Boston to convert into a charitable hospital for children. Impressed with the experiments taking place in France where indigent, sick children were removed from their homes and placed under the care of physicians, he sought to introduce that practice in Boston. While many people supported the idea, the actual building that he purchased proved unsuitable. With this large building on his hands, Lawrence decided to offer it to the Boston Society of Natural History at cost, and, of course, a contribution of five thousand dollars came with the offer. But he had not given up on the idea of building a hospital. Lawrence was instrumental in opening up a children's infirmary on Washington Street in Boston, and soon thirty beds were filled. Many more children, often those of Irish immigrants, sought care there.[35] To be concerned with social questions in antebellum America also meant taking a stand on slavery. Though usually eschewing overt and obvious political causes, like most manufacturers, he could not avoid the issue of slavery. Though antislavery, he believed that abolitionists were doing more harm than good, and he supported letting slavery survive in the Deep South while preventing its spread westward. If the slaves were freed, he believed they should be sent to Africa. Accordingly, he supported the American Colonization Society, denouncing abolitionists as "hot heads."[36]

His brother Abbott Lawrence also gave liberally of his wealth. To Harvard University in 1847, he donated fifty thousand dollars that served as seed money for the Lawrence Scientific School. He was told that the gift "enriches your descendants in a way that mere money can never do, and is a better investment than any you have ever made."[37] Professor Louis Agassiz, a leading scientist of the day, held the department's first chair. Abbott Lawrence also donated fifty thousand dollars to build model lodging houses where "persons of respectable character and moderate means might, economically and in comfort, find a home." In his will he gave another fifty thousand dollars to Harvard and ten thousand dollars to the Boston Public Library.[38] One friend said of the brothers that they realized "the responsibilities which are inseparable from wealth, and, [recognized] their obligations to the Giver, to dispense, as in His sight and for His greater glory, the bounties held by them in trust."[39]

LAWRENCE, MASSACHUSETTS

While Amos and Abbott shared a philanthropic impulse, they never relinquished their pursuit of profitable business ventures. Throughout their lives, their partnership in the commission firm of A & A Lawrence continued even after Amos Lawrence became quite ill and unable to actively engage in business. They worked together to find and explore additional economic opportunities for investment. One of the most notable was the Essex Company. All four Lawrence brothers were principle investors in this firm that became the foundation stone of the new town of Lawrence, Massachusetts.[40] Their philanthropic inclinations and profit-oriented business sense came together in Lawrence as they attempted to create a company town and factory that reflected their view of an idyllic community. Yet the limits of their moral capitalism became obvious quickly, as, just as in the Slater communities, the town was unable to avoid class conflict and the disciplinary features that came to characterize the new capitalism.

The development of this new city followed a pattern first seen in Waltham, Massachusetts, later modified in Lowell and altered to fit the changing economic needs of the industry when Lawrence was conceived. In constructing their company town, Abbott and Amos were influenced by the first textile mills and communities created in Waltham by Francis C. Lowell and Nathan Appleton and other members of the Boston Associates. The Lawrence brothers, too, became involved with the Boston Associates. They chose to invest in manufacturing rather than commerce, for they believed the former to be a more stable type of investment that avoided much of the speculation that characterized trade. Even when they invested outside of the textile industry, as in the transportation sector, they viewed railroads as an accessory to their business.[41] As a state-chartered corporation, the Boston Associates took seriously the quasi-public responsibilities that were part of the original compact of American corporations.

This belief in public responsibility initially extended to the treatment of the workforce, and the Lawrences hoped to replicate this sense of shared community in Lawrence. Like the Slaters, they looked to forms of community that would not only tie workers and owners together but would avoid the worst aspects of British industrialization. Unlike the family system of labor of the Slaters, they took as their model the mills in Waltham, which originally attracted unskilled young women to live in their communities. Girls resided in boardinghouses operated by matrons, and the young women were paid higher wages than in other textile mills. Though initially very successful and profitable, the system began to break down by the early 1830s; despite the amenities granted to them, the young women went on strike, and innovations and competition in the textile industry demanded cheaper labor.

The Lawrences in the 1840s hoped to avoid such class problems and sought to replicate the early tranquil conditions of Waltham. The first firm launched in Lowell, the Merrimack Manufacturing Company, was capitalized at six hundred thousand dollars, with investors purchasing shares for one thousand dollars each. The company offered a number of services: mill and housing construction, waterpower development, and road building. Additional subscriptions increased the company's capital, and the funds were used to construct supplementary mills. With such growth, a new company was created to develop the remaining land and water privilege sites. The Locks and Canals Company sold land and leased waterpower sites to new companies wishing to locate in Lowell. But their services did not stop there: they supplied the machinery, built the mills and housing units, and laid out the roads. As Robert Dalzell observed, the "Locks and Canals Company, ownership of which had passed to the stockholders of the Merrimack Company on a share-for-share basis, had thus assumed the function of selling what amounted to complete, prepackaged textile mills to groups of interested investors."[42]

These turnkey operations apparently could be adopted wherever sufficient waterpower resources and land were available. One suitable site was on the Connecticut River at Hadley Falls. There the Hadley Falls Company set up operations as a land developer and power provider. Out of this grew the new town of Holyoke, Massachusetts. Those who came to find work in Holyoke were not the Lowell-style girls but instead were immigrant families. Rather than a model community, Holyoke became a shantytown. Contemporaneously another new town, Lawrence, was under construction across the state on the Merrimack River, and the Lawrences hoped to avoid Holyoke's fate.[43]

Incorporated in 1845, the Essex Company received a state charter to construct a dam across the Merrimack River; this would generate waterpower to be used for manufacturing and mechanical endeavors. Waterpower sales or leases together with real estate sales and development would constitute the business of the firm. To facilitate development, the company handled a wide array of services all designed to turn a profit and to emulate the success of the Lowell enterprises. The Essex Company became at once a machine company, a real estate agent, a housing contractor, and an urban planner. To achieve their vision, the investors nominated Abbott Lawrence as president of the firm and hired Charles Storrow, a civil engineer and railroad manager who was well know to many of the firm's shareholders, to exercise oversight of the project. Amos Lawrence, for example, had given him a loan of five hundred dollars to finish his engineering program in Paris.[44] Once hired, the board of directors left Storrow in charge of both the long-term planning and the day-to-day operations of the company. He served simultaneously as treasurer, agent, and chief engineer of the company, accountable only to the directors, and he also sat on that board. But the 1840s proved to be a trying time for manufacturers. The country had just come out of a major depression and teetered on the edge of another downturn. Labor strikes, changing fashion demands, domestic and foreign competition, and an unstable political climate made the initial start-up of another textile town problematic.

From the outset, the stockholders left Storrow to guide the new town's development. Though dreaming of an industrial utopia, Amos Lawrence, long an invalid, could not assume a major role in the company's operation, and his brother Abbott, although titular head of the company, was involved in national policies and politics. In 1849 Abbott embarked for England to serve as envoy to Great Britain. Only Samuel Lawrence, then residing in nearby Lowell, served as the family's eyes on the project.[45] Storrow moved ahead determined to make Lawrence a model town. Paternalism combined with a utopian vision of class harmony guided his decisions. Writing in 1848, he said, "Where else can you find as here the elements of society ready to be molded into a good or an evil shape, nothing to pull down, all to build up; a whole town composed of young people to influence and train as you would a school."[46]

Reminiscent of Webster and Slatersville, Lawrence retained a rural atmosphere: trees, commons, parks, broad streets, and wandering animals. But unlike the early villages designed by the Slaters, the Lawrence brothers constructed three-story boarding houses for their workers, a workforce comprised initially of young girls and women. Like the Lowell girls, the activities of the females were closely monitored; they were required to attend church, join the library association, and contribute to a health fund. For the latter two services, funds were deducted from the workers' pay. Yet there were problems from the very beginning of the town. The construction workers who built the dam and erected the many buildings continued to live in Lawrence after their work was completed. They often rejected labor and social discipline and formed a sharp contrast to the more pliable young women. Lawrence would not become another Lowell or lay claim to being a peaceable, idyllic factory village such as the Slatersville of the early nineteenth century.[47]

Already by 1846, most of the arrivals to Lawrence were not wholesome farm girls or staid Yankee families but male construction workers hired to excavate the dam and canal and construct boardinghouses to accommodate workers. The company also hired Irish immigrants to supplement the labor force. In 1847 Storrow sought to incorporate the town, a move designed to relieve the firm from responsibility for providing essential services such as schools or jails. Opposition arose from nearby towns that objected to Lawrence's boundaries. Many local residents, dissatisfied with the condition of the community, demanded that the name of the town be changed. Yet Storrow pushed the matter through the legislature and on April 17, 1847, Lawrence, Massachusetts was officially incorporated. By 1848, while Storrow was still entranced by his utopian dreams about an idyllic community, Lawrence was populated by 3,600 people who lived in a boomtown complete with gamblers, drunkards, speculators, and criminals. At this time, the town featured three large manufacturing firms, machine shops, boardinghouses, a gas works, banks, churches, schools, a library, and a train station. By 1855 the town's mills contained 10 percent of the state's spindles, and the community had become a major center of industry and immigration.[48]

The economic situation in Lawrence was precarious from the start, and the town soon had a reputation for shoddy working conditions and an unhealthy living environment. A report issued by the town's school committee in 1853 showed just how far from the model town ideal Lawrence had fallen. The chief issue involved truancy, and the report noted that there were some two hundred boys and girls between the ages of five and fifteen who failed to attend school. These "street marauders," as they were called, "spend their time in prowling about shops, alleys and backyards, pilfering swill, fuel, old-iron, and such more valuable articles as happen to be unprotected."[49] The problems evident in Lawrence were brought to national attention when the Pemberton Mill collapsed in 1860. Constructed in 1853 under the direction of an assistant engineer employed by the Essex Company, this mill employed over nine hundred people. At the time of the incident, it was estimated that anywhere from six hundred to eight hundred people were working in the mill. At five o'clock in the afternoon, the mill began to collapse, and within a minute the building had crashed to the ground taking the operatives with it. The *Hartford Times* reported that some two hundred to three hundred people were either dead or missing, while the *Hartford Courant* placed the number closer to five hundred. What followed the collapse represented a second disaster. Fire broke out at around nine thirty that evening and engulfed the ruins making further rescues almost impossible. When a more accurate account of the victims was taken, about 115 people were dead or missing and another 165 wounded. In the aftermath of the collapse, a coroner's jury concluded that the pillars used to support the floors were defective, and supervision of the construction site and examination of the building materials were inadequate. Public opinion turned on the company, particularly its owners and the textile industry in general. The *New York Times* reported that the mill was known to be defective, and the collapse represented "a reckless sacrifice of life upon the altar of a mean and criminal cupidity." Southern spokesmen used the incident to criticize Northern manufacturers and to highlight the owner's abusive treatment of wage laborers. Nevertheless, within a year, the mill was rebuilt and back in operation.[50]

This tragedy was not faced by Amos and Abbott Lawrence. Both men had died, Abbott in 1855 and Amos three years earlier.[51] But this disaster did nothing to help their reputations, and it would have been particularly hurtful to them. The Lawrence brothers valued their good name above all other assets they possessed. The end results of a life's work, they believed, should be contentment, self-respect, and a nod from one's peers for a job "well done." But the town bearing their name was quickly becoming a synonym for poor working conditions, and their children did little to change its image. By the time of this scandal, Amos A. Lawrence was left to deal with the public relations fallout for the Lawrence clan. His tepid response was indicative of his lack of sympathy for the Catholic immigrants who were becoming the dominant force in this city.[52]

Amos Adams Lawrence would inherit much from his father and his uncle besides wealth. He would not only become a major manufacturer but an important philanthropist and political figure, especially concerning the issue of slavery in the antebellum era. Amos Adams Lawrence would adopt Abbott and Amos Lawrence's perspective that saw the economy as more than a means for profit. Rather than pursue speculative ventures, Amos and Abbott chose instead to adopt a steady, deliberate pace concerning business, an interest in community, and a respect for New England's values and institutions. They believed that the United States was different from Europe, and it could avoid many of the latter's pitfalls, such as its overwhelming poverty and harsh class conflicts. Like most Americans, they saw themselves as working men, emphasizing the virtues of labor and personal and community responsibility exemplified in their philanthropic pursuits.[53] Amos Adams

Lawrence would elaborate a more clear-cut philosophical approach than his father and uncle, as he would develop in a systematic way the notion that a manufacturing society must rely on a meritocratic system that allowed advancement through hard work. Institutions of higher education that rewarded the talented, virtuous, and hardworking, regardless of class situation, were keys to this possibility, for they guaranteed the perpetuation of the elite that he had witnessed in Boston. Amos Adams Lawrence would become a major advocate of a sin-free, virtuous, and Protestant America but ignored the exclusionary and disciplinary aspects of such a society.

Chapter 7

Amos Adams Lawrence

The "Puritan Warrior" and the Destiny of America

While Samuel Colt was crafting his alternative persona as Dr. Coult, immersing himself in the emerging U.S. popular culture and learning from his cousin Roswell that business required an adaptable set of moral principles, and Horatio Nelson Slater and John Fox Slater were serving as apprentices in their fathers' factories, another future leader of the New England textile industry was following a different path animated by religion, education, and enterprise. Amos Adams Lawrence entered Harvard College in 1831, graduating in 1835. Unlike Colt, his vision of an industrialized America would be akin to the shining city on a hill, not a global empire but a self-sufficient Christian Republic that eschewed sin, practiced virtue and industry, respected obedience and authority, and provided education for those men most deserving of it. Lawrence, nevertheless, differed from the Slaters' view of the nation in supporting a less paternalistic, more meritocratic society. Rather than small-town values, the beliefs of an educated urban elite should guide the country.

Although Amos Adam's father, Amos Lawrence, had never attended college, he was a great believer in education, endowing Williams College and contributing to many other educational institutions and religious organizations. While an astute businessman, he did not believe that his sons had to follow in his footsteps as long as they pursued a respectable occupation. As we saw in the last chapter, he also was not shy about giving his children advice on matters from the importance of hard work to career choices. He wrote to his eldest son William, "I have no wish that you pursue trade. . . . I would rather see you on a farm, or studying any profession."[1] Amos Adams heeded at least some of his father's advice but saw himself as a new kind of businessman. In his senior year of college, he wrote, "My present design is to be a merchant, not a plodding, narrow-minded one pent up in a city, with my mind always in my counting-room, but . . . I would be at the same time a literary man in some measure and a farmer."[2] Amos Adams realized this goal after graduation. He not only owned a farm outside of Boston but became one of the richest and most powerful businessmen in New England. Beginning as a commission merchant in 1843, he was the main selling agent for many textile mills in New England. By 1845 he was on the board of directors of several textile companies and the director of the Suffolk Bank, the American Insurance Office, the Boston Water Power Corporation, and the Middlesex Canal. He also managed the Lawrence family properties. He continued his father's philanthropic pursuits as he attained wealth, donating time and money to educational and Christian organizations. It is estimated that he gave over one million dollars to charitable pursuits during his lifetime.[3] But Amos Adams's greatest legacy was as a central figure in the struggles around slavery that tore the Union apart during his lifetime. His assistance to the New England Emigrant Aid Society, support of John Brown, and various political activities defined his career. Amos Adams Lawrence's business, political, and philanthropic pursuits were informed by his religious beliefs, which influenced his life path as much if not more than his economic interests. He distrusted the popular culture of Barnum and the young Dr. Coult as anarchistic and immoral, advocating education as a cure for these "dissolute" attractions.

Childhood and College

Amos Adams Lawrence, the second son of Amos Lawrence and Sarah Richards, was born in July 1814. But the death of his mother and the physical and mental pain such a loss caused his father made the young boy's life difficult. Until his father remarried in 1821, Amos Adams lived in Groton with his grandmother. Thereafter, the family united and resided in Boston. Throughout his life, Amos Adams Lawrence glorified his dead mother and often criticized his stepmother from whom he increasingly became estranged.[4] Despite Lawrence's religious devotion and extensive educational background, in many ways, Amos Adams's personality was like that of Samuel Colt. Like Colt, his unstable early family life may have led to an insecurity that manifested itself in a desire to make his own way despite his father's wealth and a wish to be publicly known and recognized as well as rich. As did Colt, he had a vision of America that he felt should be implemented and that he actively pursued on a public stage. But he viewed America as a republic rather than an empire. Lawrence also advocated a strict, Protestant moral code of systematic, sober, controlled conduct and virtuous action to attain these goals. If Colt was the epitome of an expressive, adventurous individualism that knew few boundaries on its conduct, Amos Adams Lawrence was the embodiment of that American individualism that sought to connect strong religious beliefs, virtuous conduct, and good works.

Amos Lawrence Sr. made sure that his son had an excellent education. Tutored and educated first in Boston, he was sent away to the Franklin Academy at the age of thirteen. This, however, proved to be an unhappy experience. The headmaster, Mr. Putnam, was often angry and unpredictable and was a strict disciplinarian. Rather than study, young Amos preferred the freedoms provided by the outdoors. His academic training stood second to his love of nature and enjoyment of riding, skating, and walking in the nearby woods.[5]

While he might ridicule his headmaster, calling him "Old Put," and neglect his studies, Amos Adams still had to submit to the control of his father. Amos Lawrence Sr. was a meticulous man, an embodiment in many ways of the calculating Protestant businessman made famous by Max Weber. Amos Sr. urged his son to keep an accurate accounting of all expenses: "Get the habit firmly fixed of putting down every cent you receive and every cent you expend. In this way you will acquire some knowledge of the relative value of things . . . Among the numerous people who have failed in business within my knowledge, a prominent cause has been a want of system in their affairs by which to know when their expenses and losses exceeded their profits."[6] Again and again, Amos Lawrence insisted that his son keep precise records for everything from trips, fares, haircuts, clothing, and food to entertainment. Still, not trusting his son, he periodically reviewed the boy's diary and made comments on the entries. After one such examination in April 1830, Amos Lawrence scolded his son and advised him to look at the following comments every time he opened the book to make an entry: "First you cannot write so well as you did 18 months ago because you are careless in writing and seemingly do not make your entries here as soon as you receive or pay money; the habit of putting-off is a slip shod habit and whoever allows himself in it will be liable to come to want."[7] Described as "no scholar," he nevertheless entered Harvard in 1831 only to leave shortly thereafter and spend several years searching for his life goals.

Amos Adams's wanderlust was bothersome to the goal-oriented values of his father. But Amos Adams was not alone in disappointing his father in the turbulent 1830s. His older brother, William Lawrence, also appeared to be somewhat cavalier about the choice of a career and his personal principles. His father wrote to him, "You ought to have some steady pursuit is quite certain. No young man can have any standing in this community without it, only you had better be engaged in printing little stories than doing nothing: persons having no duties become a small consequence, however large their property. Whatever you undertake ought to be pursued with a determination to make yourself to be respected and respectable—whether it is trafficking or tinkering, is of much less consequence than to have no pursuit." If William planned to remain in Boston, he needed to change his behavior, for "men having no pursuit here occupy a very small space in the public estimation." Apparently the warning failed in its desired effect, and Amos Lawrence once again had to admonish his son. "As I have before said, I had rather you would engage in the most common business than not to be in any business. An idle man here can have no standing in society. No matter how much money he has, he must work with his head or his hands, else he may as well at once be content to be set down as a useless encumbrance."[8] Furthermore, in Amos Sr.'s view, young William was setting a bad example for his brother Amos Adams.[9]

Continuously ill, by March 1836, Amos Lawrence, Sr. pleaded with his sons to do something useful with their lives, including working for the family business: "If either of my sons were qualified to enter my business with credit to the concern, it would be a great satisfaction to me to have them there, and thus one object would be secured." Business was expanding and "what an opening this is for an ambitious man!"[10]

This time of uncertainly proved to be crucial to the moral and political formation of Amos Adams. During his time away from Harvard, Amos Adams had been introduced to politics, intense religious debates, and discussions on class, intemperance, and asceticism. One particularly eventful episode during this period was his chance to see President Andrew Jackson. This was so exciting to young Amos Adams that he followed the president around New England. He first saw Jackson in a Boston procession and then again in Andover: "We escorted him out of town, took a stage coach and followed him to

Lowell, where we arrived just in time to see the famous procession of factory girls."[11] Even more fascinated by politics, he went to Washington, DC in the spring of 1834 where he saw Davy Crockett, Henry Clay, Martin Van Buren, and John Quincy Adams. While sitting in the House gallery, Lawrence heard Adams offer a petition to end slavery. Impressed with Adams's eloquence, his debating skills, and his intellect, Lawrence wrote, "I never heard such argument expressed so eloquently before, and never expect to again." But the highlight of the visit was a meeting with President Jackson whom he described thus: "Here sat the grand mover of the machine that supports some and crushes others."[12]

This introduction to politics convinced Amos Adams that he wanted to be more than the stereotypical businessman concerned solely with profit. He began to develop a clear and consistent philosophy of wealth, privilege, and individualism that could guide his behavior and, he believed, serve as a template for others. His Harvard years were a period when he not only crafted a vision of his life but also decided to put his beliefs into action, to be somewhat of a renaissance man who combined the practicality of business with a knowledge and appreciation of literature and a respect for nature. He realized that his father's business would one day pass to him and that he only had to "have mercantile tact enough to carry on the immense though safe machine which my father and uncle have put in operation, it will turn out gold to me as fast as I could wish: and to be rich would be my delight."[13] Although he believed that some people were born to privilege, he argued that true wealth implied more than money. He imbibed the new democratic spirit of Jacksonian America, especially the post-Puritan Protestantism that swept the country in the 1830s. Its liberal emphasis on enlightenment and benevolence informed Amos Adams's end-of-year prayer in 1837: "Great God, regard me in kindness and illumine my mind with heavenly light that may I distinguish truth from error. . . . Extend thy truth to the ends of the world and cause to cease violence and prejudice, and hasten the time when religion shall possess all minds."[14]

For Lawrence, education and hard work were the keys to creating a virtuous and compassionate society: "Real good fortune is to be in the sphere of mental improvement."[15] Man's nature can be improved if he would just have the will to better himself. Herein lies his defense of wealth and his analysis of poverty. In Lawrence's view, the reason for poverty was a lack of will. He contended that the only thing that many of the poor enjoy is sensual pleasure; they are content to be idle. "Sensual delight is almost the only kind the ignorant can enjoy," wrote Lawrence. "Their chief pleasure seems to be in the good feeling of their bodies, intellectual labour has no delights for them."[16]

This emphasis on the unequal partition of virtue legitimated the existence of different classes and informed his view regarding the division of labor. For Lawrence, the division of labor was a defense of the class system. The division of labor "divides society into classes so that it can be more easily governed, & hence conduces through good laws to order & tranquillity." Yet he was well aware of the problems awaiting the wealthy if they did not appreciate the circumstances of the working or poorer classes. He warned the rich not to despise the poor or to undervalue their services. "Unless the poor show plainly a design of making war contrary to law & justice against their opulent neighbours, as they sometimes do under the disguised names of 'defenders of Liberty,' 'democrats,' or 'working men' (in our own country) they cannot be said to be hated by the rich, the latter feel no enmity toward them."[17]

According to Lawrence, social mobility was possible for the hard worker, for the industrious person can move forward although his advancement might be gradual. Through industry, temperance, frugality, and books, there was "room for improvement" in his circumstances. He cautioned such men that they will not be poor for long and that "there is little cause of quarrelling with those who are better off, they have not conspired to make him poor." Yet Lawrence also recognized that just as too much idleness was bad, too much work was also injurious to the practice of virtue: "Working day after day without thinking is proof enough that human nature may be moulded into almost any shape & that man may be brutalized by employment as well as by idleness." To survive, workers must "assume some steady employment, some trade."[18]

Amos Adams Lawrence also believed in the community responsibilities of a wealthy man. In an early version of "The Gospel of Wealth," written while still at Harvard, Amos Adams equated riches and a virtuous benevolence, if properly understood. He wrote,

> If any one has any love for his fellow creatures, any love of the worthy respect of the neighborhood, they will be willing and glad to be rich. . . . A good man will willingly endure the labor of taking care of his property for the sake of others whom he can so much benefit by it, but his thoughts and fears will not be perpetually on the alert that he may not lose a dollar and may not make all he can. If one can be rich and yet for his private ease will not be, he is almost as loving of himself as he who heaps up only to count his dollars, and refuses the demands of charity.[19]

These were such lofty pronouncements from a Harvard boy who considered his studies dull, who failed to attend lectures or to submit his work on time, who enjoyed practical jokes and violating campus regulations, and who became a member of the Royal Navy, a club for the weakest scholars on campus. He admitted to being idle, something he condemned in others.[20]

This gap between aspirations, philosophy, and behavior haunted Amos Adams throughout his twenties. At the age of twenty-eight, Amos Adams believed that he had "passed the greater part of my life and [was] not distinguished even in [his] own city."[21] By then, Amos Adams Lawrence had served as a dry goods commission merchant for Almy, Patterson, and Company and as a purchasing agent for the Seamen's Aid Society. In 1838 he opened his own firm and sold raw silk, broadcloths, and satinets on commission but shortly after closed it and went into the commission business with Amory Appleton. His timing was not propitious, for the business of the later 1830s meant depression and slow trade. His father gave him money and property, but Amos Adams languished. He closed down his various business affairs and traveled to Europe where he remained for about one year.[22]

The trip helped to consolidate his philosophy and crystallized many of his ideas about slavery, poverty, Catholicism, education, and the role of women in society and the family. Poverty for many, he came to believe, was a direct result of Catholicism. The church served to bankrupt the people by forcing them to support the construction and maintenance of so many magnificent structures. People were not encouraged to work and to accumulate wealth for themselves. He believed that Catholics were "a lazy set of brutes."[23] The English impressed him with their sincere opposition to slavery. Almost everywhere in England, discussions focused on slavery and the desire of the British people to see its end. Yet for all the British condemnation of slavery, they continued to treat a portion of their own population, the Irish, with contempt. In Ireland Amos Adams saw wretched poverty, rampant disease, and ragged and desperate men, women, and children looking to survive. Just as in Europe, noted Lawrence, where poverty was a result of the Catholic church and a compliant government, Irish poverty resulted from a similar connection. Only this time, the government was British, and the compliant churches were both Catholic and Protestant.[24]

Necessity and a guilty conscience forced Amos Adams to yet again face his economic future. Once home from his European travels, he joined the firm of Lawrence and Stone, but that connection was soon severed: "Mr S[amuel] L[awrence] told me the other day that

Mr. Stone had concluded that he could not continue in business with me, as I am very timid and nervous when there comes any trouble. This is a bad failing to come in contact with Mr. Stone's rashness against which I have been warned."[25] Thus, another partnership was ended, but several more, this time with lasting results, would emerge.

Economic Triumph

Like many in the Colt family, Amos Adams's economic success was aided by an advantageous marriage. On March 31, 1842, he married Sarah Appleton, the daughter of William Appleton, a noted businessman. In part through Appleton's connections, the following year he made another advantageous relationship when he entered into partnership with Robert M. Mason to distribute goods made by the Cocheco Company. The days of wanderlust and procrastination gave way to ones devoted to family and business. Lawrence was determined to succeed: "I deem this a highly important step in my career, and I pray that I may be true to the new duties I have undertaken, and may not allow indolence or timidity to hinder me from taking my full share of the labor which will fall upon me."[26]

For Amos Adams Lawrence, the obvious entrance into the textile business would have been through his family's firm, A. & A. Lawrence. But when his father retired, he was determined to start his own business. Almost thirty years old, he enthusiastically set out to reorganize the Cocheco Cotton Manufacturing Company, turn a profit, and make his firm the foremost selling house in America. He succeeded. His responsibilities expanded, and he became a director and president of the Cocheco Company and subsequently a selling agent, director, and treasurer of another textile concern, the Salmon Falls Company.[27] By the 1850s Amos A. Lawrence owned stock in seventeen textile firms, two machine shops, two railroad companies, three waterpower firms, commercial office space, and a vast amount of residential property scattered throughout New England.[28] These included Bay State Mills, Boott Mills, Dwight Company, Jackson Company, Lancaster Mills, Lawrence Mills and Machine Shop, Middlesex Company, Suffolk Company, and the Lowell Machine Shop, among others. To this list he added railroad bonds, interest in waterpower companies, notes and mortgages, and other real estate.[29] Although late to enter business, he realized he had a talent for money making.

His penchant for detailed accountings of his financial dealings, inherited from his father, served him well. Ever the record keeper, he maintained a small business diary where he recorded all of his real estate holdings. The diary was divided first by county and within that classification by town. For each community he wrote the name of those who rented property from him. For example, his entries for Worcester County included an alphabetical listing of towns beginning with Ashburham and ending with Worcester. In Worcester County alone, he owned property in at least twenty-five towns including Webster. There, Henry Bugbee, a local shoe manufacturer, was listed as a renter.[30] But it was his sales commission business and his two textile mills that furnished much of his wealth.

Like Samuel Slater and Sons, Amos A. Lawrence joined the production of textiles with distribution and sales. At the time Lawrence became involved in the Cocheco Company, it was losing money. As the company's president and director, he turned the firm around through cost-cutting measures and the centralization and rationalization of business practices. Soon it was returning a 6 percent profit. Lawrence and his Cocheco partners then expanded and purchased the Salmon Falls Company where he served variously as treasurer and director. By the end of the 1850s, his stock in Cocheco and Salmon Falls was valued at fifty thousand dollars and forty-three thousand dollars respectively.[31] His selling house of Mason and Lawrence became the exclusive agent for the Cocheco Company and the Salmon Falls mill.

His economic interests expanded, and by 1868 he had become interested in the manufacture of hosiery and knit goods. With the purchase of the Ipswich Mills in 1868, he sought to manufacture and sell cotton stockings for $1.50 per dozen. At this price, he was able to appeal to a broad range of consumers. Lawrence expanded his holdings the following year with the purchase of the Gilmanton and the Ashland Mills, both New Hampshire firms. Initially the knit goods trade was an expensive money pit costing Lawrence eighty thousand dollars in losses; for the next twenty years he competed with and usually lost to British and French manufacturers. Yet by the 1880s the firm was turning a profit. The introduction of tariffs on foreign goods, a "Buy American" attitude on the part of consumers, and modern production techniques allowed Lawrence to outsell his foreign competition and made him one of the largest knit goods producers in the country.[32]

While he held an interest in these and other mills, it was his selling house that consumed much of his time and skills. Textile manufacturers usually relied on selling houses located in New York, Boston, Providence, Philadelphia, and New Orleans to handle the sales and distribution of their yarn, thread, and cloth. Rather than sell their products directly from the factory to a myriad of jobbers and retailers, they consigned them to commission agents. These independent selling agents generally dealt with transportation costs and schedules, set prices, and increasingly influenced the style, quality, and amount of cloth produced. For a fee, commission agents loaned manufacturers money, provided insurance, and even collected bad debts. While relieving manufacturers of the problems associated with distribution to a wide and ever-growing market, the use of these middlemen had drawbacks. Manufacturers increasingly ceded control over the style, quality, quantity, price, and production schedule to middlemen. If their selling agents were knowledgeable about the fashion, type, pattern, and color of cloth that customers wanted and they were able to communicate directly and swiftly with their manufacturing clients, the partnership usually prospered. But fashion was a fickle business, and some selling houses were unable to predict with accuracy new fashion trends or to judge the market, assess the credit worth of their customers, and interact easily with their clients. Such relationships could lead to disaster.[33]

Over time, manufacturers such as Nathan Appleton, Horatio Nelson Slater, and Amos A. Lawrence began to control distribution as well as production and were able to retain their positions in the ever-competitive textile industry.[34] Their selling houses usually handled only those companies that they had an interest in or owned outright. Amos Adams vigorously pursued the control of selling and production. With an office in Boston, he handled broadcloths, cassimeres, and silks. He maintained control even as his companies expanded and changed ownership. Lawrence worked with different partners, including Robert Mason, Henry B. Mather, John D. W. Joy, and eventually in 1871 with his son Amory A. Lawrence. When Lawrence and Mason became partners, they acquired several important accounts, becoming the exclusive selling agents for the Cocheco Manufacturing Company and the Salmon Falls Manufacturing Company. These two companies remained with Lawrence throughout much of his business career, and he held both a financial interest and an administrative position in each of them.[35]

This dual standing allowed his selling house to direct production without interference from manufacturers. But Lawrence was flexible in his business dealings. When Lawrence's firm represented other manufacturers such as Arlington Mills, another approach had to be undertaken. With this firm, Lawrence had to work with manufacturers to develop a production and marketing plan. Because he did not know the woolen end of the textile business as well as others, he hired Alfred Ray, previously employed as a purchasing manager in the dress department at Marshall Field & Company, to manage the account. To retain his services and thus the Arlington account, Lawrence made Ray a partner in Lawrence & Company. This solved several problems: Ray went from a salaried employee, making twenty thousand dollars annually plus commissions, to a partner; now Lawrence had the clout to force Arlington to submit to his production and marketing demands if they wanted to keep the fashion advice offered by Ray. Arlington as well as Cocheco and Salmon Falls were under his influence and control.[36] Amos A. Lawrence was an astute businessman who wanted to maintain control of his economic future. He had to be in the dominant position vis-à-vis mill owners and agents.

As with other manufacturers, however, his managerial skills and strategies were tested when labor and management collided over living and working conditions in these small textile towns and villages. In his New Hampshire factory villages, he had a chance to try something different from the Lowell model. He noted that he wanted to begin "right in Salmon Falls."[37] Like the Slater system, the factory at Salmon Falls relied on family labor, and the town that grew up around the factory exhibited many of the characteristics of Webster or Slatersville. The community had been planned to meet family needs. On the hillside opposite the mill, a grassy tree-lined mall ran up the hill, and radiating out from it were two rows of houses, each accommodating from two to four families. In addition, a four-story boardinghouse had been built to house single women who worked in the mill. This was part of the property purchased by Amos Adams Lawrence. He brought his organizational skills to town planning. He laid out a grid-style street pattern south of the mall, and along a newly designed Front Street, he encouraged businessmen to set up shop and serve his hands. Soon dry-goods merchants, bonnet makers, and boot and shoe dealers sold their goods along Front Street. A bank, a dentist, and a druggist opened, but not a saloon. Liquor was not allowed in his mill town. Up the hill, one could observe the class awareness of the new owner. New three-story boarding houses were constructed on the lower part of the hill, and then duplexes that would accommodate overseers and foremen could be found further up the hill. The third level, higher still, was reserved for the homes of the new merchants who served the town. Finally, a church stood at the top of the hill, but it was restricted to Protestant sects only. Catholics had to worship elsewhere. Whether Protestant or Catholic, workers were expected to attend church services.[38]

Yet Lawrence was never as interested in the conditions of his workers as was John Fox Slater, for example. He became even less interested as immigrant workers, many of them Catholic Irish and French Canadian, began to dominate his workforce. On January 10, 1860, Lawrence noted in his diary, “Pemberton Mill at Lawrence fell down in one sudden ruin while in operation. The pay-roll shows 960 persons employed. While the multitude confined in the ruins were being dug out, a fire started and finished the horrible catastrophe.”[39] Five stories high, this was the “model mill in the model city.”[40] In response to the tragedy, Lawrence and his friends subscribed two thousand dollars for relief and gave another three thousand dollars that they saved by canceling a dinner meeting of the New England Societies.[41] Such subscriptions were petty sums at best.

Amos Adams Lawrence was a very successful businessman who helped to create a modern version of the selling house that merged the concerns of production and marketing with an eye to changes in the market. He exhibited many classic traits of Weber's Protestant ethic, from his systematic, calculating control of his conduct and accounting affairs to his belief that virtuous conduct was a key to economic success. Yet his true calling and passion was not business. His moral values and desire to find a political solution to the problem of slavery overrode his utilitarian economic activity. From his devotion to the settlement of antislavery pioneers in Kansas through the New England Emigrant Aid Company to his attempts to run for political office and guide the affairs of the nation, Lawrence's moral and religious values were of central importance to his identity.

Slavery and the New England Emigrant Aid Company

Determined not to be consumed by his business, Lawrence took an active interest in reform movements, politics, and philanthropy. Like his father, Amos Adams Lawrence became a foremost philanthropist. He not only knew how to make money, but he had decided views on how and where it should be spent. A friend considered him “an illustrious example of the true use of one of the most important trusts committed to man: the use of wealth.”[42] One use of his riches focused on education. As early as April 1845 Lawrence offered to endow a university in Wisconsin that came to bear his name. To his alma mater Harvard he gave seventy-five thousand dollars to build a hall for the Theological School, and to Liberia he gave one thousand dollars to establish a college that might prove a lure for free African

Americans. Charities included the Boston Prison Discipline Society, the Young Men's Benevolent Society, and the Massachusetts General Hospital, among others, as well as many small gifts to individuals.[43] He recognized the significance of public institutions for the health of the community. His approach to business placed the pursuit of profit in a larger moral context, circumscribed by a view of life as much more than the quest for money. A good life entailed a community that shared the same virtuous values. No doubt Amos Adams did not always live up to his own moral dictates, especially when faced with how to react to fierce economic competition or a business downturn. Yet Lawrence, like other manufacturers in the Early Republic, was on an economic path that had no sure guidelines for behaviors or clear code of responsibilities for entrepreneurs.

Though interested in philanthropy, by the 1840s the slavery question consumed him. Like most Boston businessmen, during the 1830s and 1840s Amos Adams opposed the extension of slavery but was content to let slavery remain in the South. He feared the abolitionism of William Lloyd Garrison, which he saw as a radical attempt to dismember the Union. However, the annexation of Texas in 1845 began a process of radicalization for Amos Adams that would culminate in his support of free labor in Kansas and wholehearted advocacy of the Union in the Civil War. Amos Adams, like many other New England merchants, feared that allowing Texas statehood would not only expand the reach of slavery but provoke war with Mexico. He was right on both counts. Though the United States quickly won the war with Mexico, receiving two-fifths of Mexico's land in the Guadalupe Hidalgo Treaty of 1848, Amos Adams and his father recognized that future conflict around slavery was all but inevitable. After the Mexican War, Amos Lawrence Sr. wrote, "God's curse will assuredly rest upon the iniquity of our nation. We have acquired military renown in this war at the cost of our national character for justice and truth."[44]

Like Abraham Lincoln, Amos Adams initially favored the return of freed slaves to Liberian Africa, funding several individuals who supported colonization.[45] Yet the Mexican War and its aftermath radicalized Amos Adams. These events of the 1840s and 1850s led Amos Adams to become involved in his most famous venture, the New England Emigrant Society, an organization born out of the Kansas question. Passage of the Fugitive Slave Act in 1850 exacerbated splits already evident around the country. As a Whig, Lawrence's primary object at this time was the preservation of the Union. In his own home state of Massachusetts, political debates among Free-Soilers, Antimasons, the Liberty Party, abolitionists, and Know Nothings intensified over the issue of slavery. Lawrence procrastinated, avoided the issue, and instead counseled respect for law and order and stressed the necessity to preserve the union. But that stance was revisited when Senator Stephen Douglas introduced the Kansas Nebraska Bill, an act that would essentially repeal the Missouri Compromise and open the new territories to slavery. Passed in 1854, this bill ignited the rage of many Americans. After passage of the law, Amos Adams wrote, "We went to bed one night, old-fashioned, conservative, compromise, Union Whigs, and waked up stark mad Abolitionists."[46] His acceptance of Southern slavery based on constitutional principles soon turned into a moral crusade against the extension of slavery to the West. A group of New Englanders, including Amos Adams's uncle Abbot Lawrence and Eli Thayer, founded a new organization called the Emigrant Aid Company. Incorporated in Connecticut and capitalized at five million dollars, this company sought to assist immigrants who wanted to settle in the Western territories or states. On the board of directors were Abbott Lawrence, Thayer, and Henry Wilson, among other prominent men. Later the board was expanded to include well-known Connecticut residents, among them John Hooker, Timothy Dwight, and Charles Ives.[47]

In Massachusetts a similar law of incorporation was passed. The Massachusetts Emigrant Aid Company's board included some of the same men who participated in the aforementioned Connecticut association: Eli Thayer and Henry Wilson. Absent from the Massachusetts based New England Emigrant Aid Company was Abbott Lawrence, but his nephew Amos Adams Lawrence joined the organization about six months later. Almost immediately Lawrence and Thayer became the primary managers with Lawrence recruiting men and soliciting money for the new organization and Thayer planning its course of operation.[48] Lawrence believed that the battle in Congress was lost, the expectations that politicians could solve the slavery question was dead, and only businessmen like himself who put their time and money into saving Kansas could successfully address the question of slavery in the territories and states. Lawrence thought that as the moral conscience of the country, New Englanders had a duty to spread their vision of America's future as a Christian nation that valued free labor, education, upward mobility, frugality, and hard work to everyone. For him the company was a "public, patriotic, and benevolent effort" whose investors should expect "a little glory, a great deal of abuse, and the satisfaction of having done your duty, and served your country and race."[49] In this view, he was supported by many of New England's clergymen, including Lyman Beecher, Horace Bushnell, and Calvin

Stowe. In July 1855 these clergymen sent a letter to religious leaders throughout the region urging each one of them to become lifetime members of the Emigrant Aid Company by purchasing one share of stock at $20.00 per share. The money would be used to continue the work of the association, which they believed supported freedom, religion, education, and temperance. The goal was to raise $150,000.[50] Although Lawrence worked tirelessly to ensure the society's success, and despite the pledges made by the clergy, funding continued to be a problem with the company throughout its existence.

Lawrence used a variety of novel means to attract settlers to Kansas, including public meetings, booster circulars, brochures, songs, and poetry. His song-writing contest proved especially popular. The winner of that contest was the famous Lowell girl, Lucy Larcom. Her song, "Call to Kansas" won the fifty-dollar prize, and she wrote of her delight to Lawrence: "Your announcement was a surprise to me. When I wrote the song, the only reward I thought of, was the pleasure of writing something which should be worthy to be sung in so good a cause. And I intend that the amount of the Premium, if I receive it, shall yet return in some form to the cause of humanity."[51] The latter sentiment would have pleased Amos Adams Lawrence, and the hint that she might consider moving to the territory "when they are in need of teachers" delighted him even more.[52] She evoked the notions of New England's Pilgrim past, family and Yankee virtues of liberty, honesty, and piety. The poet, John Greenleaf Whittier, echoed her sentiments. His short poem, "The Kansas Emigrants," brought to mind the great Puritan migration to the New World—a move designed to embed Christian love, harmony, a sense of community, and shared values in a crude wilderness. The concluding stanza read,

> We'll tread the prairie as of old
> Our fathers sailed the sea,
> And make the West, as they the East,
> The homestead of the free![53]

His poem was printed on cards and distributed to those making the journey west. Booster pamphlets also flooded the North describing Kansas as an idyllic garden, replete with fertile soil, genial climate, pure water, and abundant natural resources. They stated that "all the Indian tribes are friendly to the Free State Men." The brochures made much of the opportunities for farmers, artisans, shopkeepers, businessmen, and teachers. Young men and women and male householders and widows were encouraged to make Kansas their home.[54] Lawrence initially recruited among those close to home. Among the first settlers to leave for Kansas under the umbrella of the company were men and women from the textile towns of Lawrence, Lowell, and Pawtucket. From Lawrence, Massachusetts, for example, a thirty-eight-year-old stonecutter and his wife, a twenty-nine-year-old operative and his wife, and a young male operative set out for Kansas.[55]

Amos Adams Lawrence placed his money, time, and managerial expertise in the venture. He considered his position as treasurer of the Emigrant Aid Company as difficult if not more so than his position as treasurer of one of his textile mills. He sometimes had to sell his textile stock to subsidize the society. He once stated that Kansas represented the commitment of his heart and his fortune.[56] He did not see economic benefit in this scheme, and he was aware of how a concern for profit might undermine its integrity. For example, though he was encouraged to turn this cause into a speculative land venture, he refused. He discouraged his friends from investing in this company hoping to reap a big profit. "Keep your money for your own use, rather than do anything of that sort. The value of land stock companies is the most delusive of all stocks," he told a clergyman who asked his advice about stock subscriptions. Yet he and his colleagues were not able to convince members of the Boston community to support this venture out of pure philanthropic motives. He was often alone in providing money for this enterprise. E. B. Whitman wrote, "From all quarters attention is drawn towards Boston and its liberal and philanthropic & Merchants and Capitalists, and the question is significantly asked 'Why doesn't Boston take the lead boldly and with its accustomed liberality?' 'Let her but do this and the country will respond in its proportion.'"[57] But the response was not forthcoming. S. C. Pomeroy, a general agent for the company, sympathized with Lawrence: "I have been sorry that you have had to advance so much money for the company. If the many promises are to evaporate perhaps its best to have it known for my part I do not wish to invest money where there is none in the Treasury."[58] For Lawrence, the society was a moral crusade that could establish a virtuous community in Kansas. Like the early Pilgrims and Puritans who founded townships in New England, the town was to be the basic settlement pattern adopted by the emigrants to Kansas. Churches, schools, newspapers, and sawmills were promised to the settlers. To further the analogy, Lawrence suggested that a college be built. "In it shall burn the light of liberty, which shall never be extinguished till it illuminates the whole continent," wrote Lawrence. There was just one caveat: "It should be for boys, and not for girls." Later he explained, "I have no faith in the utility of giving diplomas to women, except for good housewifery, for courage, and for rearing good families of children." Coeducational institutions, he said, would "never be first-class colleges."[59] Men had their place in society, and so did women.

Lawrence believed that just as the Puritans founded Boston, just as they set themselves apart as God's chosen people and constructed institutions to support their beliefs, the settlers from the New England Emigrant Aid Company who traveled to Kansas would set themselves apart as moral, freedom-loving people and build churches and colleges to perpetuate their beliefs. By September 1854 two parties had left New England for the Kansas territory. They established a town site that they subsequently named Lawrence after their benefactor. Joseph Savage, a member of the second party, described his early days at the site: "Before pitching our tents for the night, we like pilgrims at the end of their journey, went for the first time to bathe our wearied limbs in the turbid waters of the Kaw [Kansas River]. As we first cast our longing eyes over its surface, and felt the cooling embrace of its waters, a feeling of ownership and affection sprang up in our hearts, for on its banks were soon to be our homes."[60] But their optimistic rhetoric was tempered by the realities of Kansas, and the only homes the first settlers saw "were of most primitive style, of pole and thatch. Most of the people for some weeks boarded in common, and, in such a dwelling, sleeping upon the ground on buffalo robes and blankets."[61]

They lived in a dangerous situation because of the increasingly violent conflicts over slavery. The disappointment experienced by a number of settlers and the fear of the proslavery Missourians who swept into Kansas were communicated to Mr. Lawrence. He learned that some emigrants stayed only a short time before returning to New England, complaining that the common necessities of life including lumber materials, flour, groceries, and other supplies were insufficient or unavailable. Other disgruntled people complained that in an "uncongenial climate, [they were] starving to death." Complaints from the settlers were countered by grumblings from company officials and local businessmen. The town's newspaper editor warned Lawrence that the "Missourians are preparing to make another descent on Lawrence, and my opinion is they will not be restrained on their next visit, but will destroy everything in their reach." He felt powerless against them; the military left the settlers without protection, and he stated that the Lawrence men "are cowardly wretches who came here and are frightened to death at the sight of a revolver." Furthermore, they hardly stay overnight before "they take to their heels" and leave.[62]

The problems faced by the settlers were mirrored in the politics of the region. The first territorial election proved disappointing. In March 1855 proslavery advocates won, set up a government, and forced Free State men to accept slavery or leave the territory. The Free Staters refused such a choice. They asked that guns, especially Sharps rifles, be sent to Lawrence and other Free State communities. Lawrence complied with their request; "when farmers turn soldiers they must have arms." He paid one thousand dollars for rifles to be sent to Kansas sufferers. But more guns were needed when the proslavery governor, Wilson Shannon, ordered the militia to attack the town of Lawrence, the Free State headquarters. Six hundred men defended the town, and the militia retreated. In the context of this turmoil and turn toward more violence, Lawrence received another request for arms. The settlers ordered an additional two hundred Sharps rifles. Anger among them was high, as appeals for support to the U.S. government went unheeded, and Lawrence began to question his own part in this venture. He was concerned that the Free State settlers would rise up against the federal government, and for him such a treasonous action was unthinkable. He wrote, "However wrong in our opinion, there never can be good reason for resisting our own government, unless it attempts to destroy the power of the people through the elections, that is, to take away the power of creating a new administration every four years. . . . We are a law-abiding people, and we will sustain our own government 'right or wrong.'"[63]

Yet conflict continued to escalate in Kansas and around the country. In May 1856 Lawrence, Kansas was ransacked by proslavery elements; Senator Charles Sumner was assaulted on the floor of the U.S. Senate for a speech he delivered entitled "The Crime against Kansas"; and John Brown, his four sons, and several other men murdered five proslavery advocates at Pottawatomie Creek in retaliation for the Lawrence sacking. All three of these events shook Lawrence to the core and caused him to reevaluate his stand on the relationship between government and slavery, the preservation of the Union, the values and standards of slaveholders, and the role violence should play in the struggle against slavery. To Lawrence, John Brown was a "Puritan warrior," a Kansas hero who deserved his moral and economic support. Of Charles Sumner, whose abolitionist policies sometimes frightened him, Lawrence wrote, "Mr. Sumner's speech on the 'Kansas Crime' alone entitles him to the gratitude of every man who has an American heart, whatever may be his politics."[64]

By 1856 Lawrence encouraged Kansas residents to violate some laws because they were unconstitutional and to prepare for a revolution if honest elections were not forthcoming. For Lawrence, the country was poised between liberty and slavery, and a civil war might be the only way to settle the matter. But the Kansas situation eased, and in the spring of 1857 Lawrence resigned as treasurer of the New England Emigrant Aid Company. His tenure as treasurer had been costly, for he had expended both wealth and psychic resources in this venture. [65]

But Lawrence's commitment to the slavery issue remained the guiding focus of his life. He considered several alternative ways to defeat the system. He was attracted to the ideas of his friend Elihu Burritt who proposed a plan that would "make freedom equally aggressive and strike at the very vitals of slavery in the Southern States." His plan called for free labor and more specifically German immigrant labor to grow cotton in the South and to sell it to Northern manufacturers such as Lawrence at a profit; these immigrant workers would serve as an example to other white farmers that they, too, could prosper growing cotton with their own labor and not with the use of slaves.[66] To attack slavery in the South also had an appeal to Lawrence, and it was embodied in the person of John Brown. At the time of Harpers Ferry, it was widely believed that Amos Adams Lawrence was deeply involved in the attack. He admired Brown, had contributed money for the support of Brown's family, and met with Brown on May 28, 1859, just five months before the infamous raid on the federal arsenal. Furthermore, the Sharps rifles that Brown used were those that Lawrence had sent to Kansas earlier. Just as Lawrence tried to deny his connection with Brown in the Pottawatomie Massacre and afraid of facing charges of treason, he disavowed any involvement with Brown in the Harpers Ferry raid as well. But he did try to assist Brown after he was captured and put on trial. After Brown's arrest in 1859, he called Brown a brave man who stood up against slavery, and he aided his legal defense fund. Writing to Governor Wise of Virginia, he argued that "Brown is a Puritan whose mind has become disordered by hardship and illness. He has the qualities which endear him to our people, and his sudden execution would send a thrill of horror through the whole North. From his blood would spring martyrs, all eager to die in the cause of human liberty." Appealing to the governor as a man "who loves the whole country" and as a law-and-order man like himself, he asked for a fair trial.[67] His support went unheeded and Brown was executed.

Lawrence's stand as a supporter of the Union and as a man of law and order stood in contrast to many of his deeds. While he proclaimed national unity and preservation of the Union, his leadership on the Kansas questions, his participation in the New England Emigrant Aid Company, and his support of John Brown suggested otherwise. While alienating those who wished to accommodate the South with such actions, he estranged others with his views on abolitionists, immigrants, Mormons, education for women, and the Catholic church. Despite making many enemies, Lawrence was attracted to the political arena to realize his goals, and he sought to change the country through political action.

Politics

As Lawrence immersed himself in the slavery question in the 1850s, policy issues consumed more of his time, and he increasingly became disenchanted with the existing parties. Local and state politics was chaotic in this turbulent era, with a plethora of parties trying to attract the attention of potential candidates and voters. These included everything from single-issue parties championing temperance, labor, or abolition, a decaying Whig bloc, a broken Democratic Party, and the Know Nothings to an emerging Republican Party and a nonpartisan citizen's ticket. Lawrence searched for a group that supported his views on national union and Free-Soil principles. The Whig Party was no longer an option, and Lawrence was not yet ready to join the Republicans. His first major step was toward the American Party, better known as the Know-Nothing Party. This organization capitalized on the growing dissatisfaction with the current political situation and garnered strength throughout the country. Its proponents stressed nativism and often sidestepped abolitionism. That was fine with Lawrence, for according to Eli Thayer, he "was as far removed from sympathy with radical Abolitionists as any man in the Union."[68] Lawrence considered himself a supporter of the nation, and he felt comfortable with this new party. The party reciprocated. It nominated him for governor of Massachusetts in 1856, but he declined and withdrew his name.[69] In a letter published in the *New York Times*, he wrote that he did not covet public office "and hope[d] the crisis will not arise which will make it otherwise," but under certain circumstances, he would be willing to enter the political field. In the event that the proslavery contingent in Kansas succeeded or Congress failed to protect American manufacturers from foreign competition or elected officials deviated from such basic American principles as fairness, industry, and opportunity, "I shall not hesitate to offer myself as a volunteer to serve in any capacity, even the humblest, for the maintenance of all our rights," wrote Lawrence.[70] Induced to run in 1858 for governor, he knew that he had no chance of winning. Well before the election, he wrote, "If put up to run against Mr. Banks, I shall be beaten soundly," and he was right.[71]

This defeat did not stop Lawrence, and he was soon back in the political arena. He took another chance on finding a political solution to the slavery question. He worked to develop a national union coalition party that drew together a broad range of conservatives from around the country, all of whom advocated conciliation with the South and not destruction of the Union. Known as the Constitutional Union Party, its members worked to minimize the slavery issue, to curtail support for rabid abolitionists, to promote respect for the Constitution and its laws, and to discourage secession talk. He wanted people to "learn to discriminate between hatred of slavery and hatred of the South."[72] At home, he helped to organize Union Clubs, held meetings, and delivered speeches on these topics. And he even went so far as to accept this party's nomination for governor of Massachusetts in 1860. But his state and his country had moved beyond reconciliation. The prospects for this party were almost nil. One friend lamented, "I hope you will, some time or other before you die, belong to some respectable organization, having some definite principles, so that I can vote for you." The Republican Party trounced the Union Party, and Amos A. Lawrence came in third out of the four candidates who ran for the office.[73] Lawrence had no choice but to support the federal government in the coming war.

THE CIVIL WAR AND ITS AFTERMATH

Republican John A. Andrew was inaugurated governor of Massachusetts on January 5, 1861, and he began to prepare the state for war. Andrew made considerable effort to reach out to the Boston elite, many of whom had opposed him in the election. In that effort, he was successful. For his officer corps, he chose to recruit among the Harvard-educated elite. He attributed to them ability, integrity, honor, and reliability. Such men considered it bad form to disagree with their commander-in-chief in public, an attitude that Andrew strongly encouraged. Among this group, Andrew searched for officers to command the new black regiments he wanted to field. For these units, he tried to find ambitious young men of military experience and firm antislavery principles who had faith in the capacity of African American men for military service. He stated, "Such officers must be necessarily gentlemen of the highest tone and honor; and I shall look for them in those circles of educated Anti-Slavery Society, which next to the colored race itself have the greatest interest in the success of this experiment."[74]

As a member of this elite, Amos A. Lawrence believed that it was his duty to bear arms for Massachusetts and the Union. His contributions would be financial and organizational, however. He offered to join the military, but was told that he could best serve the Union through organizing drill clubs, soliciting funds to aid Andrew Johnson in securing Tennessee for the Union, offering a home for invalid soldiers, and recruiting soldiers for the cavalry. Governor Andrew authorized Lawrence "to recruit a battalion of four companies of cavalry . . . for three years or the war."[75] Like Connecticut, Massachusetts required each town to fill a quota of men for service. In the early months of the war, recruitment had been easy as men volunteered for service. But by 1862, many men were looking for ways to avoid military service. States resorted to bounties and military drafts to secure all the soldiers demanded by the federal government. In this climate, Lawrence tried to recruit men for his battalion. Money was used as his recruitment tool. He sent agents throughout the countryside into factories and shops, prisons, and even Canada to find men willing to enlist. Bounties of between $100 and $175 were offered to them. To get the money for these bounties, Lawrence made a deal with town officials who were unable to fulfill their own military quotas with local men. Selectmen and other town officials would pay him a fee, and in exchange he would allow local residents to charge a recruit to their military quota. From city officials in Cambridge, New Bedford, and Boston, he received $15,000, $25,800, and $30,000 respectively to settle the quota dilemma in 1862. As a bounty broker, Lawrence was successful. He and his associates collected so much money that they were able to pay all outstanding claims and to use the surplus for future recruiting schemes.[76]

One such plan came to fruition in February 1863 when Governor Andrew asked Lawrence to join an advisory committee to organize and recruit black soldiers for military service. Lawrence responded positively, and soon the committee had recruited enough black soldiers to form the Fifty-Fourth Regiment. While there was some opposition to black fighting units, Lawrence looked pragmatically at the situation. The African American recruits would add to the pool of available soldiers, thus diminishing the draft of whites, and the participation of blacks would increase their self-respect. The Fifty-Fourth proved to be an excellent fighting force, which also alleviated some of the apprehension about recruiting African Americans for service.[77]

Throughout the war, Lawrence continued to give liberally to a number of causes: the treatment of Northern prisoners, rifle clubs, pensions for Civil War veterans, the Freedman's Relief Committee, the U.S. Sanitary Commission, and the care of African American refugees. Following the war, his philanthropic gifts continued. He spearheaded a move to build a memorial hall to Harvard's fallen soldiers. He wrote, "It seems to be the least that we can do, who did not go to the war, to commemorate the virtues of those who did go, and especially of those who marched and fought and died while we were comfortable at home."[78]

In the postbellum era, Amos A. Lawrence concentrated more on his home, family, philanthropy, and business than on public service or politics. His interest in the hosiery and knit-goods industry occupied much of his time. He administered several different companies, and as a founder and later president of the Association of Knit Goods Manufacturers, he guided the development of the entire industry. As well, Lawrence & Company continued to prosper, and in 1883 his selling house acquired its largest and most prestigious client, the Pacific Mills Corporation. Just as he had brought in Alfred Ray to work with the Arlington mills account, he took in additional partners including his own son Amory to help with this account. Whatever spare time he had was usually devoted to the society of his family and friends. His only major concession to politics was to join the Republican Party.[79]

Following his death in 1886, memorial services were held around the country for him. The president of Lawrence University in Wisconsin, B. P. Raymond, said of him, "He had the genius for money making; the genius that foresees the future . . . that creates the very conditions under which a great and profitable business may thrive," and that he had a great mission to use his wealth for the public good. Education and religion received his largest donations. In Raymond's view, Lawrence recognized the limits of pecuniary gain. He knew that "gold alone, and gold as an end, projects such iron walls. Under its destroying influence, the spiritual horizon narrows; the Intellect shrivels; the sensibilities become insensate; the conscience becomes seared and the currents of sympathy dry up."[80]

Lawrence was praised for his kindness, gentleness, generosity, simplicity, and sacrifice. Such kind words had an element of truth to them. Amos Adams Lawrence had sacrificed some of his wealth in the service of the New England Emigrant Aid Society, and his moral values often trumped his economic interests when the two conflicted. Especially regarding slavery, his views became increasingly resolute, and by the outbreak of the war he was ready to forfeit even his life for the cause.

Yet, like John Fox Slater, his views on slavery allowed him to rationalize his treatment of workers and justify his defense of wealth. As did John Fox Slater, Amos Adams equated slavery with not only bondage but also with sin on the part of the slave owners, while wage labor represented economic freedom. Even if poor, the wage earner could reach economic success through industry, hard work, and virtuous conduct. Slavery offered no such possibility. It was a stain on the American conscience that needed to be eliminated. Like John Fox Slater, Amos Adams's views on slavery and wage labor allowed him to treat his workers poorly, for in his view they had choices about where and how hard to work. Slavery was in a different moral and economic category than wage labor. Yet for Amos Adams, slavery was not the only major moral problem facing America. He believed that Catholicism degraded free men in a different manner than slavery. Catholicism encouraged sloth and idleness, and the Church took the earnings of laborers to build magnificent buildings and statues that only increased the wealth and power of priests and bishops. If workers chose to be Catholic or came from Catholic countries, little could be done to improve their moral standing, and they could be treated as disposable commodities. Slavery had to be eliminated, but Catholicism, too, had to be contained if America was to become an ethical community and a true shining light for the rest of the world. Unsurprisingly, Lawrence had barely any sympathy for his Irish and French Canadian immigrant workers and did little to help them, even in the wake of the Pemberton Mill collapse.

Despite these views, Lawrence saw himself as a virtuous and generous man. Like John Fox Slater, Lawrence believed in the gospel of wealth and became a major philanthropist. Like Slater, he was a believer in the power of education, but here differences between the two become clear. Lawrence, the Harvard-educated product of the Boston elite, endowed universities and his alma mater, while John Fox Slater gave money for the creation of common schools. Amos Adams viewed education as a meritocratic means of ensuring that the small number of virtuous and talented poor boys could achieve success. He shared little of Slater's paternalistic care for the poor and no sympathy for the education of women. For Lawrence, higher education allowed the best of the poor to rise above their birth. He echoed John Adams who believed such institutions could teach the values and beliefs necessary to maintain the rule of a natural aristocracy that would guarantee a country guided by wise and moral men. Through his political activity, philanthropic giving, and economic enterprise, he attempted to spread his vision throughout the entire nation.

Conclusion

America is often praised or criticized for its commitment to capitalism, but the roots of this commitment, what it means and where it came from, have rarely been examined in depth. This study has explored the cultures of capitalism that characterized the rise of American manufacturing, exemplified in the biographies of Samuel Colt, Horatio Nelson and John Fox Slater, Amos Adams Lawrence, and their extended families. Colt, the Slaters, and Lawrence were key figures in the emergence of American manufacturing and capitalism in the nineteenth century. They shaped the weapons and textile businesses, the two major manufacturing industries of antebellum America. These men shared many beliefs and practices, from a search for business practices that could result in a more efficient workplace to a belief in the sanctity of hard work as a key to economic success. All these men helped implement a new manufacturing society increasingly based on rational and contractual forms of power, which differed from the traditional types of social control prevalent in the agriculturally based world of antebellum America. Yet they pursued their economic activity in dramatically different ways, and they were far from entrepreneurs concerned solely with profit. The entrepreneurial and cultural values of Colt, the Slaters, and Lawrence both reflected and influenced the new capitalist economy and the very meaning of the nation. Their life experiences, beliefs, and different models of business demonstrate that American capitalism was economically and organizationally diverse from its inception. These men represented different visions of capitalist enterprise and promoted disparate conceptions of the type of society that the United States could become in the future.

Samuel Colt advocated a combination of casino and crony capitalism, loudly proclaiming the benefits of a laissez-faire philosophy and an unregulated market economy while simultaneously scheming to procure government contracts for his weapons. He was an avid exponent of American westward expansion, and he believed that the United States could become a dominant force within the world. His innovations in the manufacture of guns, from the use of interchangeable parts to a rudimentary assembly life, were models of a new type of economic firm that attempted to grow quickly and moved beyond local markets, taking risks on a national and international scale. His revolutionary marketing techniques tied patriotism to American individualism, connecting guns to adventure and excitement in one of the first advertising campaigns based on appeals to lifestyle and emotions rather than simply the cost and quality of a product. As a proponent of America as an empire, he helped redefine American patriotism, advocating a bellicose, militaristic understanding of the nation's greatness different from the Jeffersonian vision of an agrarian-based, inward-looking republic.

The Slaters, in particular Horatio Nelson Slater, also were economic innovators, introducing cost accounting and double bookkeeping on a major scale into their firms. Their cultural values were very different from those of Colt, however. They initially adopted a paternalistic view of their workers and America as a whole, envisioning a nation where manufacturing would be embedded within the small-town values of family, Protestant religious beliefs, and individual virtue. For John Fox Slater in particular, these paternalistic and religious values translated into a belief that the wealthy had philanthropic responsibilities to their communities and the nation as a whole. These ideas informed his opposition to slavery and his concern for the plight of African Americans after the Civil War. The Slaters looked askance at rapid American economic development, preferring steady growth to a casino capitalism without limits. The Slaters would gradually change their understanding of the American economy, however, as their organization of the workplace moved from the family system of labor to a contract-based system that prefigured many of the elements of a disciplinary society based on controlling individuals through rational mechanisms such as detailed work and behavioral rules of conduct. As national and even global markets emerged after the Civil War, and immigrants began to replace native born workers, the Slaters became more aggressively expansionist, adopting the values of opulence and greed that characterized the Gilded Age.

Amos Adams Lawrence, too, had a strong Protestant vision of America, but his conception was much more nationally oriented than that of the Slaters. Though a pioneer in the merging of manufacturing and selling houses within the economic domain, Lawrence's major concerns were cultural and political. His actions in support of a free Kansas in the political arena in the antebellum United States were attempts to advance his cultural agenda of a sin-free America where Protestant values of individual virtue, thrift, sobriety, and hard work would become so widespread that they would eliminate the dual scourges of slavery and Catholicism. His support of educational institutions was guided by this vision, as he believed that a natural aristocracy, represented by businessmen like those of the Boston elite, should guide the country. For Lawrence, higher education combined with a manufacturing economy provided the meritocratic conditions whereby talented poor young men could achieve economic success through hard work and systematic conduct.

The respective backgrounds and family histories of these men help to explain their different approaches to economic, social, and cultural life. Samuel Colt grew up in an unstable family environment. His father gained and lost a lot of money during his lifetime, and Colt experienced an economic deprivation that neither the Slaters nor Lawrence had to face. Colt had to venture out into the world on his own at an early age, dependent solely on his mechanical aptitude and, more important, his ability to charm influential people. Colt also learned to embrace risk at an early age, drawing on the experiences of his great uncle Peter Colt and especially following the example of his cousin Roswell Colt. Samuel Colt never suffered from a lack of confidence, for he developed a grand vision of America with men like himself at the center, a patriotic genius/inventor who united the populist values of egalitarianism and individualism with manufacturing entrepreneurship.

The Slaters inherited their businesses from their successful fathers and were apprenticed at a relatively young age to work in their textile mills. They adopted a slow and steady approach to economic growth compared to Colt, in part because they felt the pressure of the legacy of the Slater name. Their manufacture of fine and fancy goods also was oriented toward a domestic and local market rather than a global one. Finally, unlike Colt, religious beliefs were central to their lives and guided many of their actions, from John Fox Slater's philanthropic activities and antislavery beliefs to the their distrust of nonnative immigrants, especially Catholics.

Amos Adams Lawrence, too, inherited his fortune. But his path was different from the Slaters, for his father, Amos, was not especially attracted to business and wanted his son to pursue different arenas of activity. Amos Adams not only considered himself a new kind of renaissance businessman, but he also struck out on his own to make his fortune. Make a fortune he did, but he was aided by his elite contacts. His membership in an urban upper class was reinforced by his attendance at Harvard and his many political and social connections. Like his father, Lawrence was concerned with the moral fiber of the nation as much as his own economic profit, and he saw the creation of elite cultural and educational institutions as a means of attaining his vision of a good America.

These men were very different in outlook and economic practice, and their biographies and beliefs demonstrate that capitalism has always been diverse, from economic practices to the relationship of industry to moral values. In the antebellum era, the manufacturing decisions of Colt, the Slaters, and Lawrence were influenced by family ties, state actions and the potential for government contracts, and their particular moral values, as well as market exigencies. Theoretically, the vastly disparate lives and beliefs of these early and influential American entrepreneurs clearly calls for a rethinking of the role of culture in the study of the history of entrepreneurs and business. Contemporary historians analyze American entrepreneurship and the rise of manufacturing utilizing the categories of the economist, such as market growth, competition, and management strategies. As we have demonstrated, this model is limited in many ways. In antebellum America, an agrarian republic rather than a full-fledged capitalist society predominated, and the market was often subservient to custom and local concerns. In this era, entrepreneurial practices differed greatly. Family firms were the norm; mercantile practices were still in use; and efficiency and profit were often subservient to cultural and moral values. Business and entrepreneurial history has not benefited from the cultural turn that has characterized much recent scholarship in history and other disciplines. Many historians outside of business history contend that language, beliefs, or in the contemporary lexicon culture do not simply reflect material and social circumstances, nor are they a set of traditions transmitted from one generation to the next. Rather, culture is plural, a porous set of concepts and practices. Its very definition is dependent on the contingent, constantly shifting outcomes of struggles over meanings as well as economic interests.

For example, the beliefs and practices of early entrepreneurs cannot be understood without an examination of the complex culture of antebellum America. As demonstrated by the actions of Colt, the Slaters, and Lawrence, the economic behavior of the rational actor, *homo economicus*, was conditioned by the moral and cultural context of the era.[1]

Naomi Lamoreaux is a welcome exception to this rule, as she is one of the few business historians who has explored the role of culture in the rise of modern capitalist enterprise. She argues that custom and tradition form the backdrop for economic activity. As she writes, "Economic actors never make decisions solely on the basis of prices and quantities in the market; their choices are always shaped by their preferences and their perceptions of available options, which in turn are largely structured by the cultural systems in which they operate."[2] Lamoreaux notes that the concern for family welfare often influenced early entrepreneurial activity in the United States and that merchants and manufacturers, like farmers, were constrained by the values of the communities in which they lived. She contends that because of conditions of economic uncertainty in the antebellum era, institutions such as the family provided trust networks that could allow economic activity to take place. Thus, in Lamoreaux's view, family and community connections are not necessarily "antithetical to capitalist enterprise."[3] However, economic interest invariably takes precedence over customary behavior because of the rise of market forces and the concomitant social changes that occur in their wake. Lamoreaux states, following the economist Peter Temin, "The shift toward instrumental behavior that occurs during any period of rapid change, if sustained for a significant time, will force accommodating changes in the institutional structure in the form of a shift from community to market—that is, from a culture in which transactions are predominantly governed by custom to one in which they are mainly governed by price."[4]

Her analysis of culture and economic activity is accurate in many ways. For example, the cultural and religious values of paternalism influenced how Colt, the Slaters, and Lawrence treated their workers. Yet Lamoreaux's conception of culture is too passive, unconscious, and constraining to fully analyze its role in the rise of manufacturing and capitalist enterprise. We view culture as contested terrain, where battles over ideas and beliefs provide different opportunities for shaping economic and social life. While Lamoreaux constructs a dichotomy of traditional culture guided by custom and the instrumental action of the market, we contend that culture and market behavior intersect in complex ways, and especially in the antebellum era the practice and meaning of capitalism was disputed and far from clear. The Slaters, Colt, and Lawrence were all trying out different approaches to manufacturing, attempting to create a symbiosis between their firms, a new manufacturing economy, and their respective visions of American culture. They combined utilitarian, rational decision making with cultural values in diverse ways, as they tried to embed the new manufacturing economy within their evolving conceptions of America. They experimented with different forms of organization within their firms and company towns that would yield profits and remain consistent with their cultural values. Moreover, they clearly believed that Americans were not simply motivated by rational, instrumental action. Colt's advertising campaigns were in large part based on the idea that people will purchase a gun because of the images and emotions that a weapon can evoke. For the Slaters and Lawrence, people were ethical creatures guided by moral values rather than instrumentally rational ones. Their souls could only be saved through the teaching and example of virtuous conduct, and manufacturing enterprises had to accommodate and serve this worldview. Colt, the Slaters, and Lawrence also did not simply follow a cultural template that was handed down to them but consciously pursued their cultural beliefs and economic interests, tying them together in many ways. Colt was mindful of the connection of empire and the manufacture of weapons, while the Slaters and Lawrence were clearly aware of the ways the Protestant religion could create virtuous, obedient, and productive workers. They were interested in politics not only for protection of their own economic interests but also as a means to implement their conception of American culture on a wide scale.

The paucity of conceptions of complex cultural activity in the study of entrepreneurial history dovetails with the seeming hegemonic vision of a single global capitalism today. As capitalism is equated with low-cost labor and global megacorporations, alternative visions of capitalist economic organization have faded. This belief in a single model of capitalism often results in radical criticisms of government regulations and programs and calls for the privatization of public services, implicitly constructing the nineteenth century in the era before state regulation as a golden age of economic and social activity. While in areas from worker safety to child-labor laws this was clearly far from a utopian age, we have also demonstrated that capitalism has always been bound up with government actions. From Colt's pursuit of contracts for his guns to the Slaters' and Lawrence's support of the tariff for cotton manufacturers and the enormous wealth the Slaters gained through supplying the Union in the Civil War, governments have always helped direct the economic activity of entrepreneurs. Moreover, innovation and change for Colt and the Slaters was dependent on their particular cultural milieu and the conditions within their industries, whether it was the teeming activity of the government supported manufacturers in the Connecticut Valley or the geography and entrepreneurial culture of New England that allowed the Slaters and Lawrence to build their firms. The men who constructed the textile industry shared technical information through trade association meetings and other venues, while the mechanics of the industrial revolution often belonged to fraternal societies, sharing information about how to solve mechanical issues and problems.[5]

Moral values have also invariably been central to entrepreneurial activity, from the freewheeling individualism of Colt, to the sober, religiously informed beliefs of the Slaters and Lawrence. Indeed, calls for privatization today are as much demands for a particular moral vision as a call for economic efficiency, as the rigors of the market are supposed to ensure hard work and virtuous conduct on the recipients of this discipline, from the poor to public school teachers. Yet whether it is social capital that provides the trust that is the glue holding together economic life or values of individual competence, fairness, and justice that underlie contractual and market activity, capitalism has always depended on values beyond economic efficiency and self-interest.[6] The intricate web of relationships within the Colt, Slater, and Lawrence families provided the trust that allowed their firms to become powerful and profitable. Moreover, the economic success of Colt, the Slaters, and Lawrence was inextricably connected to nonmarket values, from Colt's populist understanding of the appeal of weapons to the Protestant values of the Slaters and Lawrence that influenced how they approached their firms.

This is not to say that the study of American manufacturing should eschew concerns with market activity, instrumental action, and the like. We have paid close attention to the role of these factors in the rise of these capitalist enterprises. Yet as capitalism is not defined only by economic criteria like prices, wages, and the like, so *homo economicus*, the rational agent, cannot encompass the complexities of market behavior, and business history must reconsider its enthrallment to such conceptions. Market activity is always bounded by cultural and moral values, from familial concerns to ideals of virtuous conduct, which inform, legitimate, and circumscribe any quest for economic efficiency. Businesses and culture are constantly interacting with one another, and Colt, the Slaters, and Lawrence not only revolutionized American manufacturing. Their cultural values helped to shape the very image and definition of America in the nineteenth century, and many of the ideas and practices that they developed, from cost accounting to religious education to the advocacy of empire, are still important today. Yet neither the Colt, Slater, nor Lawrence model of manufacturing and society was particularly attractive. It is a sign of the imaginative paucity of our time that many contemporary entrepreneurs and politicians look to this nineteenth-century era of unregulated industrial capitalism as a golden age to be emulated today.

Notes

Introduction

1. Susan Strange, *Casino Capitalism* (New York: Blackwell, 1997). See also Paul Krugman, "Crony Capitalism U.S.A.," *New York Times*, January 15, 2002.
2. Alfred D. Chandler, Jr., *The Visible Hand: The Managerial Revolution in American Business* (Cambridge: Belknap, 1977), 51.
3. Alexis de Tocqueville, *Democracy in America*, vol. 2 (New York: Doubleday, 1990), 137.
4. Quoted in William Hosley, *Colt: The Making of An American Legend* (Amherst: University of Massachusetts Press, 1996), 88.
5. Mark Noll, *America's God: From Jonathan Edwards to Abraham Lincoln* (New York: Oxford University Press, 2002).
6. James L. Huston, "Economic Landscapes Yet to be Discovered: The Early American Republic and Historians' Unsubtle Adoption of Political Economy," in *Whither the Early Republic: A Forum on the Future of the Field*, ed. John Lauritz Larson and Michael A. Morrison (Philadelphia: University of Pennsylvania Press, 2005), 78.
7. James D. McCabe, Jr., *Great Fortune, and How They Were Made; or the Struggles and Triumphs of our Self-Made Men* (Cincinnati: E. Hannaford, 1871).
8. Hosley, *Colt.*
9. Robert F. Dalzell, Jr., *Enterprising Elite: The Boston Associates and the World They Made* (Cambridge: Harvard University Press, 1987); Thomas H. O'Connor, *Lords of the Loom: The Cotton Whigs and the Coming of the Civil War* (New York: Scribner, 1968); Richard H. Abbott, *Cotton*

and Capital: Boston Businessmen and Antislavery Reform, 1854–1868 (Amherst: University of Massachusetts Press, 1991); William F. Hartford, *Money, Morals and Politics: Massachusetts in the Age of the Boston Associates* (Boston: Northeastern University Press, 2001); Frances Gregory, *Nathan Appleton: Merchant and Entrepreneur, 1779–1861* (Charlottesville: University Press of Virginia, 1975); Bradford P. Raymond, *Memoir of Abbott Lawrence* (Appleton: Post Pub. Co., 1886); Hamilton A. Hill, *Memoir of Abbott Lawrence* (Boston: Little, Brown and Company, 1883); William B. Lawrence, *Extracts From the Diary and Correspondence of the Late Amos Lawrence with a Brief Account of Some Incidents in His Life* (Boston: Gould and Lincoln, 1855); and William B. Lawrence, *Life of Amos A. Lawrence with Extracts from His Diary and Correspondence* (Boston: Houghton, Mifflin, 1888).

10. Charles Sellers, *The Market Revolution: Jacksonian America, 1815–1846* (New York: Oxford University Press, 1991); Arthur M. Schlesinger, Jr., *Age of Jackson* (Boston: Little, Brown and Company, 1945); Christopher Clark, *Roots of Rural Capitalism* (Ithaca: Cornell University Press, 1990); and Winifred Rothenberg, *From Market-Places to a Market Economy* (Chicago: University of Chicago Press, 1992).
11. Robert D. Cuff, "Notes for a Panel on Entrepreneurship in Business History," *Business History Review* 76 (2002): 131 and Naomi R. Lamoreaux, Daniel M. G. Raff, and Peter Temin, "Beyond Markets and Hierarchies: Toward a New Synthesis of American Business History," *American Historical Review* 108 (2003), 404-433.

CHAPTER 1

1. The Colt family discussed in this book represent two lines of descendents from Deacon Benjamin Colt (1698–1754); two of his sons were Lt. Benjamin Colt (1738–1781) and Peter Colt (1744–1824). Among the children of Lt. Benjamin Colt was Christopher Colt, Sr. (1780–1850). He resided in Hartford, Connecticut, where he married Sarah Caldwell in 1805, became a widower, and later married Olive Sargeant in 1823. Christopher Colt and Sarah Caldwell had four sons: John Caldwell Colt (1810–1842), Christopher Colt, Jr. (1812–1855), Samuel Colt (1814–1862), and James B. Colt (1816–1878). The other son of Deacon Benjamin Colt was Peter Colt. Among his many children was Roswell Colt (1779–1856).
2. Alexis de Tocqueville, *Democracy in America*, trans. George Lawrence (Garden City: Doubleday, 1969), 615.
3. Cathy Matson, "Introduction: The Ambiguities of Risk in the Early Republic," *Business History Review* 78 (2004): 599.
4. Emile Durkheim, *The Division of Labor in Society* (New York: Free Press, 1984), 149–75; and Francis Fukuyama, *Trust: Social Virtues and the Creation of Prosperity* (New York: Free Press 1995).

5. Stephanie Coontz, *Marriage, a History* (New York: Viking, 2005), 167.
6. John Demos, *Past, Present and Personal: The Family and the Life Course in American History* (New York, Oxford University Press, 1986), 99–102.
7. Peter Colt, "The Peter Colt Narrative," ed. Ralph Giddings (typed transcript, Connecticut State Library, n.d.), 4–24.
8. Ibid., 16–17.
9. Ibid., 18.
10. Franklin Bowditch Dexter, *Biographical Sketches of the Graduates of Yale College with Annals of the College History* (New York: Holt, 1903), 3: 65–66.
11. Floyd M. Shumway, "Early New Haven and Its Leadership" (PhD diss., Columbia University, 1968), 271–72.
12. Ibid., 250; Dexter, *Biographical Sketches*, 65–67.
13. E. James Ferguson, "Business, Government, and Congressional Investigation in the Revolution," *William and Mary Quarterly* 16 (1959): 293–97.
14. Albert E. Van Dusen, *Connecticut: A Fully Illustrated History of the State from the Seventeenth Century to the Present* (New York: Random House, 1961), 158–59; John D. R. Platt, "Jeremiah Wadsworth, Federalist Entrepreneur" (PhD diss., Columbia University, 1955), 5–11.
15. Colt, "Peter Colt Narrative," 19.
16. Charles J. Hoadley, *The Public Records of the State of Connecticut From May 1778 to April 1780* (Hartford: Case, Lockwood and Brainard, 1778), 111.
17. Platt, "Jeremiah Wadsworth," 9–21. See also Ferguson, "Business, Government and Congressional Investigation," 313.
18. *Connecticut Courant and Weekly Intelligencer*, February 24, 1784. For his efforts he received five hundred pounds sterling annually. See Wadsworth and Carter to Colt, Williamsburg, December 30, 1781. Colt Family Letters, Peter Colt, 1775–1877, Connecticut State Library. Hartford, CT. Hereafter cited as Peter Colt Letters.
19. Wadsworth Correspondence, December 18, 1783, December 28, 1783, February 21, 1784. Quoted in Margaret E. Martin, "*Merchants and Trade of the Connecticut River Valley, 1750–1820*," in *Smith College Studies in History*, vol. 24 (Northampton: Department of History, Smith College 1939), 41.
20. *Connecticut Courant and Weekly Intelligencer*, July 8, 1783; *Connecticut Courant and Weekly Intelligencer*, July 22, 1783; and *Connecticut Courant and Weekly Intelligencer*, July 29, 1783. See also Gaspare John Saladino, "The Economic Revolution in Late Eighteenth Century Connecticut" (PhD diss., University of Wisconsin, 1964), 80–83.
21. *Connecticut Courant and Weekly Intelligencer*, October, 26 1789; *Connecticut Courant and Weekly Intelligencer*, December 31, 1789.

22. Chester McArthur Destler, "The Hartford Woolen Manufactory: The Story of a Failure," *Connecticut History* 14 (1974): 10–12.
23. Ibid., 14, 16–25.
24. Samuel McKee, Jr., *Alexander Hamilton Papers on Public Credit, Commerce and Finance, "Report on Manufactures, December 5, 1791"* (New York: n.p., 1934), 266.
25. Peter Colt to Alexander Hamilton, Paterson, NJ, 28 February 28, 1793 in *The Papers of Alexander Hamilton*, vol. 14, ed. Harold Syrett (New York: Columbia University Press, 1969), 266.
26. Peter Colt to Alexander Hamilton, Paterson; June 30, 1793 in *The Papers of Alexander Hamilton*, vol. 14, ed. Harold Syrett. See also Pierre C. L'Enfant to Alexander Hamilton, New York, October 16, 1793 in *The Papers of Alexander Hamilton*, vol. 15, ed. Harold Syrett (New York: Columbia University Press, 1969), 363–65.
27. Peter Colt to Wife, Williamsburg, April 28, 1782, Peter Colt Letters (see note 18 for full citation); Peter Colt to Sally Colt, New York, January 12, 1797, Peter Colt Letters.
28. Martin, "Merchants and Trade," 181–82.
29. Colt, "Peter Colt Narrative," 21–22; and W. M. Halsted to His Honor, Oliver Spencer Halsted, Chancellor of the State of New Jersey and Ordinary and Surrogate General in the Same, Chancery, NJ, 1844.
30. Colt, "Peter Colt Narrative," 12.
31. *Connecticut Courant and Weekly Intelligencer*, April 10, 1805.
32. *Connecticut Courant and Weekly Intelligencer*, January 20, 1784. See also Martin, *Merchants and Trade*, 120.
33. Martin, *Merchants and Trade*, 85, 182–83, 189–92, 200–202, 212; *Connecticut Courant and Weekly Intelligencer*, June 24, 1793; and *Hartford Courant*, January 24, 1857. These enterprises represented only a portion of his interests. He invested fifteen thousand dollars in the Connecticut Land Company, an enterprise that owned part of the Western Reserve in Ohio. This land, which bordered Lake Erie, was given as compensation for land previously claimed and annexed by Connecticut in the Wyoming Valley of Pennsylvania. As with other ventures, Caldwell took a leadership position, becoming one of three trustees of the enterprise. Investments in river improvement projects, aqueducts, and turnpikes followed
34. Martin, *Merchants and Trade*, 127–28; *Connecticut Courant and Weekly Intelligencer*, May 3, 1785; *Connecticut Courant and Weekly Intelligencer*, April 5, 1790; and *Connecticut Courant and Weekly Intelligencer*, January 24, 1857. See also P. H. Woodward, *One Hundred Years of the Hartford National Bank of Hartford, Connecticut* (Hartford: Case, Lockwood and Brainard, 1892), 16–17, 34.
35. *Connecticut Courant and Weekly Intelligencer*, May 10, 1802; *Connecticut Courant and Weekly Intelligencer*, June 18, 1806; *Connecticut Courant and Weekly Intelligencer*, April 13, 1808; *Connecticut Courant and Weekly Intelligencer*, May 23, 1810; and *Connecticut Courant and*

Weekly Intelligencer, May 12, 1812. See also Martin, *Merchants and Trade*, 214; and Jack Rohan, *Yankee Arms Maker, the Story of Samuel Colt and His Six-Shot Peacemaker* (New York: Harper and Brothers, 1935), 4–5.

36. *Hartford Courant*, October 21, 1887.
37. *Hartford Courant*, June 28, 1869.
38. Rohan, *Yankee Arms Maker*, 6–7; Martin, *Merchants and Trade*, 66.
39. Christopher Colt to Samuel Colt, Hartford, December 5, 1834, Samuel Colt Papers, Box 1, Connecticut Historical Society. Hereafter cited as CHS Colt MSS. Those remaining at home were her own children, Olive, William, and Maria. See also Olive Colt to Samuel Colt, Hartford, October 23, 1834, CHS Colt MSS, Box 1.
40. *Hartford Courant*, March 24, 1841.
41. *An Authentic Life of John C. Colt, now Imprisoned for Killing Samuel Adams in New York on the Seventeenth of September 1841* (Boston: Dickinson, 1842), 24–25.
42. Christopher Colt to Samuel Colt, Hartford, December 5, 1834, CHS Colt MSS, Box 1.
43. Olive Colt to Samuel Colt, Hartford, October 23, 1834, CHS Colt MSS, Box 1.
44. Olive Colt to Samuel Colt, Hartford, December 5, 1834, CHS Colt MSS, Box 1.
45. Christopher Colt to Samuel Colt, Hartford, December 5, 1834, CHS Colt MSS, Box 1; and Mrs. C. Colt to Samuel Colt, Hartford, June 10, 1832, CHS Colt MSS, Box 1.
46. *Authentic Life of John C. Colt*, 22, 27, 40–43.
47. Andie Tucher, *Froth & Scum: Truth, Beauty, Goodness, and the Ax Murder in America's First Mass Medium* (Chapel Hill: University of North Carolina Press, 1994), 100–106.
48. Samuel Colt to Christopher Colt, Sr., Lowell, September 1834, CHS Colt MSS, Box 1.
49. Olive Colt to Samuel Colt, Hartford, November 26, 1836, CHS Colt MSS, Box 1.
50. Jay Coughtry, *The Notorious Triangle: Rhode Island and the African Slave Trade, 1700–1807* (Philadelphia: Temple University Press, 1981), 48. See also J. Stanley Lemons, "Rhode Island and the Slave Trade," *Rhode Island History* 60 (2002): 95–104. For a detailed discussion of the DeWolf family and their various business ventures see De Wolf Papers, Reels 9, 10, and 11. Papers of the American Slave Trade, Part 2: Selected Collections, Series A: Selections from the Rhode Island Historical Society, Providence, RI.
51. George Howe, *Mount Hope: A New England Chronicle* (New York: Viking Press, 1958 [1959]), 204–6.
52. Lemons, "Rhode Island and the Slave Trade," 97, 100–101.

53. Howe, *Mount Hope*, 229–38. See also Allecia H. Middleton, *Life in Carolina and New England During the Nineteenth Century as Illustrated by Reminiscences and Letters of the Middleton Family of Charleston, South Carolina and the DeWolf Family of Bristol, Rhode Island* (Bristol: Priv. print 1929), 36; and Christy Millard Nadalin, "The Last Years of the Rhode Island Slave Trade," *Rhode Island History* 54 (1996): 46–48.
54. Howe, *Mount Hope*, 237.
55. Edward Dickerson to Samuel Colt, February 17, 1853, CHS Colt MSS, Box 7.
56. U.S. Bureau of the Census, *United States Federal Population Census, Manuscript Schedules, Eighth Census of the United States, Hartford, Connecticut, 1860* (Washington, DC, 1860). Hereafter cited as Federal Population MSS
57. James Colt to Samuel Colt, Hartford, October 2, 1854, Records of the Colt Patent Fire Arms Manufacturing Company, 1826–1979, Box 10, Connecticut State Library. Hereafter cited as CSL Colt Records; and James Colt to Samuel Colt, Hartford, October 10, 1854, CSL Colt Records, Box 10.
58. J. D. Alden to Samuel Colt, June 5, 1855, CSL Colt Records, Box 10 and Harry Branch to Samuel Colt, Hartford, June 15, 1855, CSL Colt Records, Box 10.
59. James Colt to Samuel Colt, Hartford, June 13, 1855 CLS Colt Records, Box 10.
60. Ibid. See also *Hartford Courant*, September 18, 1901. Brach was not impressed with his charge: "the oldest boy is loafing about here but he will get no sympathy from me or assistance for he is old enough to take care of himself, but too darned lazy to work. He is the only black sheep in the flock and I don't know that he is much to blame considering how he has been handled." See Harry Brach to Samuel Colt, Hartford, June 15, 1855, CSL Colt Records, Box 10; and Federal Population MSS.
61. Christopher Colt to Samuel Colt, New York, February 24, 1834, CHS Colt MSS, Box 1.
62. Christopher Colt to Samuel Colt, Hartford, January 9, 1836, CHS Colt MSS, and Christopher Colt to Samuel Colt, Hartford, September 21, 1837, CHS Colt MSS.
63. *Hartford Courant*, February 27, 1849.
64. Elbert B. Smith, "Thomas Hart Benton: Southern Realist," *American Historical Review* 58 (1953): 795.
65. James Colt to Samuel Colt, St. Louis, July 26, 1854, CSL Colt Records, Box 10; and James Colt to Samuel Colt, St. Louis, August 10, 1854, CSL Colt Records, Box 10.
66. James Colt to Samuel Colt, St. Louis, September 24, 1855, CSL Colt Records, Box 10.
67. "I am not alone Sam where I say that nothing however desperate would surprise me with regard to him. I may be too cautious and the growl of

the bear may be more than the bite, but as I said before—I am not alone in thinking him desperate." See Harry Brach to Samuel Colt, Hartford, 15 June 15, 1855, CSL Colt Records, Box 10.

68. James Colt to Samuel Colt, St. Louis, September 2, 1855, CSL Colt Records, Box 10.
69. James Colt to Samuel Colt, St. Louis, September 24, 1855, CSL Colt Records, Box 10.
70. James Colt to Samuel Colt, St. Louis, September 28, 1855, CSL Colt Records, Box 10. See also *New York Times*, July 29, 1881.
71. Olive Colt to Samuel Colt, Ware Cottage, June 15, 1830, CHS Colt MSS, Box 1; and Frederick Tuckerman, *Amherst Academy: A New England School of the Past, 1814–1861* (Amherst, Amherst Trustees, 1929), 77–87.
72. Capt. Bassett to Christopher Colt, Norwich, January 18, 1832, CHS Colt MSS, Box 1.
73. Ibid.
74. Samuel Colt to Christopher Colt, New York, September 13, 1834, CHS Colt MSS, Box 2.
75. Olive Colt to Samuel Colt, Hartford, November 26, 1836, CHS Colt MSS, Box 1; and Christopher Colt to Samuel Colt, Hartford, January 9, 1836, CHS Colt MSS.
76. Robert Tucker, ed., *The Marx-Engels Reader* (New York: Norton, 1978), 475.

CHAPTER 2

1. *Hartford Courant*, June 5, 1856.
2. Martin Rywell, *Samuel Colt: A Man and His Epoch* (Marriman: Tenn.: Pioneer Press, 1952), 84.
3. Ibid., 25–30; Philip K. Lundeberg, *Samuel Colt's Submarine Battery: The Secret and the Enigma* (Washington, DC, Smithsonian Institution Press, 1974), and Kenneth Silverman, *Lightning Man: The Accursed Life of Samuel F. B. Morse* (New York: Knopf, 2003), 215–16.
4. Scott A. Sandage, *Born Losers: A History of Failure in America* (Cambridge: Harvard University Press, 2005).
5. Merritt Roe Smith, *Harpers Ferry Armory and the New Technology* (Ithaca: Cornell University Press, 1977).
6. Robert V. Remini, *Life of Andrew Jackson* (New York: Harper and Row, 1988), 223; and Sean Wilenz, *The Rise of American Democracy: Jefferson to Lincoln* (New York: WW Norton, 2005), 312 n.
7. Anthony F. C. Wallace, *The Long, Bitter Trail: Andrew Jackson and the Indians* (New York: Hill and Wang, 1993), 3–13, 50–70.
8. Jack Rohan, *Yankee Arms Maker* (New York: Harper and Brothers, 1935), 26–50. See also Charles Rosenberg, *The Cholera Years: The*

United States in 1832, 1849, and 1866 (Chicago: University of Chicago Press, 1962), 37–39.

9. James Cook, *The Arts of Deception: Playing with Fraud in the Age of Barnum* (Cambridge: Harvard University Press, 2001), 3. See also Benjamin Reiss, "P. T. Barnum, Joice Heth and Antebellum Spectacles of Race," *American Quarterly* 51 (1999): 78–107. According to Reiss, Heth was a major attraction in New York City and was popularized by the penny press. "These periodicals, the first entirely commercial serial publications in America, were perhaps the most compelling voices of Jacksonian individualism. Their brash displays of hostility for the culture mavens of the upper classes (and for each other), their sympathies for the urban working and upwardly mobile classes, their freedom from political patronage . . . marked their distinctiveness from the more genteel 'six-penny' papers." Ibid., 82. See also P. T. Barnum, *Life of P. T. Barnum Written by Himself Including his Golden Rules for Money-Making Brought Up to 1888* (Buffalo: Courier Company, 1888), 37–42.
10. Benjamin Reiss, *The Showman and the Slave: Race, Death, and a Memory in Barnum's America* (Cambridge: Harvard University Press, 2001), 28.
11. Ibid., 28–29. See also Jackson Lears, *Fables of Abundance: A Cultural History of Advertising in America* (New York: Basic Books, 1994).
12. *Albany Microscope*, 26 October 1833, quoted in William L. Kellner, "On Samuel Colt and the Patent Arms Manufacturing Company of Paterson, New Jersey," (M.A. Thesis, Fairleigh Dickinson University, 1968), 10.
13. T. Adolphus Trollope, "Some Recollections of Hiram Powers," *Lippincotts Magazine of Popular Literature and Science* XV (February 1895), 208–9; Daniel Aaron, *Cincinnati, Queen of the West, 1819–1838* (Columbus: Ohio State University Press, 1992), 276–9; Rohan, *Yankee Arms Maker*, 38–50.
14. Ibid., 84. On the imagery of the Centaur in the West, see Louis S. Warren, "Buffalo Bill Meets Dracula: William F. Cody, Bram Stoker, and the Frontiers of Racial Decay," *American Historical Review* 107 (October 2002): 1124–56.
15. Michael Schudson, *Discovering the News: A Social History of American Newspapers* (New York: Basic Books, 1978), Reiss, *Showman and the Slave*, 36; see also, Andie Tucher, *Froth & Scum: Truth, Beauty, Goodness, and the Ax Murder in America's First Mass Medium* (Chapel Hill: University of North Carolina Press, 1994).
16. Amy Gilman Srebnick, *The Mysterious Death of Mary Rogers: Sex and Culture in Nineteenth-Century New York* (New York: Oxford University Press, 1995).
17. Ibid., 100–107.
18. Ibid., 101. Philip Hone, close friend of Roswell Colt and former mayor of New York, regularly attended the trial. See Philip Hone, *The Diary of*

Philip Hone, 1828–1851, ed. Allan Nevins (New York: Dodd Mead and Company, 1927), 2:579.

19. Christopher Colt to Roswell L. Colt, Hartford, July 30, 1835. Samuel Colt Papers, Box 1, Connecticut Historical Society. Hereafter cited as CHS Colt MSS.
20. Ibid., Roswell Colt to Samuel Colt, Paterson, NJ, February 12, 1836, CHS Colt Mss, Box 1.
21. Roswell Colt to Messr. Hutchinson and Onderdonk, New York, March 2, 1839, Roswell Colt Collection, Box 5, Historical Society of Pennsylvania Philadelphia, PA. Hereafter cited as Roswell Colt Collection. See also, Robert Herz, "The S.U.M.: The History of a Corporation," (M.S., New School for Social Research, 1939), 48–53.
22. D. Stanton Hammond, "The Colts of Paterson," *Proceedings of the New Jersey Historical Society* 79 (1961): 196.
23. Roswell Colt to John Deveaux, Paterson, NJ, January 1, 1840. Roswell Colt Collection, Box 3. See also Peter Colt, "The Peter Colt Narrative," ed. Ralph Giddings (typed transcript, Connecticut State Library, n.d.).
24. Samuel Taylor to Roswell Colt, Baltimore, January 23, 1819, Roswell Colt Collection, Box 7.
25. Herz, "The S.U.M.," 74.
26. N. Biddle to Roswell Colt, Philadelphia, April 8, 1837, Roswell Colt Collection, Box 10.
27. Hone, *Diary*, I:x–xii. See also, Herbert Kriedman, "New York's Philip Hone: Businessman-Politician-Patron of the Arts and Letters" (PhD diss., New York University, 1965).
28. Roswell Colt to John Colt, Paterson, NJ, December 6, 1843, Roswell Colt Collection, Box 3; Nicholas Biddle to Roswell Colt, Philadelphia, November 8, 1838, Roswell Colt Collection, Box 10.
29. Nicholas Biddle to Roswell Colt, Philadelphia, June 20, 1838, Box 10.
30. March 21, 1842.
31. May 30, 1838.
32. November 8, 1838.
33. 13 December 1838.
34. Herman Cope, Superintendent, Bank of the United States, Suspended Debt and Real Estate Department to Roswell Colt, September 2, 1840, Roswell Colt Collection, Box 4, and Roswell Colt to Herman Cope, April 20, 1842, Roswell Colt Collection, Box 3.
35. Roswell Colt to John Deveaux, Paterson, NJ, January 1, 1840, Roswell Colt Collection, Box 3; Coster and Carpenter to Roswell Colt, New York, April 8, 1836, Roswell Colt Collection, Box 4; and for details of his losses at Paterson, see Communication to the Senate and House, Roswell Colt Collection, Box 9. See also Herz, "The SUM," 74.
36. Simson Hart to Roswell Colt, Farmington, September 8, 1831, Roswell Colt Collection, Box 5.

37. L. R. Trumbull, *A History of Industrial Paterson* (Paterson: C.M. Herrick, 1882), 168.
38. William Hosley, *Colt: The Making of an American Legend* (Amherst: University of Massachusetts Press, 1996), 84.
39. Samuel Colt to Roswell Colt, New York, February 25, 1834, Roswell Colt Collection, Box 4.
40. Ibid.; Roswell Colt to Samuel Colt, New York, October 15, 1838, Roswell Colt Collection, Box; and Roswell Colt to Dudley Selden, New York, January 23, 1838, Roswell Colt Collection, Box 3. See also Samuel Colt to Christopher Colt, aboard ship, February 3, 1838, Colt Family Papers, 1793–1961, Box 2, Special Collections, University of Rhode Island, South Kingston, RI. Hereafter cited as Colt Family Papers.
41. "I have bargained, sold, assigned and transferred, and hereby do bargain, sell, assign, and transfer to him one other eighth part or portion of said improvements together with the benefit to arise there from and from any Patent or patents to be issued on account thereof in the United States, and in order that the said Joseph D. Selden may be fully secure in the benefits intended to be transferred to him by this instrument for the consideration aforesaid, it is declared and understood by me that the said Joseph D. Selden shall be entitled to have and claim from me one eighth part of all the benefits arising from the improvements made by me in the construction or manufacture of fire arms of every description." Samuel Colt's Conveyance to Joseph Selden, Paterson, NJ, August 8, 1835, CHS Colt MSS, Box 1.
42. Kellner, "On Samuel Colt," 17–19; and Samuel Colt to Christopher Colt, New York, January 7, 1836, Colt Family Papers, Box 2. Immediately after the signing, Colt sold half of his share to Dudley Selden for five hundred dollars plus interest, payable December 1, 1835. Over the next several years, Samuel Colt came to regret this transaction and to distrust Dudley Selden. The relationship soured, and Colt made repeated attempts to regain control over his own business ventures. It took about a decade before Selden agreed to sell Colt his stake in the business. Sam vowed not to dispose of any more of his patents.
43. H. Ellsworth to Christopher Colt, Washington, DC, September 22, 1835, Colt Family Papers, Box 1.
44. Roswell Colt to Samuel Colt, Paterson, NJ, February 12, 1836, CHS Colt MSS.
45. Doron S. Ben-Atar, *Trade Secrets: Intellectual Piracy and the Origins of American Industrial Power* (New Haven: Yale University Press, 2004), 192–94.
46. Kellner, "On Samuel Colt," 21.
47. Frederic Cople Jaher, *The Urban Establishment: Upper Strata in Boston, New York, Charleston, Chicago and Los Angeles* (Urbana: University of Illinois Press, 1982), 179–85; Hone, *Diary*, I:338, 2:533, 606, 863; Edward Pessen, *Riches, Class, and Power Before the Civil War* (Lexington,

MA: D. C. Heath, 1973; Kellner, "On Samuel Colt," 22–23; and List of Stockholders, Colt Family Papers, Box 1.

48. Rywell, *Samuel Colt*, 37.
49. Kellner, "On Samuel Colt," 26.
50. Samuel Colt to Christopher Colt, May 30, 1836, Colt Family Papers, Box 2; and Samuel Colt to Christopher Colt, April 11, 1836, Colt Family Papers, Box 2.
51. Kellner, "On Samuel Colt," 26–34.
52. Ibid., 38.
53. Samuel Colt to Jesse Hoyt, Paterson, NJ, October 2, 1837, CHS Colt MSS, Box 2.
54. Dudley Selden to Samuel Colt, New York, April 14, 1837, CHS Colt MSS, Box 2.
55. Quoted in Dudley Selden to Samuel Colt, New York, February 20, 1837, CHS Colt MSS, Box 2.
56. Kellner, "On Samuel Colt," 48–49.
57. Ibid., 47.
58. Ibid., 46–52. See also Rywell, *Samuel Colt*, 48.
59. Trumbull, *A History of Paterson*, quoted in Kellner, "On Samuel Colt," 61–62.
60. R. B. Lee to Samuel Colt, Ft. Monroe, August 9, 1837, CHS Colt MSS, Box 1.
61. Kellner, "On Samuel Colt," 40, 45.
62. Rywell, *Samuel Colt*, 56.
63. Ibid., 54; Kellner, "On Samuel Colt," 42.
64. Peter Temin, *The Jacksonian Economy* (New York: WW Norton, 1969), 113–20; Reginald C. McGrane, *The Panic of 1837: Some Financial Problems of the Jacksonian Era* (Chicago: University of Chicago, 1924), 91–131; and Bray Hammond, *Banks and Politics in America from the Revolution to the Civil War* (Princeton: Princeton University Press, 1957), 326–68, 405–50.
65. Samuel Colt to Christopher Colt, New York, January 22, 1840, CHS Colt MSS, Box 2.
66. Edward J. Balleisen, "Vulture Capitalism in Antebellum America: The 1841 Federal Bankruptcy Act and the Exploitation of Financial Distress," *Business History Review* 70 (1966): 476–78.
67. Lundeberg, *Samuel Colt's Submarine*, 7, 16.
68. Hosley, *Colt*, 22.
69. George DeKay to Samuel Colt, New York, October 12, 1842, CHS Colt MSS, Box 6.
70. Samuel Colt to Secretary of the Navy, New York, October 13, 1842, CHS Colt MSS, Box 6.
71. Samuel Colt to William McNeill, New York, October 16, 1842, CHS Colt MSS, Box 6.
72. Lundeberg, *Samuel Colt's Submarine*, 47–52.

73. Alexis de Tocqueville, *Democracy in America* (New York: Doubleday, 1990), 11: 98–100.
74. F. O. Matthiessen, *American Renaissance: Art and Expression in the Age of Emerson and Whitman* (New York: Oxford University Press, 1941). See also Robert D. Richardson, *Emerson: The Mind on Fire* (Berkeley: University of California Press, 1996); and Ralph Waldo Emerson, *The Essential Writings of Ralph Waldo Emerson*, ed. Brooks Atkinson (New York: Random House, 2000).
75. Samuel Colt to William Colt, 1844, quoted in Rywell, *Samuel Colt*, 83–84.
76. David Hounshell, *From the American System to Mass Production, 1800–1932* (Baltimore: The Johns Hopkins University Press, 1984), 47–50; Hosley, *Colt*, 67–68.

CHAPTER 3

1. John Davis, *The Great Exhibition* (Stroud: Sutton, 1999), 161.
2. Richard Slotkin, *The Fatal Environment: The Myth of the Frontier in the Age of Industrialization, 1800–1890* (New York: Atheneum, 1985), 183–84.
3. Samuel Colt, "On the Application of Machinery to the Manufacture of Rotating Chambered-Breech Fire-Arms, and the Peculiarities of those Arms," *Institution of Civil Engineers* (1851): 8.
4. Ibid., 11.
5. Robert Tucker, ed., *The Marx-Engels Reader* (New York: WW Norton, 1978), 476.
6. *Hartford Daily Times*, August 18, 1859.
7. William Hosley, *Colt: The Making of an American Legend* (Amherst: University of Massachusetts Press, 1996), 14, 74.
8. *Hartford Daily Times*, December 11, 1851.
9. *Hartford Daily Times*, July 24, 1852.
10. Hosley, *Colt*, 77–79.
11. Ibid.
12. Gene Silvero Cesari, "American Arms-Making Machine Tool Development, 1798–1855" (PhD diss., University of Pennsylvania, 1970), 186–93.
13. Ibid., 152.
14. David A. Hounshell, *From the American System to Mass Production, 1800–1932: The Development of Manufacturing Technology in the United States* (Baltimore: The Johns Hopkins University Press, 1984), 46–50.
15. Slotkin, *Fatal Environment*, 111.
16. Hosley, *Colt, 26–27, 33.*
17. Merritt Roe Smith, *Harpers Ferry Armory and the New Technology: The Challenge of Change* (Ithaca: Cornell University Press, 1977), 28, 92, 117, 246. See also David R. Meyer, "Formation of Advanced

Technology Districts: New England Textile Machinery and Firearms, 1790–1820," *Economic Geography* 74 (1998): 40.

18. Cesari, "American Arms-Making," 64.
19. Smith, *Harpers Ferry Armory*, 127, 135.
20. Ibid., 196–209, 219.
21. David A. Hounshell, "The System: Theory and Practice," in *Yankee Enterprise: The Rise of the American System of Manufacturers*, ed. Otto Mayr and Robert C. Post (Washington: Smithsonian Institution Press, 1981), 127–47.
22. Cesari, "American Arms-Making," 124, 151–58, provides an extensive discussion of Lawrence, his relationship with Robbins, and the Sharp's Rifle Company. See also Matthew Roth, *Connecticut: An Inventory of Historic Engineering and Industrial Sites* (Washington, DC: Historic American Engineering Record, 1981), xi–xxi, 54–55.
23. Smith, *Harpers Ferry Armory*, 288–90.
24. Hosley, *Colt*, 49, 59.
25. Paul Uselding, "Elisha K. Root, Forging, and the 'American System,'" *Technology and Culture* 15 (1974): 543.
26. Roth, *Connecticut*, 78–79.
27. Uselding, "Elisha K. Root," 549, 563, 567.
28. Hounshell, *From the American System to Mass Production*, 49.
29. Coltsville Historic District, National Historic Landmark Nomination, (May 8, 2005 [February 8, 2007]), 22–30. Connecticut Commission on Culture and Tourism, Hartford, CT. Hereafter referred to as Coltsville.
30. Ibid., 28; Hounshell, *From the American System to Mass Production*, 19–21, 49–50.
31. Alexis de Tocqueville, *Democracy in America* (New York: Doubleday, 1990), 2: 51.
32. Slotkin, *Fatal Environment*, 87.
33. David Nye, *America as Second Creation: Technology and Narratives of New Beginnings* (Cambridge: MIT Press, 2003), 2–11.
34. John Kasson, *Civilizing the Machine: Technology and Republican Values in America, 1776–1900* (New York: Penguin, 1976), 6–10, 39–41.
35. Ibid., 146–48.
36. Samuel Colt to the Connecticut Historical Society, Hartford, November 30, 1855, Samuel Colt Collection, Box VII, Connecticut Historical Society, Hartford, CT. Hereafter cited as CHS Colt MSS.
37. *Hartford Daily Times*, September 11, 1852.
38. Hosley, *Colt*, 84–85.
39. *Hartford Daily Times*, November 15, 1847.
40. *Hartford Daily Times*, November 15, 1847.
41. *Hartford Daily Times*, November 15, 1847.
42. *Hartford Daily Times*, February 24, 1849.
43. *Hartford Daily Times*, February 10, 1852.
44. Hosley, *Colt*, 83–85.

45. *Hartford Daily Times*, January 5, 1852 and December 1, 1852.
46. Colt Advertisements, *The Knickerbocker Magazine*, May 1860, 569–73.
47. Hosley, *Colt, 80.*
48. Colt Advertisements, *The Knickerbocker Magazine*, May 1860, 569–73.
49. To view this particular advertisement, see Connecticut History on the Web, http://www.connhistory.org/graphics/WWSEII/ads3.gif.
50. *Hartford Daily Times*, August 13, 1852;and October 24, 1851.
51. The cultural belief in the sanctity and virtue of productive labor fit in well with the conditions of the small farmers who dominated the American economy, but it also provided a justification for a market society. While the labor theory of value was based on the idea that the worker should receive the fruits of his labor, it did not result in a theory of the exploitation of wage labor, as with Marxist economics. From the perspective of the American version of the labor theory of value, the market economy would create a just, roughly equal distribution of wealth to a degree commensurate with talents, and such a distribution would result in an approximate equality of condition, given abundant land and widespread commercial agriculture. This perspective drew on the republican and individualistic beliefs prominent in the United States, for it saw inequality due to the corruption and idleness of politicians, and the use of wealth for dissolute purposes. Republicans and Whigs in the Jacksonian era expanded the labor theory of value to include all of those who were gainfully employed, including bankers, financiers, and bondholders, and they presented themselves as workers on the side of labor. The real problem generating inequality, they argued, was the despotic and corrupt Democratic Party led by Andrew Jackson and his followers.
52. Sean Wilentz, "America's Lost Egalitarian Tradition," *Daedalus* 131 (2000): 66–81.
53. Peter Baldwin, *Domesticating the Streets* (Columbus: Ohio State University Press, 2003).
54. Hosley, *Colt*, 109–11.
55. Coltsville, item number, 7, 1–2; and Roth, *Connecticut*, 50–52.
56. Cesari, "American Arms-Making," 214–20.
57. Coltsville, item number, 8, 5.
58. Hosley, *Colt*, 121–23.
59. Class differences were evident, as the housing for the skilled labor was much more spacious and accommodating than that for semi-skilled workers. See Coltsville, item number, 7, 2–3.
60. Hosley, *Colt*, 116–19.
61. Coltsville, item number, 1, 11–13.
62. Ibid., 18.
63. Hosley, *Colt*, 111–14.

64. *Hartford Daily Times*, October 27, 1860 and January 8, 1861.
65. "Mechanics, Working Men of Conn. Read, Read, Read!" Broadsides, 1860, M486W. CHS Colt MSS.
66. Hosley, *Colt*, 102–3.
67. Ibid., 92–94.
68. Martin Rywell, *Samuel Colt: A Man and an Epoch* (Harriman, TN: Pioneer Press, 1955), 45.
69. Coltsville, item number, 3, 8.
70. Edwin E. Marvin, *A History of the Fifth Regiment of Connecticut Volunteers* (Hartford: Wiley, Waterman and Eaton, 1889), 5–6.
71. Hosley, *Colt*, 94–97.

CHAPTER 4

1. Much of the material on the early Slater years is based on the following: Barbara M. Tucker, *Samuel Slater and the Origins of the American Textile Industry, 1790--1860* (Ithaca: Cornell University Press, 1984), 33–86. See also George S. White, *Memoir of Samuel Slater, the Father of American Manufactures Connected with a History of the Rise and Progress of the Cotton Manufacture in England and America with Remarks on the Moral Influence of Manufactories in the United States* (Philadelphia: n.p., 1836), 97, 281. In this work, White recounts a rumor concerning Slater: "the British government employed a person to assassinate Mr. Slater, by means of an infernal machine." The author, however, considers this a "Canterbury tale." White is the person who labeled Slater the "Father of American Manufactures" and the "Arkwright of America."
2. White, *Memoir of Samuel Slater*, 264.
3. Ibid., 75; Brendan Francis Gilbane, "A Social History of Samuel Slater's Pawtucket, 1790–1830" (PhD diss., Boston University, 1969), 3–11; and David R. Meyer, "Formation of Advanced Technology Districts: New England Textile Machinery and Firearms, 1790–1820," *Economic Geography* 74 (1998): 37–38.
4. Louis McLane, "Report of the Secretary of the Treasury (22nd Cong., 1st sess., House Executive Document no. 308)," *Documents Relative to the Manufactures in the United States* (Washington: 1833 repr. New York: Burt Franklin, 1969), 931. Hereafter referred to as McLane Report.
5. See for example Gordon Wood, "Afterword," *The Republican Synthesis Revisited: Essays in Honor of George Athan Billias*, ed. Milton Klein, Richard Brown, and John Hench (Worcester: American Antiquarian society, 1992), 143–51.
6. Tucker, *Samuel Slater*, 47–57; White, *Memoir of Samuel Slater*, 76, 83; David J. Jeremy, *Transatlantic Industrial Revolution: The Diffusion of Textile Technologies Between Britain and America, 1790–1830* (Cambridge: MIT Press, 1981), 84–86.

7. Henry-Russell Hitchcock, *Rhode Island Architecture* (Providence: Rhode Island Museum Press, 1939), 39.
8. Tucker, *Samuel Slater*, 71–86.
9. Ibid.
10. Jeremy, *Transatlantic Industrial Revolution*, 87.
11. Gilbane, "A Social History," 140–42.
12. White, *Memoir of Samuel Slater*, 215. The rest of Slater's assets were as follows: part owner of mills in Pawtucket and Smithfield, houses in Pawtucket, Seekonk, Hartford, and Boston, buildings in Providence, and farms in Attleborough, Saybrook, and Pelham. For a complete listing of Slater's mill property, see Tucker, *Samuel Slater*, 93.
13. James Lawson Conrad, Jr., "The Evolution of Industrial Capitalism in Rhode Island, 1790–1830: Almy, the Browns, and the Slaters" (PhD diss., University of Connecticut, 1973), 325.
14. McLane Report, 951.
15. Conrad, "Evolution of Industrial Capitalism," 324–25.
16. Tucker, *Samuel Slater*, 93–96. and McLane Report, 276–77.
17. McLane Report, 928–29, 931
18. The property he conveyed to these creditors and used for collateral included the following: "a block of buildings on South Main street; a cotton factory with all its machinery, engine, two dwelling houses, and land on which they all stand; also one other building and a dwelling house, all in Providence; also certain parcels of land in Smithfield; also certain parcels of land with dwelling houses, a cotton factory, mill privilege, machinery, etc. etc., in Attleboro and Seekonk, also one half of Union Bank in Pawtucket, also about two thousand acres of land in Oxford, Dudley & Douglas, in Massachusetts, with all the cotton factories, mills, rights, of water, dwelling houses, stories and buildings thereon, machinery, etc., . . . also one half of the Jewett City Manufacturing Company's works consisting of mills, cotton factories, rights of water dwelling houses, stores etc." "A Financier of the Old School," *Proceedings of the Worcester Society of Antiquity* V (1879), 9–10.
19. Tucker, *Samuel Slater*, 107–10.
20. Jeremy, *Transatlantic Industrial Revolution*, 90–91; and Peter J. Coleman, *The Transformation of Rhode Island, 1790–1860* (Providence: Brown University Press, 1963), 83,
21. Jeremy, *Transatlantic Industrial Revolution*, 87–88; William R. Bagnall, *Textile Industries of the United States* (Cambridge: 1893), 398.
22. Susan Berry, "The Architecture of Power: Spatial and Social Order in Seven Rhode Island Mill Villages" (PhD diss., University of California, 1992), 35.
23. Jeremy, *Transatlantic Industrial Revolution*, 96–99.
24. Gilmore left and subsequently perfected his machines at the Lyman and Coventry mills. See James L. Conrad, Jr., "'Drive That Branch': Samuel Slater, the Power Loom, and the Writing of America's Textile History,"

Technology and Culture 36 (1995): 1–28. See also Gail Fowler Mohanty, "Putting Up With Putting-Out: Power-Loom Diffusion and Outwork for Rhode Island Mills, 1821–1829," *Journal of the Early Republic* 9 (1989): 191–216 and Gary B. Kulik, "The Beginnings of the Industrial Revolution in America: Pawtucket, Rhode Island, 1672–1829" (PhD diss., Brown University, 1980), 336–60.

25. Berry, "Architecture of Power," 63.
26. M. S. Franklin, "The Houses and Villages of North Smithfield, Rhode Island," *Pencil Points* 21 (1935): 49–63.
27. Robert Ross MacMurray, "Technological Change in the American Cotton Spinning Industry, 1790–1836" (PhD diss., University of Pennsylvania, 1970), 135.
28. R. Rogerson to John Slater, Boston September 2, 1814. Slater Correspondence, Rhode Island School of Design, Providence, quoted in Berry, "Architecture of Power," 40.
29. E. A. Buck, "*An Historical Discourse Delivered at the Semi-Centennial Anniversary of the Slatersville Congregational Church, Sept. 9, 1866* (Woonsocket: S. S. Foss, 1867), 39.
30. Ibid., and Albert Donnell, *An Historical Address Delivered at the Centennial Celebration of the Congregational Sunday School at Slatersville, Rhode Island, September 13, 1908* (Woonsocket: Charles E. Cook, 1908), 33.
31. Buck, *An Historical Discourse*, 8.
32. Buck, *An Historical Discourse*, 23–25; Donnell, *An Historical Address*, 16–17.
33. Buck, *An Historical Discourse*, 12–17.
34. Ibid., 7.
35. Many of his factory families practiced a form of fundamental emotional religious devotion. "Meetings were often exceedingly boisterous. Shoutings were to be heard within and without while strong men would be falling until some half dozen at a time were lying together upon the floor." See Buck, *An Historical Discourse, 11, 24 and* Catharine Williams, *Fall River: An Authentic Narrative,* ed. Patricia Caldwell (New York: Oxford University Press, 1993), 111.
36. Daniel Feller, *The Jacksonian Promise: America, 1815–1840* (Baltimore: The Johns Hopkins University Press, 1995), 96–97. See also Mark Noll, *America's God: From Jonathan Edwards to Abraham Lincoln* (New York: Oxford University Press, 2002).
37. Buck, *An Historical Discourse*, 12–14, 18.
38. Ibid., 41.
39. Anne M. Boylan, *Sunday School, the Formation of an American Institution, 1790–1880* (New Haven: Yale University Press, 1988), 6–11; Tucker, *Samuel Slater*, 75–76, 168.
40. Donnell, *An Historical Address*, 19; Buck, *An Historical Discourse*, 14–20.

41. Buck, "*An Historical Discourse*, 22, 25, 29–31.
42. John Slater to Almy and Brown, September 13, 1808, Almy and Brown Papers, Rhode Island Historical Society, Providence, RI. See also Richard M. Bayles, ed., *History of Providence County, Rhode Island* (New York: W.W. Preston, 1891), 2:491.
43. Liquor License, 1828, Jewett City Cotton Manufacturing Company, Box 21. Slater Company Records. 1795–1892. Archives and Special Collections. Thomas J. Dodd Research Center, University of Connecticut, Storrs CT. Hereafter cited as Slater Company Records.
44. Buck, *An Historical Discourse*, 10.
45. William H. Jordy, *Buildings of Rhode Island* (New York: Oxford University Press 2004), 245; and Berry, "Architecture of Power," 66–67.
46. John Slater to John Slater 2nd.Smithfield, January 15, 1834, Samuel Slater and Sons, v. 236, Samuel Slater Collection, Baker Library, Harvard University, Cambridge, MA; and Joseph Almy to John Slater 2nd, Slatersville, April 7, 1837, Samuel Slater and Sons, v. 236, Samuel Slater Collection, Baker Library, Harvard University, Cambridge, MA. Hereafter referred to as Slater MSS.
47. Bayles, *History of Providence County*, 2:497.
48. Although the economy was in decline, Slater tried to keep them in good repair. In 1832 he was concerned about the health of workers in his Jewett City mill and instructed his agent, "To have each & every cellar now owned by me at Jewett City, thoroughly cleansed from all decayed vegetable & other substances as are prejudicial to the health of the inhabitants; also to have the sink drains thoroughly cleansed & all other filth around each dwelling house carefully removed. Also, to have the privy's thoroughly cleansed & strew lime around each sink drain frequently & into each privy. Also see that each tenement is thoroughly whitewashed, windows cleaned & kept clean & have every thing done that can be consistently & which is conducive to health. . . . and as suitable persons ought to have the charge of this to enforce its fulfilment. I recommend that yourself, Capt. Carpenter & Mr Simons, the watchman, be the committee to examine each tenement *immediately* on receipt of this. [Furthermore,] also have both mills kept perfectly clean & have the window boards & sashes wash'd with soap suds-then have them wash'd with lime water made tolerable thick-frequently & have the floors kept as clean as you consistently can & have the privy's attached to each mill cleaned out well & frequently & have the walls in the privy well washed in each room, then while they are wet heave on lime . . . which will no doubt be conducive to the health & comfort of the help employed." John Slater to John Fox Slater, Smithfield, March 22, 1838, Slater Company Records, Box 17.
49. Thomas H. O'Connor, *Lords of the Loom: The Cotton Whigs and the Coming of the Civil War* (New York: Scribner, 1968), 20–22.
50. Kulik, "Beginnings of the Industrial Revolution in America," 275.

51. McLane Report, 931.
52. Robert V. Remini, *The Life of Andrew Jackson* (New York: Harper and Row, 1990), 226.
53. Paul Goodman, *Towards a Christian Republic: Antimasonry and the Great Transition in New England, 1826–1836* (New York: Oxford University Press, 1988), 10.
54. Ibid., 12–13.
55. John L. Brooke, *The Heart of the Commonwealth, Society and Political Culture in Worcester County, Massachusetts, 1713–1861* (New York: Cambridge University Press, 1989), 322, 328.
56. Ibid., 336. Alongside his immediate family, Abraham and Isaac Wilkinson—twin sons of Oziel Wilkinson and brothers-in-law to Samuel Slater—he led the Antimasonic cause in Pawtucket. They bankrolled a newspaper, *The Pawtucket Herald*, which publicized their views. Their pronouncements could be quite vitriolic. In an 1832 debate, Abraham Wilkinson called a local Masonic lodge a "Slaughter House" and "an abominable bloodstained, stinking Order." Wilkinson sued a Mason charging that Masonic judges and juries worked together for the benefit of their brethren. He asked, "Would not a mason, on trial, have secret means of communication with a masonic judge or juror, which one not a mason could not have?" This fear of anti-republican secret societies intersected with the new Christian populist militancy to fuel the antimason movements. Antimasons believed they were correct, righteous and "were Christian Republicans unfurling the banner of 'genuine' Christianity and 'true' republicanism." See Goodman, *Towards a Christian Republic*, 209, 214.
57. Fletcher to Samuel Slater, Jewett City, January 27, 1824, Slater Company Records, Box 17.; Samuel Slater to Fletcher, North Providence, May 3, 1824, Slater Company Records, Box 17; Samuel Slater to Fletcher, North Providence, October 23, 1824, Slater Company Records, Box 17; and Samuel Slater to Fletcher, Oxford, February 14, 1826, Slater Company Records, Box 17,
58. Samuel Slater to Fletcher, North Providence, December 29, 1823, Slater Company Records, Box 17.
59. John Slater to John Bacon, Smithfield, August 7, 1825, Slater Company Records, Box 16.
60. Foss for John Slater to Sanford Meech, Smithfield, December 22, 1828, Slater Company Records, Box 16.
61. Foss for John Slater to Sanford Meech, Smithfield, January 21, 1830, Slater Company Records, Box 16
62. McLane Report, 982–85.
63. Foss for John Slater to Henry Carpenter, Smithfield, May 16, 1831, Slater Company Records, Box 16 and Foss for John Slater to Charles Hyatt, Smithfield, June 17, 1831, Slater Company Records, Box 16.

64. Foss for John Slater to Collier, Smithfield, May 16, 1831, Slater Company Records, Box 16.
65. Foss for John Slater to Collier, Smithfield, March 29, 1831, Slater Company Records, Box 16.
66. *Memorial of John F. Slater, of Norwich, Connecticut* (Norwich, 1885), 7.
67. *Memorial of John F. Slater*, 11; and Buck, *An Historical Discourse*, 38.
68. White, *Memoir of Samuel Slater*, 242; and Samuel Slater to son John Slater, 2nd, North Providence, March 30, 1821, Slater MSS, Samuel Slater and Sons, v. 235.
69. Samuel Slater to C. Farnum, North Providence, August 22, 1825, Slater Company Records, Box 17. See also White, *Memoir of Samuel Slater*, 241–42.
70. Slater MSS, Samuel Slater and Sons, v. 237, Samuel Shove, Jr. to Thomas G. Slater, May 5, 1834, Slater MSS, Samuel Slater and Sons, v. 237.
71. John Whipple to Horatio N. Slater, Sutton, September 7, 1844, Slater MSS, Samuel Slater and Sons, v. 237.
72. Samuel Slater to John Slater 2nd, North Providence, March 30, 1821, Slater MSS, Samuel Slater and Sons, v. 235.
73. S. & J. Slater, John Slater to John Forsyth, Secretary of State, Providence, December 6, 1837, Slater MSS, Samuel Slater and Sons, v. 235.

CHAPTER 5

1. *Pawtucket Chronicle*, May 1, 1835, quoted in Brendan F. Gilbane, "A Social History of Samuel Slater's Pawtucket, 1790–1830" (PhD diss., Boston University, 1969), 207. The genealogy for the Slaters is as follows: The Slater family begins with William Slater of Belper, England. Two of his sons, Samuel Slater (1768–1835) and John Slater (1776–1843) migrated to Rhode Island and entered the textile business. Samuel had nine children including the following: Georgbe B. Slater (1804–43), John Slater 2nd. (1805–38), Horatio Nelson Slater (1808–88), and Thomas G. Slater (1812-c. 1845). His brother John Slater had several children including John Fox Slater (1815–84) and William Slater (1817–82).
2. George White to Horatio Nelson Slater, Canterbury, CT, May 1, 1835, Horatio Nelson Slater Papers, Box 1, Slater Mill Historic Site, Pawtucket, RI. Hereafter referred to as Horatio N. Slater Papers.
3. Scott E. Casper, *Constructing American Lives: Biography and Culture in Nineteenth-Century America* (Chapel Hill: University of North Carolina Press, 1999), 30–57.
4. Ibid., 88.
5. Max Weber, *The Protestant Ethic and the Spirit of Capitalism* (New York: Routledge, 2001) and Michel Foucault, *Discipline and Punish: The Birth of the Prison* (New York: Vintage, 1979).

6. Amy Dru Stanley, *From Bondage to Contract: Wage Labor, Marriage, and the Market in the Age of Slave Emancipation* (New York: Cambridge University Press, 1998).
7. Both Horatio Nelson Slater and John Fox Slater became wealthy men. The former man left the bulk of his estate, with an estimated value of nine million dollars, to his adopted son. His bequests were few and centered on contributions made to Brown University. Although John Fox Slater's estate was more modest, his net worth was still calculated in the millions. Bequests and gifts included one million dollars to his granddaughter, a one million dollar endowment to the John Fox Slater Trust, and millions in real estate and moveable assets to his son, William Slater. See Will of John Fox Slater, May 1884, Probate Records, Connecticut State Library, Hartford, CT. Hereafter referred to as CSL. See also *Norwich Bulletin*, May 13, 1884.
8. *Memorial of John F. Slater, of Norwich, Connecticut. 1815–1884* (Norwich, 1885), 6–7.
9. Horatio N. Slater to John Slater, Providence, February 7, 1831, Horatio N. Slater Papers, Box 1.
10. John Fox Slater to E. Stillman, Norwich, June 19, 1844, S. and J. Slater Records, Box 17, Dodd Research Center, University of Connecticut, Storrs, CT. Hereafter referred to as Slater Company Records.
11. Daniel L. Phillips, *Griswold—A History Being a History of the Town of Griswold, Connecticut From the Earliest Times to the Entrance of our Country into the World War in 1917* (New Haven: Tuttle Morehouse and Taylor, 1929), 78–80, 100.
12. Ibid., 106–7.
13. Personal Estate Owned by John Slater in Griswold, October 1, 1829, Slater Company Records, Box 21.
14. After the death of his mother, William Slater remained in Slatersville where he continued to reside until his death in 1882. He directed the Slatersville factories and guided the development of the community. Most of his father's side of the family, including Mrs. Ruth Slater and Elizabeth Slater (sister of William and John Fox Slater), continued to live in Slatersville. Ruth Slater remained in the family home on School Street. Around 1850, William Slater built a sizeable house with a mansard roof and a magnificent four-story tower in town, and his sister Elizabeth, now married to Dr. Elisha Bartlett, moved into a grand home on Green Street. While her husband was a physician and college professor, he had strong ties to the industrial community of Lowell. A Brown University graduate, he served as a physician in Lowell, Massachusetts where he took an active interest in politics, becoming the first mayor of that town as well as a member of the state legislature. Known for his medical treatises such as "The History of the Diagnosis" and "Treatment of Typhoid and Typhus," he achieved special recognition for his defense of the Lowell system of labor. He published "A Vindication

of the Character and Condition of the Females Employed in the Lowell Mills" in 1841, as a response to previously published articles in the *Boston Times* and the *Boston Quarterly Review* that challenged the health and character of female mill operatives. Bartlett argued that the company was devoted to the health and welfare of its workers. In his pamphlet: "A Vindication of the Character and Condition of Females Employed in the Lowell Mill," (Lowell, 1841), Bartlett wrote:

> "Both overseers and superintendents, pastors and Sunday School teachers interest themselves at once and warmly in her welfare and comfort . . . and thus in addition to the good offices growing out of her common relations to her employers, she is blessed with the divine charities of a Christian love."

He worked to perpetuate the belief that factory work was a positive experience and a benefit to the laborer: "The aggregate change which is wrought in the moral character and condition of the young females who come here from the country is eminently happy and beneficial. The great preponderance of influence is enlightening, elevating and improving—not darkening, debasing and deteriorating. Their manners are cultivated, their minds are enlarged, and their moral and religious principles are developed and fortified. Hundreds and hundreds of these girls will long live to refer the commencement of their best and highest happiness to their residence in this this city." See Elisha Bartlett, *Vindication of the Character and Condition of Females Employed in the Lowell Mills, against the Charges Contained in the Boston Times and the Boston Quarterly Review* (Lowell, 1841), 21.

Thirteen years her senior, Bartlett had married Elizabeth, daughter of John Slater and sister of William and John Fox Slater. When his health declined in the 1850s, the couple took up residence in Slatersville and built their home on land previously owned by her parents. Within five years Bartlett died, and William Slater, now a widower, assumed responsibility for his widowed mother and sister. They all moved in together, along with William Slater's four children. See William H. Jordy, *Buildings of Rhode Island (New York: Oxford University Press, 2004)*, 244–48. Management of Slatersville remained under William Slater's control throughout his lifetime, and the property and its administration later passed to his son, John.

15. John Warner Barber, *Connecticut Historical Collections, Containing a General Collection of Interesting Facts, Traditions, Biographical Sketches, Anecdotes, etc., Relating to the History and Antiquities of Every Town in Connecticut; with Geographical Descriptions* (New Haven: J. W. Barber, 1836), 310.
16. Phillips, *Griswold*, 162–65.
17. Labor Contracts, 1837–1838, Slater Company Records, Box 2.

18. Heman Humphrey, *Domestic Education* (Amherst: J.S. & C. Adams, 1840) in *Children and Youth in America: A Documentary History, Robert Bremner, ed., 3 vols.* (Cambridge: Harvard University Press, 1970), 1:351.
19. Labor Contracts, 1837–1838, Barclays, March 7, 1838, Slater Company Records, Box 2; Labor contract with Charles Hillman, February 24, 1838, Slater Company Records, Box 2. Labor contract with Sabin Bates, February 5, 1838, Slater Company Records, Box 2. Labor contract with Joshua Rathbone October 19, 1838, Slater Company Records, Box 2. Labor contract with Nathan Champlin, n.p., November 12, 1838, Slater Company Records, Box 2. and Labor contract with Sally Braman, March 7, 1838, Slater Company Records, Box 2.
20. Labor contract with David Terry, February 8, 1838, Slater Company Records, Box 2.
21. The 1838 agreement with Joshua Rathbone, for example, read:

> That the said Rathbone hereby agrees for his children to work for the said Slater at his Jewett City Mill from this date to April 1st 1839:
> As follows
> Mary . . . at the rate of 9/ per week
> Susan . . . at the rate of 6/ per week
> Ruth . . . at the rate of 5/ per week
> Emily Lemphere . . . at the rate of 13/ per week
> And the said Rathbone is to occupy the Old House by the pond for which he is to pay rent at the rate of eighteen dollar per year.
>
> The said Rathbone agrees that his children shall be regular in their attendance to their work and to be at the mill by the ringing in of the bell to call the help to work—to keep no hens nor sell any manure which may be made on the premises and is not to occupy the tenement no longer than he may remain in the employ of the said Slater. (Labor Contract with Joshua Rathbone, October 19, 1838, S. and J. Slater Records, Box 2)

This contract was written in October 1838 and expired the following April. Skilled workers could expect even more detailed instructions. Three of the Barclay men, James, John, and David, all mule spinners, signed a one year contract with John Slater in March 1838, which read as follows:

> The said Barclays do hereby agree to run the mules standing in the west end of the Slater Mill of 612 spindles and the pair of mules of 448 spindles standing in the same room with the other before named for the term of one year from the first day of April next at the following rate say for the largest mule, Eleven cents per hundred skeins and to furnish their own piecers or provided the said Slater furnishes piecers, the said Barclays are to pay for the same what ever the said Slater may

> have to pay and they are to run the smaller mules for twelve cents per hundred skein and the said Slater to furnish piecers for those mules for the sum of three 50/100 dollars pr week which the sd Barclays are to pay and the said John Barclay agrees to take charge of the room that is to have a general oversight to see that everything is kept in good order to see that all the waste made in the room shall be picked over every day and properly separated to see that all the mules be properly oiled and to be carefull that no unnecessary waste of oil shall be made and to have the mules cleaned whenever the superintendant of the mill shall think proper and whenever done to see it well done and they agree neither to carry nor to use in the mill any ardent spirits nor suffer the same to be brought in to the room under their charge by others during the year, and they agree to . . . be prompt to the bell and in all things as far as duty goes to use their exertions to promote the said Slaters interest.

The contract also stipulated that John Barclay was to receive an additional $.50 per week for taking charge of the mule room so long as he ran it well and did not "allow any idlers or strangers to come in to the mule room without permission first being obtained from the superintendent of the mill." They also were allowed a tenement at the rate of $26.25 per year.

See Labor contract with Barclays, March 7, 1838, Slater Company Records, Box 2.

22. General Regulations, Jewett City, January 1, 1841, Slater Company Records, Box 2. See also E. A. Buck, "*An Historical Discourse Delivered at the Semi-Centennial Anniversary of the Slatersville Congregational Church, September 9, 1866*" (Woonsocket: S.S. Foss, 1867), 24.
23. "Constitution of the Methodist Episcopal Church Sabbath School, 1861–1863," Webster, MA, United Church of Christ, Webster, Massachusetts. For a more detailed examination of the Sabbath School, see Barbara M. Tucker, *Samuel Slater and the Origins of the American Textile Industry, 1790–1860* (Ithaca: Cornell University Press, 1984), 163–74.
24. Phillips, *Griswold*, 108–12, 114.
25. Ibid., 142–43.
26. *Historic and Architectural Resources Survey of the Town of Griswold, Connecticut: Additional Materials National Register of Historic Places Nomination*, Connecticut General Assembly, 2001, 1:27, 2:JC050, 2:JC111, 2:JC112. These factory neighborhoods featured paired bay windows, gable dormers, and porches. They housed only part of the Slater labor force. The company also built duplexes throughout the hamlet, sometimes next door to or within close proximity to the substantial homes of affluent Jewett City residents. Along fashionable South Main Street, for example, a two family Slater wood frame mill house was built circa 1860. Further along the same street stood a second

empire-style frame home belonging to Andrew Burnham, director of a local bank. This two story home, with a mansard roof, also featured paired bay windows, gable dormers, and a porch with square columns.

27. U.S. Bureau of the Census, *United States Federal Population Census, Manuscript Schedules, Eighth Census of the United States* (Washington, DC, 1860); Griswold, Connecticut, 1860 (Washington, DC, 1860). Hereafter cited as Federal Population MSS 8. See also Connecticut Bureau of Labor Statistics, *Second Annual Report*, May session (Hartford, 1875), 13–21; Albert E. Van Dusen, *Connecticut* (New York: Random House: 1961), 255.
28. Federal Population MSS 8, Griswold, Connecticut, 1860.
29. *Memorial of John F. Slater*, 11–12.
30. Pierce represented New London County at the Free Soil State Convention that met in New Haven in September 1848. See *Free Soil Advocate*, September 30, 1848; *Hartford Courant*, November 8, 1859; and J. H. Beers, *Genealogical and Biographical Record of New London County, Connecticut; Containing Biographical Sketches of Prominent and Representative Citizens and Genealogical Records of Many of the Early Settled Families* (Chicago: n.p., 1905), 21–22.
31. Malcolm McG.regor Dana, *The Annals of Norwich, New London County, Connecticut in the Great Rebellion of 1861–65* (Norwich: J.H. Jewett & Company, 1873), 19, 49, 58–59.
32. Ibid., 49, 59. Slater's Union sympathies were shared by many of his workers. A number of his Jewett City textile workers joined the union forces beginning in July 1861. Eighteen-year-old Otis Horton enlisted on July 23, and he remained in the army for the duration of the war. When released from service in 1865, he returned to Jewett City and his job in the mill. A fellow operative, Thomas Coleman, enlisted at the same time and served in the same unit. He too remained for the duration of the war. Several months later, other young men joined up, and this enthusiasm continued into the next year. While some of them served out their enlistment, others were captured, wounded, died, or were discharged as disabled. See Phillips; *Griswold*; Federal Population MSS 8, Griswold, Connecticut, 1860; and U.S. Bureau of the Census, *United States Federal Population Census, Manuscript Schedules, Ninth Census of the United States*, Griswold, Connecticut, 1870 (Washington, DC, 1870). Hereafter cited as Federal Population MSS 9.
33. Federal Population MSS 8, Griswold, Connecticut, 1860 and "Norwich's Slaters Created Industry," *Norwich Bulletin*, in possession of Dale Plummer, Norwich, CT.
34. John D. Nolan, *History of Taftville, Connecticut* (Norwich: Bulletin Press, 1940), 3–8.
35. Matthew Roth, *Connecticut: An Inventory of Historic and Engineering and Industrial Sites* (Society for Industrial Archeology, 1981), *194*.

36. Connecticut Bureau of Labor Statistics, "The Strike at Taftville," *Second Annual Report of the Bureau of Labor Statistics*, May session (Hartford, 1875), 127–31.
37. Ibid.
38. Ibid., 128–30. See also *Windham County Transcript,* May 6, 1875. This newspaper stated: "We believe that as a general thing the owners of mills pay their help all that the markets will bear, and that strikes are always disastrous to those who engage in them."
39. Federal Population MSS 8, Griswold, Connecticut, 1860.
40. Federal Population MSS 9, New Hartford, Connecticut, 1870.
41. Ibid.
42. *Historic and Architectural Resource Survey of the Town of Griswold*, 2:JC096, 2:JC118, 2:JC119.
43. Of course, Slater was not the only one to employ children or to construct simple, utilitarian homes and boarding houses, nor was he the most egregious violator of child labor and compulsory school education laws. New Hartford, for example, was the destination of one of Slater's former workers, George Burdick. In 1860 he was hired as a master weaver at Slater's Jewett City factory and, together with his wife and three children, lived in company housing. By 1870, however, he had left Slater's employ and moved to New Hartford, Connecticut where he could be found in the local factory. That factory employed children as young as six years of age. Of Burdick's six children, four worked in the mills. They ranged in age from eight to sixteen. By 1871, six-year-old Solomon was employed as well. See Federal Population MSS 9, New Hartford, Connecticut, 1870; Federal Population MSS 9, Griswold, Connecticut, 1870; Bureau of Labor Statistics, *Second Annual Report* (Hartford, 1875), 15–16.
44. *Memorial of John F. Slater*, 12–13.
45. "Norwich's Slaters Created Industry."
46. Robert Tucker, ed., *The Marx-Engels Reader* (New York: W.W. Norton, 1978), 475.
47. Frances M. Caulkins, *History of New London Connecticut from the first Survey of the Coast in 1612 to 1860: with memoir of the author* (New London: H.D. Utley, 1895), 387–99.
48. Ibid., 476–77, 613; and U.S. Bureau of the Census, *United States Federal Population Census, Manuscript Schedules, Seventh Census of the United States*, Norwich, Connecticut, 1850. Hereafter cited as Federal Population MSS 7.
49. Dale Plummer, "Jail Hill Historical and Architectural Survey," (typed transcript, Otis Public Library, Norwich, CT, June 1984), xxxi–xxxvii; Van Dusen, *Connecticut*, 212.
50. It expanded through the acquisition of several other textile concerns, including the Quinebaug Company and another in Bozrah. See George D. Coit, "A Historical Sketch of the Second Congregational Sunday

School of Norwich, Connecticut Delivered Sunday Evening, December 16, 1894," (Norwich: Bulletin Print., n.d.), 6–11. Held on Sunday, the school started at 9:00 with scripture reading and prayer. A similar program was undertaken in the afternoon followed by an evening prayer meeting. See Caulkins, *History of New London*, 554–57.

51. James T. Dickinson, *A Sermon Delivered in the Second Congregational Church on the fourth of July, 1834 at the Request of the Anti-Slavery Society of Norwich and Vicinity* (Norwich: Anti-Slavery Society, 1834), 4–5.
52. John P. Gulliver and Daniel Coit Gilman, *Address Delivered at the Dedication of the Slater Memorial Building at Norwich, Connecticut, Thursday November 4, 1886* (Norwich: L. & E. Edwards, 1856), 11.
53. Caulkins, *History of New London*, 549.
54. Gulliver and Gilman, *Address*, 24–25, 29.
55. Gulliver and Gilman, *Address*, 31–41 and Bond, *A Discourse*, 27–30.
56. Luella Sampson Kellogg, *United Workers of Norwich: A History of One-Hundred Years of Community Service* (Cambridge: Word Guild, 1978), v–vi, 1–7.
57. *History of the Park Congregational Church, 1874–1949* Copy held by Local History Room, Otis Public Library, Norwich CT.
58. *Memorial of John F. Slater*, 7.
59. Ibid., 23–24.
60. Frederick C. Jaher, *Urban Establishment: Upper Strata in Boston, New York, Charleston, Chicago and Los Angles* (Urbana: University of Illinois Press, 1981), 58–64.
61. A. Whittemann, *American Philanthropists* (New York: A. Wittemann, 1887), 13.
62. Moses Pierce to Horatio Nelson Slater, Norwich, July 22, 1875, Horatio N. Slater Papers, Box 1. See also U.S. Bureau of the Census, *United States Federal Population Census, Manuscript Schedules, Tenth Census of the United States*, Norwich, Connecticut, 1880; Federal Population MSS 9, Norwich, Connecticut, 1870; and John F. Slater, will dated May 14, 1884, *Windham County Transcript, 14 May 1884.*
63. George S. White, *Memoir of Samuel Slater* (Philadelphia: n.p., 1836), 241–42; Samuel Shove, Jr. to Thomas Slater, May 5, 1834, Samuel Slater and Sons, v. 237, Samuel Slater Collection, Baker Library, Harvard University, Cambridge, MA (hereafter cited as Slater MSS); and G. A. Trimbull for Central Bank to Thomas Slater July 14, 1834, Samuel Slater and Sons, v. 237, Slater MSS. Thomas was excluded from the family business and labeled as a problem child. At the age of thirteen, he and a friend tried to run away to New York. His father sent out a team to catch them and lamented, "It is a very lamentable thing that two young boys should be so thoughtless to leave a good house for an uncertainty, but so it is" Later, Thomas Slater's interests ran more to

champagne, fine suits, fancy dinner parties, and rides in the countryside than factory operations or the counting house. See David Kingman to Thomas Slater, April 29, 1834, Samuel Slater and Sons, v. 237, Slater MSS; Thomas Slater to Wm. Tiffany, June 12, 1834, Samuel Slater and Sons, v. 237, Slater MSS; and Thomas Slater to C. A. Tourtellot, August 15, 1840, Samuel Slater and Sons, v. 237, Slater MSS.

64. Horatio Nelson Slater to Samuel Slater, Cheshire, November 16, 1819, Horatio N. Slater Papers, Box 1. See also Horatio Nelson Slater to Samuel Slater, Cheshire, August 18, 1818, Horatio N. Slater Papers, Box 1,and Horatio Nelson Slater to Samuel Slater, Cheshire, July 25, 1825, Horatio N. Slater Papers, Box 1.

65. John Slater 2nd and Samuel Slater to John Slater, North Providence, March 30, 1821, Samuel Slater and Sons, v. 237, Slater MSS. See also Sanford J. Horton, *"The Measure of a Man": Memorial Discourse Delivered in St. Peter's Church, Cheshire, Sunday evening, September 30, 1888* (New Haven. 1889), 10. I would like to thank Ann Moriarty, Archivist, Cheshire Academy, Cheshire, Connecticut, for providing me with a copy of the Discourse.

66. Horatio Nelson Slater warned Thomas, who was away in Baltimore, that

> Father is very low indeed; he has now been confined to his bed for about twelve days with a complication of diseases among which are Rhumatism, Gravel with considerable fever and latterly with a very sore throat, which resembles very much the malignant sore throat a well known disease. Either of these difficulties singly is sufficient in the degree in which he has been afflicted by it to constitute, of itself, alarming sickness. Their combined effect has reduced him for the time astonishingly in strength, and at times has been so violent that his life has been almost entirely despaired of not less than three times since last Friday. . . . I fear the chance is not equal of his recovery. Under these circumstances, it is the wish of the family that you hasten your departure from Baltimore and arrive here as soon as possible when it is hoped you may find father recovering or if that is not permitted, that you may be allowed to pay the last tribute of respect and affection to him whose memory should be dear to his son.

See Horatio N. Slater to Thomas Slater, Providence, April 18, 1833, Horatio N. Slater Papers, Box 1.

67. George B. Slater died of TB. Death certificate of George B. Slater, November 15, 1843, Vital Statistics, Deaths, Webster, Massachusetts. Town Hall, Webster, Massachusetts.

68. Letter of Guardianship, April 9, 1839, Horatio N. Slater Papers, Box 1; H. Nelson Slater Will-Investment for Elizabeth, n.d., Horatio N. Slater Papers, Box 1; and Federal Population MSS 8, 1860, Webster, Massachusetts.

69. His younger brother Thomas died in 1843. Apparently never out of debt, and only loosely connected with the family business, he was only thirty one years of age when he died. See White, *Memoir of Samuel Slater*, 241–42. Within an eight year period, Horatio Slater lost four family members. He had to manage the future fortunes of Samuel Slater and Sons alone. After the deaths of his brothers, Horatio Slater ran the community with an iron hand and as much control as he could muster.
70. *Leading Business Men of Webster, Southbridge, Putnam, and Vicinity; Embracing Also Danielsonville, East Douglass, and Oxford* (Boston: Mercantile Publication Company, 1890), 4–5. See also Tucker, *Samuel Slater*, 94–104.
71. Duane. Hamilton Hurd, *History of Worcester County, Massachusetts, with Biographical Sketcher of Many of its Pioneers and Prominent Men*, 2 vols. (Philadelphia: J. W. Lewis, 1889), Tucker, *Samuel Slater*, 126–29, 154–59; and "Two Hundred Years of Progress: Webster-Dudley 1739–1939," *Webster Times*, 1939, 10.
72. Lyman Tiffany to John Slater 2nd, Boston, November 15, 1832, Samuel Slater and Sons, v. 236, Slater MSS; Town Meeting Records, April 7, 1834, Webster Town Hall, Webster, Massachusetts; and Webster Town Hall, Webster Massachusetts,: "List of Selectmen"List of Selectmen,"
73. Waite to Samuel Slater and Sons, Webster, November 9, 1835, Union Mills, v. 185, Slater MSS; Waite to Samuel Slater and Sons, Webster, November 16, 1836, Union Mills, v. 185, Slater MSS. See also John R. Mulkern, *The Know-Nothing Party in Massachusetts: The Rise and Fall of a People's Movement* (Boston: Northeastern University Press, 1990), 16–17.
74. Slater MSS, S. and J. Slater, v. 15. There are several collections of the S and J. Slater manuscripts. This collection is within the Slater archives housed at Baker Library, Harvard University., John Slater 2nd to John Forsyth, Providence, December 6, 1837 application for passport and E. W. Fletcher to John Wright, Providence, March 1838. See also Death certificate of George B. Slater and "Two Hundred Years of Progress," 4.
75. O'Connor, *Lords of the Loom*, 36–37; Waite to Samuel Slater and Sons, Webster, November 9, 1835, Union Mills, v. 185, Slater MSS and Joseph Dorfman, "Jackson Wage-Earner Thesis," *American Historical Review* 54 (January 1949): 301, 305.
76. Storrs to H. N. Slater, Webster, November 11, 1844, Union Mills, v. 117, Slater MSS.
77. Storrs to H. N. Slater, Webster, November 13, 1844, Union Mills, v. 117, Slater MSS.
78. Town Meeting Records, March 21, 1836 WebsterTown Hall, Webster, Massachusetts. Examination of the Town Meeting records?" reveals that support for paupers and schools absorbed much of the town's early

budgets. In 1834, residents spent $921.81 and $600 respectively for those two items. By 1839, support for schools stood at $1,045.31 and support for the poor at $456.33. As the town grew, the expenditures multiplied. Town Meeting Records, April 1, 1834–March 11, 1839, Webster Town Hall, Webster, Massachusetts.

79. Paupers and pupils appeared of primary concern throughout the antebellum years. In 1826, townspeople discussed the merits of acquiring a farm for the support of the poor. Samuel Slater offered "to let them have my Phip's farm at a low rate." He concluded that "if the Town's money was judiciously laid out in a farm for the support of the lazy and indigent, I have no doubt but that it would eventually lessen the lazy and poor rates." John Slater, 2nd, Samuel Slater to son John, North Providence, March 5, 1826, Union Mills, v. 117, Slater MSS. and; John Slater 2nd. Samuel Slater to son John, North Providence, March 30, 1826, Union Mills, v. 117, Slater MSS. Eventually, both a pauper farm and a poor house were acquired. Town Meeting Records, March 3, 1851, Webster Town Hall, Webster, Massachusetts.
80. Samuel Slater and Sons, Inc., *Slater Mills at Webster: 1812–1912* (Worcester, n.d.). See also Massachusetts Statutes, ch. 23, sec. 1, 281.
81. Samuel Slater and Sons to H. N. Slater, Webster, April 4, 1845, Union Mills, v. 117, Slater MSS. See also Barton and Bacon to Samuel Slater and Sons, May 13, 1848, Union Mills, v. 188, Slater MSS.
82. Town Meeting Records, March 5, 1855, Webster Town Hall, Webster Massachusetts.
83. Town Meeting Records, April 2, 1855, Webster Town Hall, Webster, Massachusetts.
84. A. Hodges to H. N. Slater, September 12, 1839, H. N. Slater, v. 33, Slater MSS. See also Tucker, *Samuel Slater*, 165–74.
85. "Methodist Episcopal Church at the Four Corners," December 21, 1884, Congregational Church Parish Records 1838–1911, United Church of Christ, Webster, Massachusetts. Hereafter referred to as United Church of Christ MSS; Charles A. Johnson, "Camp Meeting Hymnody," *American Quarterly* 4 (Summer 1952): 111, 113–14; and William A. Emerson, *History of the Town of Douglas, Massachusetts, Earliest Period to the Close of 1878* (Boston: F. W. Bird, 1879).
86. Tucker, *Samuel Slater*, 165, 175–81; Records of Board Meetings for Webster Church, December 11, 1841, United Church of Christ MSS; and Records of Board Meetings for Webster Church, July 2, 1848, United Church of Christ MSS.
87. Tucker, *Samuel Slater*, 176–77; and Town Meeting Records, April 11, 1842, Webster, MA.
88. *Webster Journal*, September 12, 1858; Old Rent Book, Union Mills, v. 87, Slater MSS; and "Two Hundred Years of Progress," 10.
89. Administrative Sales, Sutton Manufacturing Company, v. 45, Slater MSS.

90. H. Thomas Johnson, "Early Cost Accounting for Internal Management Control: Lyman Mills in the 1850s," *Business History Review* 46 (Winter 1972): 468.
91. Expenses, January 1840–January 1841, Sutton Manufacturing Company, v. 45, Slater MSS.
92. Early Handwritten Credit Reporting Ledgers of the Mercantile Agency, Dun and Bradstreet. Rhode Island, v. 9, January 1856. Baker Library, Harvard Business School, Cambridge, Massachusetts. Hereafter referred to as Dun and Bradstreet. See also *Slater Mills at Webster*, 10.
93. Although commission agents took most of the thread and cloth produced by the Slater firm, Horatio Nelson Slater also decided to sell twine, yarn, and some thread directly to local manufacturers situated in Stafford Springs and Thompsonville, Connecticut and Worcester, Massachusetts. See Samuel Slater and Sons to John Shephard, Webster, November 10, 1840, Union Mills, v. 114, Slater MSS; N. Kingsbury to Samuel Slater and Sons, Stafford Springs, October 2, 1845, Samuel Slater and Sons, v. 196, Slater MSS; Medlicott to Samuel Slater and Sons, Thompsonville, December 10, 1853, Samuel Slater and Sons, v. 199, Slater MSS; and Phoenix Thread Mill to Silas Dinsmore, Worcester, March 19, 1846, Samuel Slater and Sons v. 196, Slater MSS. Sometimes they were even able to sell their cloth directly from the factory to the retailer.
94. Underhill and Co. to Samuel Slater and Sons, New York, March 11, 1845, Samuel Slater and Sons, v. 210, Slater MSS; Underhill and Co. to Samuel Slater and Sons, New York, July 3, 1845, Samuel Slater and Sons, v. 210, Slater MSS; Underhill and Co. to Samuel Slater and Sons, New York, July 25, 1845, Samuel Slater and Sons, v. 210, Slater MSS; and Samuel Slater and Sons to T. N. Underhill, Webster, September 7, 1843, Union Mills, v. 116, Slater MSS.
95. C. Howe to George Kimball, Webster, February 28, 1834, Union Mills, v. 185, Slater MSS; Waite to Samuel Slater and Sons, Webster, August 3, 1836, Union Mills, v. 185, Slater MSS; and Samuel Slater and Sons to T. N. Underhill, Webster, September 7, 1843, Union Mills, v. 116, Slater MSS.
96. Underhill and Co. to Samuel Slater and Sons, New York, March 17, 1846, Samuel Slater and Sons, v. 210, Slater MSS; Hacker, Leat, and Co. to Samuel Slater and Sons, March 28, 1848, Samuel Slater and Sons, v. 217, Slater MSS; and M. Caulfield to Storrs, New York, October 26, 1849, Samuel Slater and Sons, v. 190, Slater MSS. See also Dun and Bradstreet, v. 10:27, 256.
97. Dodge and Tucker to Samuel Slater and Sons, Boston, September 4, 1844, Samuel Slater and Sons, v. 222, Slater MSS; W. Hanson and Bros. to Samuel Slater and Sons, Philadelphia, February 10, 1845, Samuel Slater and Sons, v. 222, Slater MSS; Almy Patterson and Co. to Samuel Slater and Sons, Boston, September 22, 1849, Samuel Slater and Sons,

v. 227, Slater MSS; G. F. Duncombe to Samuel Slater and Sons, New York, July 28, 1853, Samuel Slater and Sons, v. 199, Slater MSS; and Fletcher to Union Mills, Providence, December 24, 1850, Union Mills, v. 187, Slater MSS.

98. *Slater Mills at Webster*, 36–37; Curtis to Horatio N. Slater, Brooklyn, December 23, 1868, Horatio N. Slater Records, Box 1.

99. Storrs to Lester, Webster, March 7, 1844, Union Mills, v. 116, Slater MSS; Fletcher to Union Mills, Providence, August 15, 1853, Union Mills, v. 188, Slater MSS; Fletcher to Union Mills, Providence, December 15, 1854, Union Mills, v. 189, Slater MSS; Fletcher to Union Mills, Providence, January 9, 1852, Union Mills, v. 187, Slater MSS; Fletcher to Union Mills, Providence, August 25, 1852, Union Mills, v. 188, Slater MSS; Fletcher to Union Mills, Providence, February 22, 1855, Union Mills, v. 188, Slater MSS; and Storrs to C. Hale, Webster, August 6, 1858, Union Mills, v. 114, Slater MSS. See also Harding to Storrs, August 27, 1849, Samuel Slater and Sons, v. 190, Slater MSS.

100. *Slater Mills at Webster*, 10; D. W. Jones to Horatio Nelson Slater, May 14, 1836, Horatio N. Slater Records, Box 1. Personal control also extended to other aspects of his business, including transportation. In the1840s, the Norwich and Worcester Railroad ran through Webster. Horatio Slater paid to have a turn out tract constructed near one of his factories. Later, to compete with the local Norwich and Worcester Railroad, Slater built and operated his own railroad, the Providence, Webster and Springfield line. Later it was operated by the Boston and Albany Railroad. See Ellery Bicknell Crane, *Historic Homes and Institutions and Genealogical and Personal Memoirs of Worcester County, Massachusetts, with a History of Worcester Society of Antiquity* (New York: Lewis Publishing Company, 1907) 2:802. "Two Hundred Years of Progress," 4; *Slater Mills at Webster*, 10; Agreement: Samuel Slater and Sons and Norwich & Worcester Railroad Company, February 5, 1850, Union Mills, v. 193, Slater MSS.

101. Tucker, *Samuel Slater*, 138, 223–27.

102. Ralph D. Vicero, "Immigration of French Canadians to New England, 1840–1900: A Geographical Analysis" (PhD diss., University of Wisconsin, 1968), 173.

103. In another incident, a rumor spread through town that a wagonload of rifles was being brought in to arm the local Irish and French Canadian parishioners. The Methodists, Congregationalists, and Baptists panicked and decided to burn down the church before they became targets of Roman Catholic attack. It turned out, however, that the church was bringing in pipes for the organ, not guns and ammunition. Guards had to be stationed around the building to insure its safety. See Tucker, *Samuel Slater*, 259–60.

104. John Jonet, for example, moved to Webster, circa. 1850 with his wife and eleven children. See Federal Population MSS 7, Webster, Massachusetts, 1850.

105. Vital Statistics, Births, Deaths and Marriages, 1832–1870. Webster Town Hall, Webster, Massachusetts.
106. Tucker, *Samuel Slater*, 259–62.
107. Norwich and Worcester Railroad to Storrs, August 28, 1855, Union Mills, v. 191, Slater MSS.
108. L. Briggs to Storrs, Masonville, February 1, 1858, Union Mills, v. 121, Slater MSS.
109. Tucker, *Samuel Slater*, 252–53.
110. Dun and Bradstreet, v. 100, September 2, 1884, 311. A local Webster resident replied to a birth announcement in the Webster paper. Horatio N. Slater, Jr., announced the birth of a son and celebrated that by giving his workers a day off. This was how one worker responded:

    In this mill town where babies aren't born with silver spoons in their mouths, the coming of Horatio has made little Mickie Korovitz awfully happy. Mickie doesn't know Horatio's family, in fact, he has no acquaintance with millionaires to speak of. But Mickie is happy because daddy is home all day. Daddy has a holiday, and with full pay, which is occasion for double rejoicing. 'Mickie's daddy works in the Slater mills. Almost everybody's daddy in Webster works in the Slater mills, because the mills have been here since 1790 and make the sustaining industry in the village. Sometimes Mickie's daddy is home all day and many days because there is no work, the mills are shut down. But then Mickie can't be very happy because there isn't so much to eat as when daddy is working all the time.' What a wonderful baby son it must be to be hailed with such a salute. Mickie always wished he could be a Prince. But now he'd about as soon be Horatio N. Slater Jr. It's just as good as being a Prince.

    See "Cause of Joy," Newspaper Clipping, Horatio N. Slater Records, Box 1.
111. Horton, *"The Measure of a Man."* See also Estate of H. N. Slater, 1891–1906, v. 35, Slater MSS.

CHAPTER 6

1. William M. Thayer, *The Poor Boy and the Merchant Prince; Or, Elements of Success Drawn from the Life and Character of the Late Amos Lawrence, A Book for Youth* (Boston: Gould and Lincoln, 1857), v–vi.
2. Ibid., v–vi, 344. See also Scott E. Casper, *Constructing American Lives: Biography and Culture in Nineteenth-Century America* (Chapel Hill: University of North Carolina Press, 1999), 121.
3. Anthony Mann, "How 'Poor Country Boys' Become Boston Brahmins: The Rise of the Appletons and the Lawrences in Ante-Bellum Massachusetts," *Historical Journal of Massachusetts 31* (Winter 2003): 44–45.

4. Amos Lawrence to Amos Adams Lawrence, Boston, December 4, 1836, Letter Book 9, Amos Lawrence Papers, Massachusetts Historical Society, Boston, Massachusetts. Hereafter cited as Amos Lawrence Papers. The Lawrence family came from Groton, MA. The head of the family was Samuel Lawrence, a farmer. He had six sons and three daughters Two of his sons were Abbott Lawrence (1792–1855) and Amos Lawrence (1786–1852). Amos Lawrence moved to Boston, set up his business, married and had three sons and a daughter. Amos Adams Lawrence (1814–1886) was his second son.
5. Amos Lawrence to Amos Adams Lawrence, Boston, July 6, 1835, Letter Book 9, Amos Lawrence Papers.
6. William R. Lawrence, ed., *Extracts from the Diary and Correspondence of the Late Amos Lawrence with a Brief Account of Some Incidents in his Life* (Boston: Gould and Lincoln, 1856), 37.
7. Mann, "Poor Country Boys," 50–53.
8. Amos Lawrence to Amos Adams Lawrence, Boston, December 5, 1836, Letter Book 9, Amos Lawrence Papers.
9. Mann, "Poor Country Boys," 61–67.
10. Offered a partnership in this house, he declined because "he did not consider the principles on which the business was conducted as the true ones." Lawrence, *Extracts from the Diary*, 29.
11. Thayer, *Poor Boy*, vii–xviii; Amos Lawrence to Amos Adams Lawrence, Boston, July 20, 1835, Letter Book 9, Amos Lawrence Papers; Amos Lawrence to Amos Adams Lawrence, Boston, July 26, 1835, Letter Book 9, Amos Lawrence Papers; Amos Lawrence to Amos Adams Lawrence, Boston, November 1, 1836, Letter Book 9, Amos Lawrence Papers; and Amos Lawrence to Amos Adams Lawrence, Boston, December 5, 1836, Letter Book, 9, Amos Lawrence Papers.
12. Lawrence, *Extracts from the Diary*, 145.
13. Edward Pessen, *Riches, Class, and Power Before the Civil War* (Lexington: D.C. Heath, 1973), 331–35.
14. Peter Dobkin Hall, *The Organization of American Culture, 1700–1900: Private Institutions, Elites, and the Origins of American Nationality* (New York: New York University Press, 1982), 72.
15. Robert F. Dalzell, Jr., *Enterprising Elite: The Boston Associates and the World They Made* (Cambridge: Harvard University Press, 1987), 102–8.
16. Arthur J. Roinick, Bruce D. Smith, and Warren E. Weber, "Lessons From a Laissez-Faire Payments System: The Suffolk Banking System (1825–1858)," *Federal Reserve Bank of Minneapolis Quarterly Review* (Fall 2002): 32–33.
17. Ibid., 35; Dalzell, *Enterprising Elite*, 235; and Arthur J. Roinick, Bruce D. Smith, and Warren E. Weber, "Suffolk Bank and the Panic of 1837," *Federal Reserve Bank of Minneapolis Quarterly Review* (Spring 2000): 3–12.

18. Dalzell, *Enterprising Elite*, 235.
19. Will of Abbott Lawrence, January 27, 1855, Probate Records; Abbott Lawrence to Nathan Appleton, Boston, April 28, 1854; Abbott Lawrence Papers, Houghton Library, Harvard University, Cambridge, Massachusetts. Hereafter cited as Abbott Lawrence, Houghton Papers. See also Nathan Appleton, *Memoir of the Hon. Abbott Lawrence Prepared for the Massachusetts Historical Society* (Boston,: J.H. Eastburn Press, 1856), 8.
20. William F. Hartford, *Money, Morals, and Politics: Massachusetts in the Age of the Boston Associates* (Boston: Northeastern University Press, 2001), 56–57.
21. Abbott Lawrence, December 31, 1831,Abbott Lawrence Houghton Papers.
22. Abbott Lawrence to Nathan Appleton, Boston, January 15, 1833 Abbott Lawrence Houghton Papers.
23. Lawrence, *Extracts from the Diary*, 257.
24. Ibid.
25. Appleton, *Memoir*, 8–11, 17; and Lawrence, *Extracts from the Diary*, 269.
26. Paul Goodman, "Ethics and Enterprise: The Values of a Boston Elite, 1800–1860," *American Quarterly* 18 (Fall 1966): 442.
27. Ibid., 437; and Lawrence, *Extracts from the Diary*, 118.
28. Lawrence, *Extracts from the Diary*, 329. See also Frank Ballard, *Stewardship of Wealth* (New York 1865), 25.
29. Lawrence, *Extracts from the Diary*, 260 and Ballard, *Stewardship of Wealth*, 36.
30. Ballard, *Stewardship of Wealth*, 36.
31. Paul C. Gutjahr, *Popular American Literature of the Nineteenth Century* (New York: Oxford University Press, 2001), 59.
32. George Trask, *Letters on Tobacco, for American Lads; Or Uncle Toby's Anti-Tobacco Advice to his Nephew Billy Bruce* (Fitchburg: George Trask, n.d.), ix.
33. Lawrence, *Extracts from the Diary*, 177, 309.
34. Ibid., 174.
35. Ibid., 231–32.
36. Ballard, *Stewardship of Wealth*, 36–37.
37. Ibid., 43–45.
38. Ibid., 48–49.
39. Ibid.
40. Samuel A. Green, *Memoir of Abbott Lawrence* (Boston: John Wilson and Son, 1908), 4.
41. Dalzell, *Enterprising Elite*, 59–69, 77.
42. Ibid., 47–49; and John Coolidge, *Mill and Mansion: A Study of Architecture and Society in Lowell, Massachusetts, 1820–1865* (New York: Russell and Russell, 1942), 18–43.

43. Constance McLaughlin Green, *Holyoke, Massachusetts: A Case History of the Industrial Revolution in America* (New Haven: Yale University Press, 1939), 18–30, 41–44 and John S. Garner, *The Model Company Town: Urban Design Through Private Enterprise in Nineteenth Century New England* (Amherst: University of Massachusetts Press, 1982), 6–7. See also James E. Vance, Jr., "Housing the Worker: The Employment Linkage as a Force," *Urban Structure Economic Geography* 42 (October 1966): 318–20.
44. Peter Ford, "'Father of the Whole Enterprise' Charles S. Storrow and the Making of Lawrence, Massachusetts, 1845–1860," *Massachusetts Historical Review* 2 (2000): 5, www.historycoperative.org.csulib.ctstate .edu/journals/mhr/2/ford. See also Duncan Erroll Hay, "Building 'The New City on the Merrimack': The Essex Company and its Role in the Creation of Lawrence, Massachusetts" (PhD diss., University of Delaware, 1986), 1–4.
45. For an extensive discussion of the company and Storrow, see Hay. See also Green, *Memoir*, 4–5.
46. Ford, "'Father of the Whole Enterprise,'" 9.
47. Donald B. Cole, *Immigrant City: Lawrence, Massachusetts 1845–1921* (Chapel Hill: University of North Carolina Press, 1963), 17–27.
48. Ford, "'Father of the Whole Enterprise.'"
49. "Lawrence, Massachusetts Annual Report of the School Committee of the City of Lawrence for the School Year 1853" *in Children and Youth in America: A Documentary History*, ed. Robert H. Bremner (Cambridge: Harvard University Press, 1970): I:468.
50. *Hartford Courant*, January 11, 1860; *Hartford Times*, January 11, 1860; and January 12, 1860; *New York Times*, January 12, 1860. See also Ford, "Father of the Whole Enterprise," 11–25 and Cole, *Immigrant City*, 30–31.
51. Throughout the years, Amos Lawrence faced a series of devastating illnesses. Beginning as early as 1810, he was stricken with a remittent fever. Thereafter, his health became precarious and he fell ill in 1818 and again in 1831. Lawrence, *Extracts from the Diary*, 40, 62, 105. For the remainder of his life, he remained in poor health, often confined to his home but still able to meet with family and friends and order his investments. Abbott's health was more robust, but he fell ill in June 1855 and died two months later.
52. William Lawrence, *Life of Amos A. Lawrence* (Boston: Houghton Mifflin, 1888), 163.
53. Dalzell, *Enterprising Elite*, 122–36.

CHAPTER 7

1. Robert F. Dalzell, Jr., *Enterprising Elite: The Boston Associates and the World They Made* (Cambridge: Harvard University Press, 1987), 65.

2. William Lawrence, *Life of Amos A. Lawrence with Extracts from his Diary and Correspondence* (Boston: Houghton Mifflin, 1888), 23.
3. Betty Farrell, *Elite Families: Class and Power in Nineteenth Century Boston* (Albany: State University of New York Press, 1993), 139; Thomas O'Connor, *Lords of the Loom: The Cotton Whigs and the Coming of the Civil War* (New York: Scribner, 1968), 69.
4. Barry A. Crouch, "In Search of Union: Amos A. Lawrence and the Coming of the Civil War" (PhD diss., University of New Mexico, 1970), 22.
5. Lawrence, *Life of Amos A. Lawrence*, 8–9.
6. Ibid., 86.
7. Memorandum Book, April 13, 1830, Box 3, Amos Adams Lawrence Papers, Massachusetts Historical Society, Boston, Massachusetts. Hereafter cited as AA Lawrence MSS.
8. The material for this paragraph was taken from Barbara M. Tucker and Kenneth H. Tucker, Jr., "The Limits of *Homo Economicus*: An Appraisal of Early American Entrepreneurship," in *Whither the Early Republic: A Forum on the Future of the Field*, ed. John Lauritz Larson and Michael A. Morrison (Philadelphia: University of Pennsylvania Press, 2005), 62–63; Amos Lawrence to William Lawrence, Boston, April 29, 1835, Letter book 9, Amos Lawrence Papers, Massachusetts Historical Society, Boston, Massachusetts. Hereafter cited as Amos Lawrence Papers. In this letter, Amos, Sr. told William that he purchased shares in the new Boott Company for him. He requested that he later share the shares with his brother. "It will be a good concern."
9. Amos Lawrence to William Lawrence, Boston, March 18, 1836, Letter Book 9, Amos Lawrence Papers.
10. Amos Lawrence to William Lawrence, Boston, March 29, 1836, Letter Book 9, Amos Lawrence Papers. Amos Adams did not want to follow his father's path exactly. Unsure of his objectives in life and freed from academic rules and regulations, Amos Adams first moved to Bedford and then returned to Andover. By 1834, he was back at Harvard. See Lawrence, *Life of Amos A. Lawrence*, 11–17.
11. Lawrence, *Life of Amos A. Lawrence*, 18.
12. Ibid., 20, 22.
13. Ibid., 23–24.
14. Ibid., 34.
15. Essay, "What is Meant by Good Fortune," c. 1835, 104, AA Lawrence MSS.
16. Ibid.
17. Essay, "What Are We to Infer as to Man's Nature or a State of Society from the Number and Variety of Pursuits, Trades, Professions &c.," c. 1835, 100, AA Lawrence MSS. See also Essay, "On the Natural Enmity Between the Rich and Poor," c. 1835, 124, AA Lawrence MSS.
18. Essay, "On the Natural Enmity Between Rich and Poor," c. 1835, 124, AA Lawrence MSS.

19. Lawrence, *Life of Amos A. Lawrence*, 23–24.
20. Crouch, "In Search of Union," 36–41.
21. Diary of Amos Adams Lawrence, August 4, 1841. Amos Adams Lawrence Diaries and Account Books, Massachusetts Historical Society, Boston, Massachusetts. Hereafter cited as Lawrence Diary MSS.
22. Crouch, "In Search of Union," 64–67.
23. Ibid, 69.
24. Lawrence, *Life of Amos A. Lawrence*, 36–48. See also, Crouch, "In Search of Union," 67–73.
25. Lawrence Diary MSS, January 2, 1842.
26. Lawrence, *Life of Amos A. Lawrence*, 50.
27. Ibid., 52.
28. Statement of Assets, c. September 1857, Box 11, AA Lawrence MSS.
29. Ibid.
30. Lawrence Diary MSS, Box 4, Rent Book, n.d. "Two Hundred Years of Progress: Webster-Dudley, 1739–*1939," Webster Times*, 1939, 8.
31. Statement of Assets, c. September 1857,Box 11, AA Lawrence MSS; Lawrence, *Life of Amos A. Lawrence*, 51–52; and Michael French, "Co-Ordinating Manufacturing and Marketing: The Role of the Selling Agent in US Textiles," *Textile History* 25 (1994): 227–28.
32. Lawrence and Company, *The Story of Lawrence and Company* (Boston: Walton Advertising and Printing Company, 1913), 3–13. This short book provides a chronology of Lawrence and Company; from 1843 to 1890, the name of the firm and the partners in the firm changed many times. See also Lawrence, *Life of Amos A. Lawrence*, 247–49.
33. Hansjorg Siegenthaler, "What Price Style? The Fabric Advisory Function of the Dry Goods Commission Merchant," *Business History Review* 41 (1967): 55–59.
34. Alfred D. Chandler, Jr., *The Visible Hand: The Managerial Revolution in American Business* (Cambridge: Belknap Press, 1977), 71–72.
35. This specialized selling house was patterned after those established earlier by such firms as A & A Lawrence or J. W. Paige and Company. The latter company had been formed in 1828 by stockholders of the Waltham, Merrimack, Hamilton, and Appleton Companies to dispose of their cloth. The firm dealt directly with jobbers and retailers often located in the large coastal towns. With its booming regional market, access to the western trade via railroads and canals, and foreign commerce, New York appeared the ideal point for distribution. This certainly was true for Mason and Lawrence. About 85 percent of their goods went to jobbers and firms in that city. See Glenn Porter and Harold C. Livesay, *Merchants and Manufacturers: Studies in the Changing Structure of Nineteenth-Century Marketing* (Baltimore: Johns Hopkins University Press, 1971), 22–28; and Chandler, *Visible Hand*, 71–72. The firm of Mason and Lawrence went through several name changes. See Lawrence and Company, *Story of Lawrence and Company*, 11–13.

36. Siegenthaler, "What Price Style?" 56–59.
37. Lawrence, *Life of Amos A. Lawrence*, 52. Lawrence wrote, "In regard to religious instruction, it seems to me that if our church does not produce the desired interest, either from want of talent in the preacher or from prejudice against the forms, there must be some kind of preaching, and some form adopted, which will."
38. Lawrence, *Life of Amos A. Lawrence*, 52–53. See also Strafford Regional Planning Commission, *Salmon Falls—The Mill Village Historic District Study for the Town of Rollingsford, New Hampshire* (Dover, 1974), 2–4.
39. Lawrence, *Life of Amos A. Lawrence*, 163.
40. Donald B Cole, *Immigrant City: Lawrence, Massachusetts, 1845–1921* (Chapel Hill: University of North Carolina Press, 1963), 31.
41. Lawrence, *Life of Amos A. Lawrence*, 163. The figures that Lawrence mentions appear high. Historians suggest there were about 670 workers in the mill at the time of collapse. There is also some disagreement concerning the number of people killed and wounded. See Cole, *Immigrant City*, 31–32.
42. B. P. Raymond, *In Memory of Hon. Amos A. Lawrence: Discourse* (Appleton: Post Publishing Company, 1886), 7.
43. Ibid., 12–15; Lawrence, *Life of Amos A. Lawrence*, 53–58; and Crouch, "In Search of Union," 114.
44. O'Connor, *Lords of the Loom*, 76.
45. Lawrence, *Life of Amos A. Lawrence*, 53–54.
46. O'Connor, *Lords of the Loom*, 98.
47. *Resolves and Private Laws of Connecticut, 1836–1857*, 3:303. For a discussion of the confusion surrounding the incorporation of the company, see Samuel A. Johnson, *The Battle Cry of Freedom: The New England Emigrant Aid Company in the Kansas Crusade* (Lawrence: University of Kansas Press, 1954).
48. An Act to Incorporate the Massachusetts Emigrant Aid Company (April 1854), 164.
49. Amos A. Lawrence to Rev. Lum, November 28, 1854, quoted in Richard H. Abbott, *Cotton and Capital: Boston Businessmen and Antislavery Reform, 1854–1868* (Amherst: University of Massachusetts Press, 1991), 30; and Amos A. Lawrence to James Blood, February 16, 1855 in Abbott, *Cotton and Capital*, 30. See also Lawrence, *Life of Amos A. Lawrence*, 80–81.
50. "Education, Temperance, Freedom, Religion in Kansas, July 24, 1855, www.territorial kansasonline.org.
51. Lucy Larcom to Amos A. Lawrence, Wheaton Female Seminary, Norton, MA, Februry 8, 1855, Box 9, AALawrence MSS.
52. Ibid.
53. John Greenleaf Whittier, *The Complete Poetical Works of John Greenleaf Whittier, Household Edition* (Boston: Houghton Mifflin, 1904), 391–92.

54. Shelley Hickman Clark and James W. Clark, eds., "Recollections of Joseph Savage, by Joseph Savage," *Kansas History: A Journal of the Central Plains* 27 (Spring–Summer 2004): 36.
55. United States Federal Population Census, Manuscript Schedules, Seventh Census of the United States, Lawrence, Massachusetts, 1850.
56. Lawrence, *Life of Amos A. Lawrence*, 85–86.
57. Ibid., 80–81. See also Whitman to Amos Adams Lawrence, Boston, April 2, 1855, Box 9, AA Lawrence MSS,
58. Pomeroy to Amos A. Lawrence, Kansas, April 6, 1855, Box 9, AA Lawrence MSS.
59. Lawrence, *Life of Amos A. Lawrence*, 116, 227.
60. Clark and Clark, "Recollections of Joseph Savage," 38.
61. Sarah T. L. Robinson, *Kansas, Its Interior and Exterior Life: Including a Full View of Its Settlement, Political History, Social Life, Climate, Soil, Productions, Scenery* (Lawrence, n.d.), 8, NetLibr e-book.
62. G. W. Brown to Amos Adams Lawrence, Kansas, April 30, 1855, Box, 9 AA Lawrence MSS. and F. A. Hunt to Amos Adams Lawrence, St. Louis, April 18, 1855, Box 9, AA Lawrence MSS.
63. Lawrence, *Life of Amos A. Lawrence*, 96–101.
64. Ibid., 123–25, 140–41; and Crouch, "In Search of Union," 171–73. Lawrence and Brown's relationship is somewhat clouded. Eli Thayer believed that Brown abused Lawrence's support. While Lawrence gave him money to pay his way to Kansas and provided $1000 to pay the mortgage on his New York home, Lawrence criticized the man saying that he deceived everybody. "He was always ready to shed blood, and he always did shed it without remorse." See Eli Thayer, *A History of the Kansas Crusade: Its Friends and its Foes* (New York: Harper, 1889), 190–93.
65. Abbott, *Cotton and Capital*, 39–49. This resignation was not the first he submitted. In September 1855, he tried to resign amid the ever increasing debt obligations incurred by the company. Within the previous twelve month period, he had given $13,000 to the organization, and repeatedly had to draw from his personal funds to pay ongoing expenses. By the middle of October, he had not been replaced and complained that bills were due. He had just paid one for $2,000 from his own purse, with three other bills due for immediate payment. See Amos A. Lawrence to Branscomb, Boston, September 26, 1855, and Amos A. Lawrence to Branscomb, Boston, October 9, 1855, and Amos A. Lawrence to Branscomb, Boston, October 19, 1855 in www.territorialKansasonline.org.
66. Elihu Burritt to Amos Adams Lawrence, April 27, 1855, Box 9. AA Lawrence MSS.
67. Lawrence, *Life of Amos Adams Lawrence*, 122–38; and Crouch, "In Search of Union," 189–92.

68. Thayer, *A History of the Kansas Crusade*, 190.
69. John R. Mulkern, *The Know-Nothing Party in Massachusetts: The Rise and Fall of a People's Movement* (Boston: Northeastern University Press, 1990), 137–53; and Crouch, "In Search of Union," 173–74.
70. *New York Times*, July 4, 1856.
71. Lawrence, *Life of Amos A. Lawrence*, 143–44; and Crouch "In Search of Union," 186–88.
72. Abbott, *Cotton and Capital*, 64.
73. Lawrence, *Life of Amos A. Lawrence*, 146. For a detailed discussion of the Constitutional Union Party, see Crouch, "In Search of Union," 198–225.
74. Richard F. Miller, "Brahmin Janissaries: John A. Andrew Mobilizes Massachusetts' Upper Class for the Civil War," *New England Quarterly* 75 (June 2002): 225.
75. Lawrence, *Life of Amos A. Lawrence*, 184.
76. Ibid., 187. See also Civil War Receipt Book, 1862–1863, Box 4, Lawrence Diary MSS,and Crouch, 268–73.
77. Crouch, "In Search of Union," 278–81. Later, Lawrence was involved in a campaign to raise money for bounties to be given to southern black men who agreed to enlist in the Union Army. Agents were sent to the South, and the men they recruited were used to fill Northern draft quotas.
78. Crouch, "In Search of Union," 281–83. See also Lawrence, *Life of Amos A. Lawrence*, 232.
79. Crouch, "In Search of Union," 269–82; and Lawrence and Company, *Story of Lawrence and Company*, 12–13.
80. Raymond, *In Memory*, 9, 27–28.

CONCLUSION

1. Paula Fass, "Cultural History/Social History: Some Reflections on a Continuing Dialogue," *Journal of Social History* 37 (2003): 39–54. See also Barbara M. Tucker and Kenneth H. Tucker, Jr., "The Limits of *Homo Economicus*: An Appraisal of Early American Entrepreneurship," *Whither the Early Republic: A Forum on the Future of the Field*, ed. John Lauritz Larson and Michael A. Morrison (Philadelphia: University of Pennsylvania Press, 2005), 59–69.
2. Naomi R. Lamoreaux, "Rethinking the Transition to Capitalism in the Early American Northeast," *Journal of American History* vol. 90 (September 2003): 440.
3. Ibid., 454.
4. Ibid., 459.
5. Ibid., 449.
6. Emile Durkheim, *The Division of Labor in Society* (New York: The Free Press, 1984): 149–75.

Index